AF567199

Secrets of Backyard Bird Photography

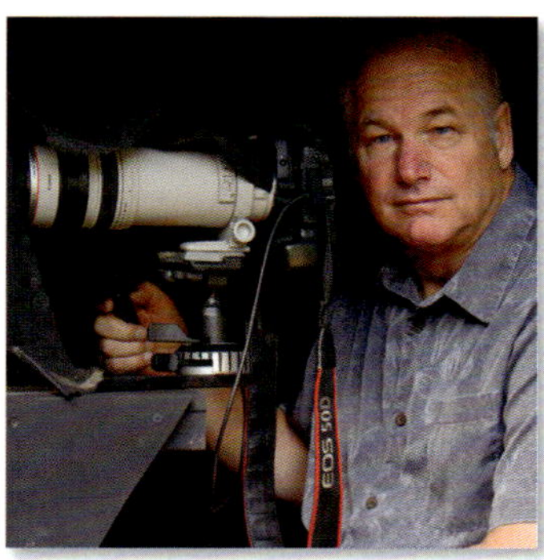

J. Chris Hansen is a wildlife and nature photographer who lives and works in the redwoods of Northern California. His images have been published in numerous outdoor magazines, including *Mule Deer* and *California Hunter*. He has a passion for bird photography and can often be found photographing in his backyard.

http://christhephotog.blogspot.com/

Secrets of Backyard Bird Photography

J. Chris Hansen

rockynook

J. Chris Hansen (christhephotog.blogspot.com)

Project Editor: Maggie Yates
Copyeditor: Maggie Yates
Layout: Hespenheide Design
Cover Design: Helmut Kraus, www.exclam.de
Printer: Friesens Corporation, Altona, Canada
Printed in Canada

ISBN 978-1-937538-55-2

1st Edition 2014

Rocky Nook Inc.
802 East Cota St., 3rd Floor
Santa Barbara, CA 93103
www.rockynook.com

Library of Congress Cataloging-in-Publication Data

Hansen, J. Chris, author.
Secrets of backyard bird photography / by J. Chris Hansen. -- 1st edition.
pages cm
ISBN 978-1-937538-55-2 (hardbound : alk. paper)
1. Photography of birds. 2. Photography--Digital techniques. 3. Single-lens reflex cameras. I. Title.
TR729.B5H36 2014
778.9'328--dc23
2014008573

Distributed by O'Reilly Media
1005 Gravenstein Highway North
Sebastopol, CA 95472

This book is printed on acid-free paper.

This book is dedicated to God, who makes all things possible,
and to my family, Lenore, Jay, and Annika, for their loving support of the writing of this book.

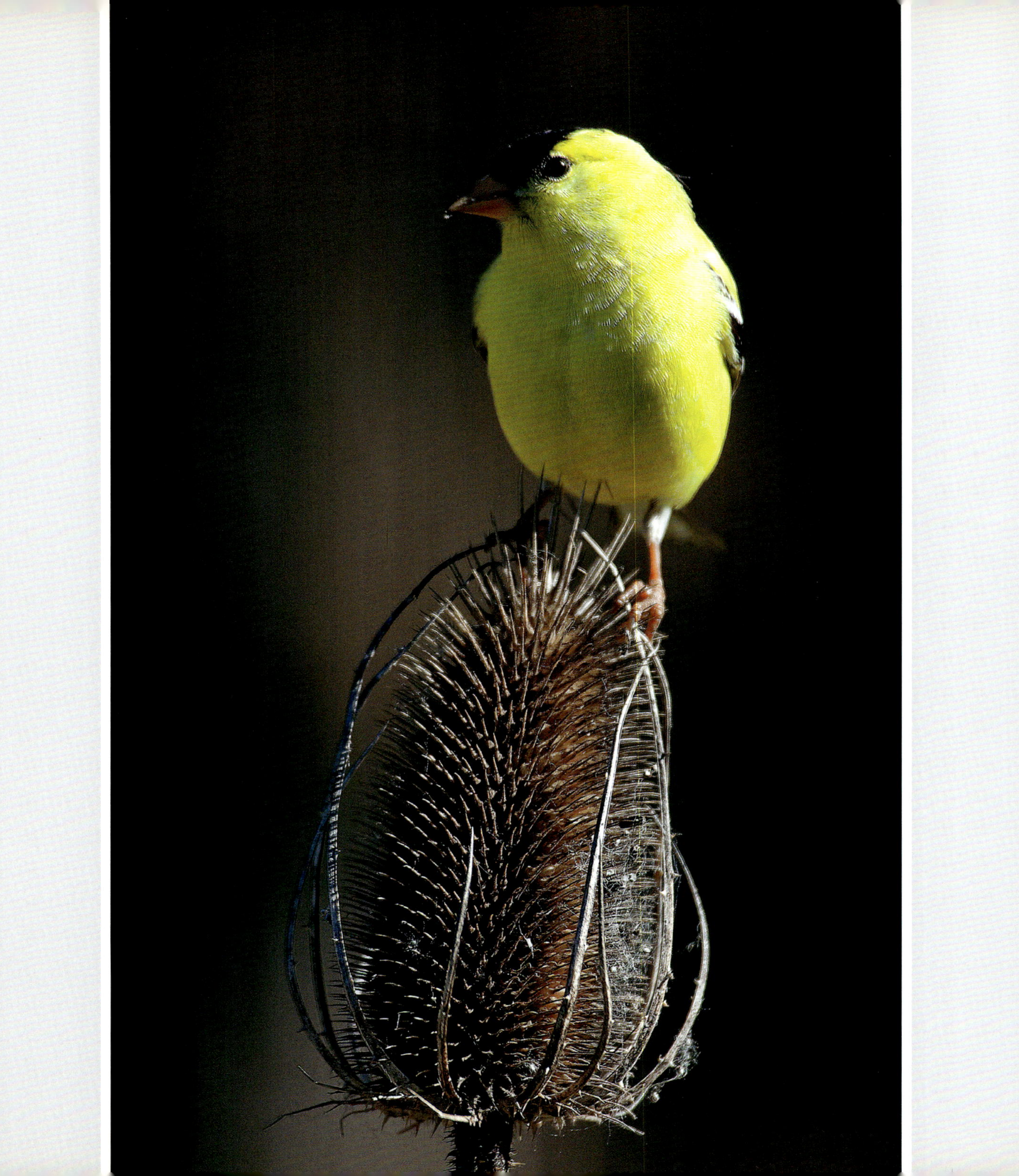

Acknowledgements

To Steve Hellman, for helping bring this book to life with his editing expertise and encouragement.
To my parents, John and Betty Hansen, for raising me with a love for the outdoors and all of God's creation.
For the team at Rocky Nook, Joan Dixon, Maggie Yates, Alison Smith, and Matthias Rossmanith,
for their professionalism and invaluable help in making this book a reality.

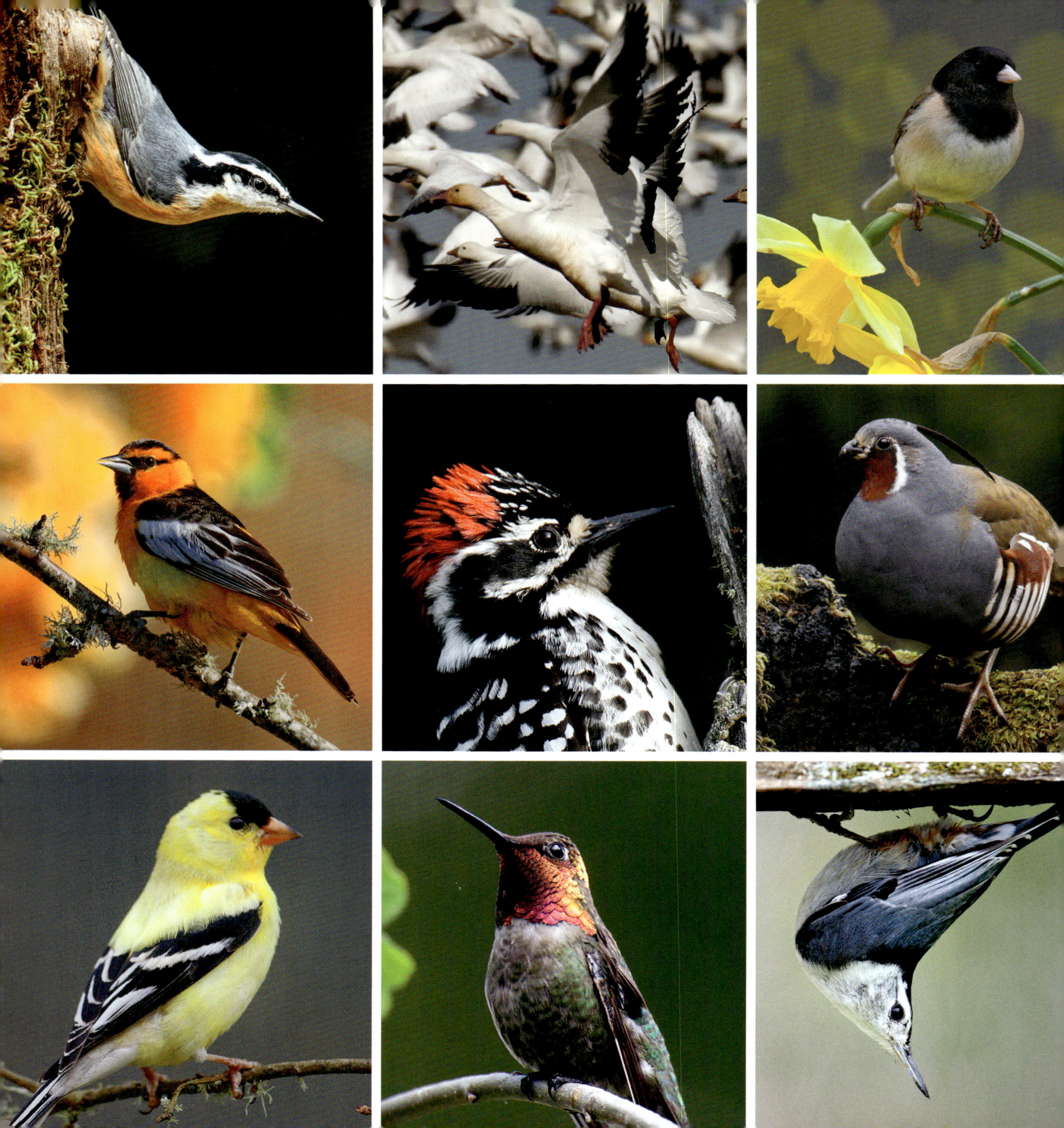

Table of Contents

Introduction		1
Chapter 1	**The Best Camera and Equipment**	3
Chapter 2	**The Basics of Attracting Birds**	7
Chapter 3	**A Few Tricks of the Trade**	23
Chapter 4	**The Use of Blinds**	37
Chapter 5	**How to Capture the Best Bird Images**	41
Chapter 6	**Photographing Hummingbirds**	47
Chapter 7	**Beyond the Backyard**	59
Chapter 8	**Showing Your Bird Photography**	65
Chapter 9	**DIY Projects**	68
	Peter Pan Feeder	68
	A Changeable Perch Feeder	70
	Small Water Feature: Bird Baths	73
	The Knothole Feeder	76
	Building a Window Blind	82
	Ground Pod for Shooting from a Windowsill	86
	Building a Large Water Feature	88
	Building a Chair Blind	93
	A Permanent Blind	98
	A Shooting Shelf for a Permanent Blind	106
Resources and Suppliers		113
Recipes for Suet		115
Conclusion		117

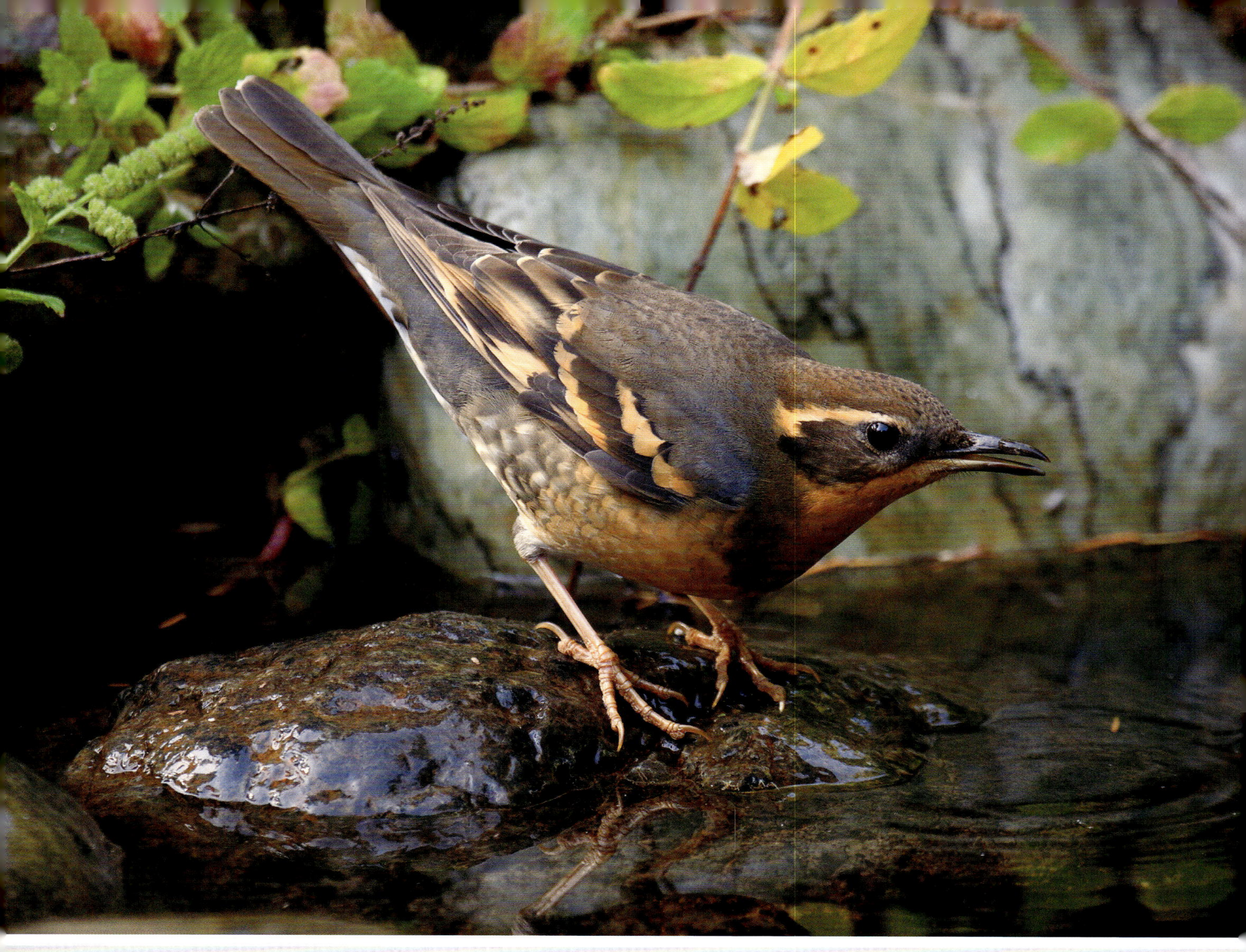

▲ *Varied thrush on rocks set in a backyard pond*

Introduction

This comprehensive guide offers a variety of techniques and projects for backyard bird photography. You will learn how to use feeders, perches, backgrounds, blinds, and the proper camera equipment to create professional-quality images. In its simplest form, photographing birds in your backyard is convenient, economical, and very rewarding; ultimately, it can become an addictive adventure.

Any type of backyard, from the wide-open space of a western ranch to a city apartment with a patio or deck, can yield excellent images of local birds. By providing perches, feeders, and water sources, and by utilizing blinds, the photographer can create an inviting environment for birds. With the help of the information in this book and some practice, you will have the tools to begin creating fantastic bird images.

The advantages of backyard bird photography are many. The primary advantage is the fact that travel is unnecessary. No flights, car rentals, or hotel rooms; no big expenses paying for meals or gas; no fighting traffic to go anywhere. When your primary location for shooting is your backyard, you don't even have to shave or put on your makeup. The birds won't care if you've shaved or not.

The second advantage of shooting in your yard is that your bird subjects are often easier to find and capture than wild birds. Because neighborhood birds are accustomed to sharing their space with people, they don't typically see us as a threat—unless you get too close. While you have to travel to the habitats of wild birds to photograph them, backyard birds are easy to find because they come to you. Your backyard *is* their habitat! This book offers ideas for ways to draw the birds into your camera range.

Shooting bird images in your own backyard is also a huge time saver. The time you would have spent traveling can now be spent in the comfort of your own location shooting images at your convenience. You won't risk spending hundreds or thousands of dollars on travel to a place where you could get rained out.

There are disadvantages to backyard bird photography, as well. The biggest problem is that you are limited to the species of birds that you can attract to your backyard. If you are shooting from your apartment in the Bronx, it is unlikely that you'll have the opportunity to photograph penguins. Another consideration is the limits of migration: you'll only be able to photograph some species of birds during certain times of year.

Another disadvantage to shooting only in your backyard is that it can be easy to fall into a rut. It's up to you to provide the spark to keep your bird photography fresh. One of the most creative aspects of backyard birding is setting up the backyard habitat. You have the opportunity to design and produce beautiful set-ups and backgrounds for your images.

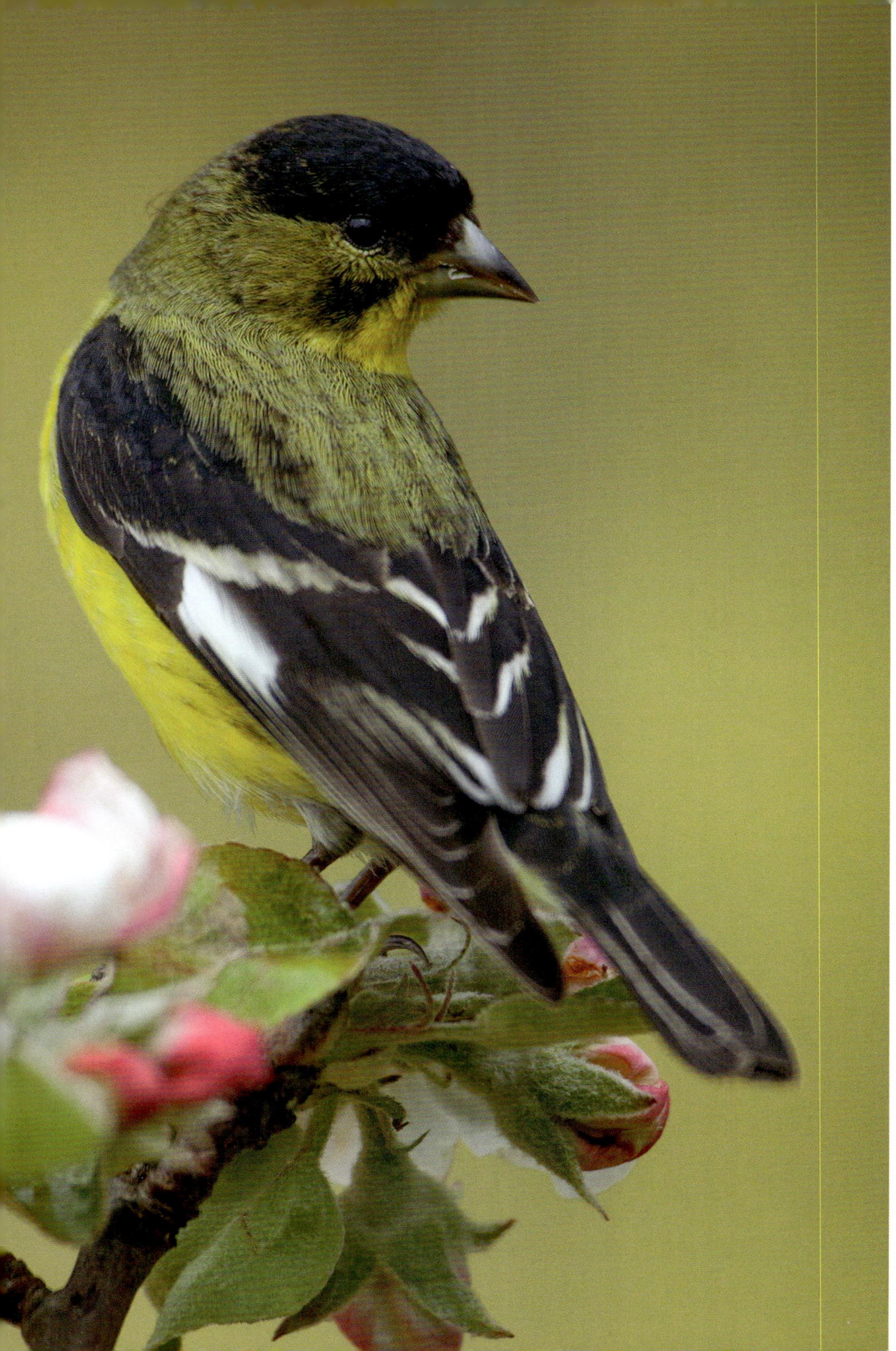

◄ *Goldfinch on blossom next to a tube feeder*

CHAPTER 1

The Best Camera and Equipment

I have found that the best camera to use is a Digital Single Lens Reflex (DSLR), with a pixel count of six megapixels or larger. These cameras have interchangeable lenses that can be purchased in varying powers of up to 800 mm. Any of the major manufactured cameras, such as Canon, Nikon, Pentax, Sigma, Olympus, Panasonic, Sony, and Fuji, will work quite well for this purpose.

As far as lenses are concerned, it is best to use a telephoto lens with a focal length of at least 200 mm or longer. The longer the zoom of your lenses, the better they are for bird photography, but the more expensive they will be. My personal favorite is a 100-400 mm telephoto zoom lens. A zoom lens allows you to move in closer or pull further away from your subject, so you don't have to change positions the way you would with a prime lens. This is advantageous when a variety of birds of different sizes visit your bird feeder set-ups, and you need a tighter (or wider) shot.

If you do not own a DSLR, a Point-and-Shoot (P&S) camera can work as long as it has a few critical features. The most important feature is that it should have little to no shutter lag. This means that when you push the shutter button to take the picture, there shouldn't be any delay until the picture is taken. If you do decide upon using a camera with shutter delay, be prepared for the frustration of a lot of missed pictures, since birds can move rather quickly.

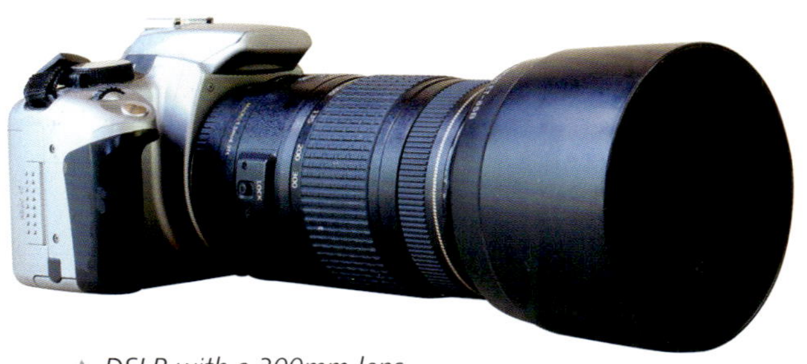

▲ *DSLR with a 300mm lens*

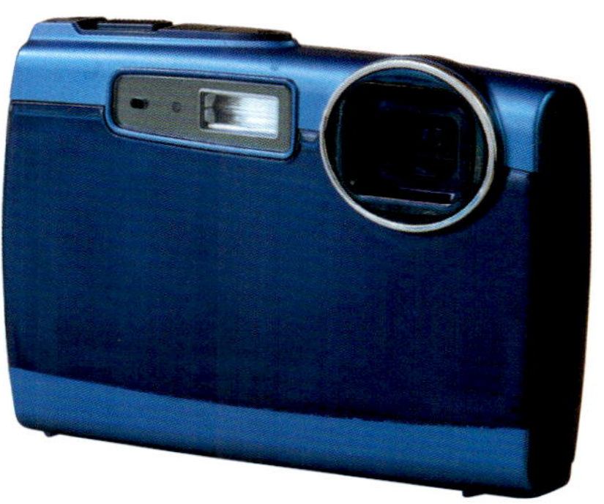

▲ *Point-and-shoot camera*

Your camera should also have a 10x optical (not digital) zoom or longer, and have a place for a tripod mount on the bottom. In terms of megapixels, the best is a camera with a minimum of six megapixels or higher.

A tripod or camera support of some kind is a must. You will spend a lot of time waiting, and when the action does occur, you are going to want your camera to be in a stable, secure position ready for you to click the shutter.

In choosing a tripod, you usually get what you pay for. I'm not saying that cheap tripods don't work—they typically just don't have a tough enough build to last very long without something

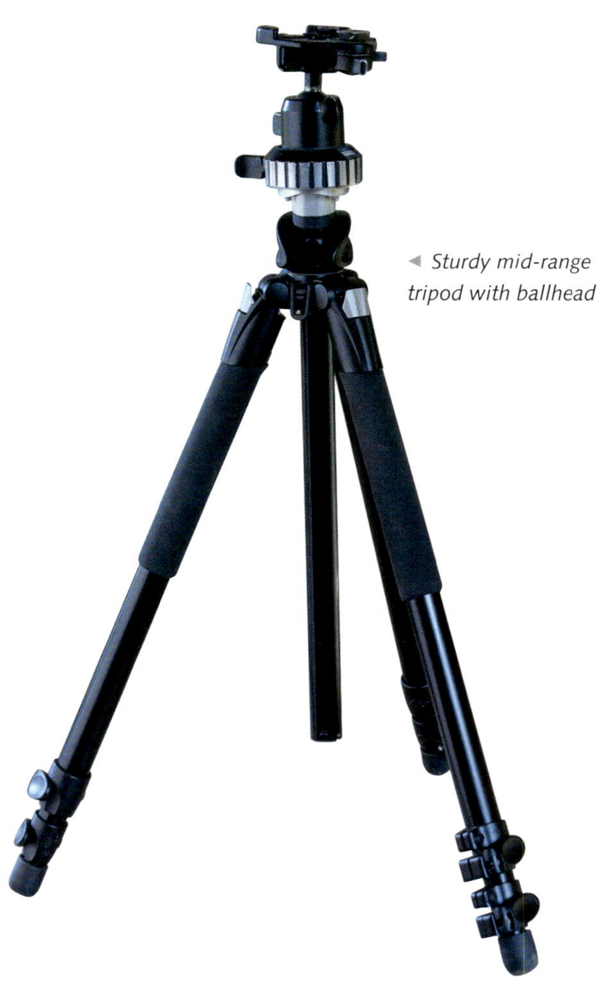

◄ *Sturdy mid-range tripod with ballhead*

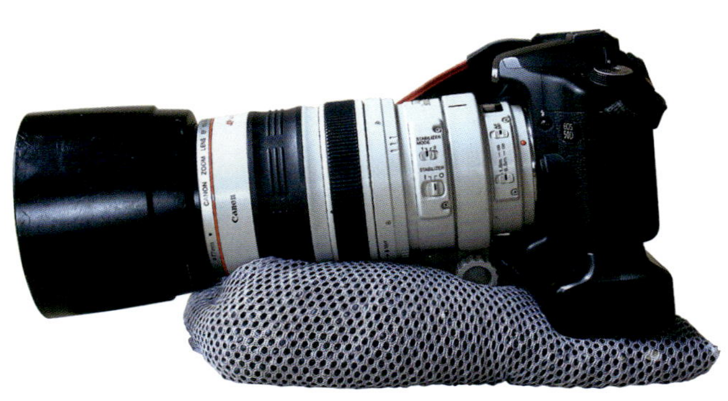

▲ *Beanbag with DSLR camera and a 400mm lens*

stripping, breaking, or some part coming loose. Do you want to trust your camera on something that may fail? Choose a tripod that is sturdy and well made. Tripods manufactured by Bogen/Manfrotto, Gitzo, Cullman, and Benbo are all considered to be reliable.

If you feel that a tripod is beyond your budget, consider using a beanbag or other similar camera support. In a pinch, a folded up jacket, sweater, or towel can be used to support and stabilize your camera.

A special warning is needed here. Never leave your tripod and camera standing up unattended. Children, pets, or a clueless person can easily knock over your equipment. I know this from personal experience.

A must-have when using any kind of zoom or telephoto lens is a cable shutter release. It minimizes the camera shake caused by pressing the shutter so you don't end up with a blurry image. DSLRs can be equipped with an electronic cable release, and some even use a remote release. P&S cameras are very limited in this department, although some do come equipped for a wireless remote.

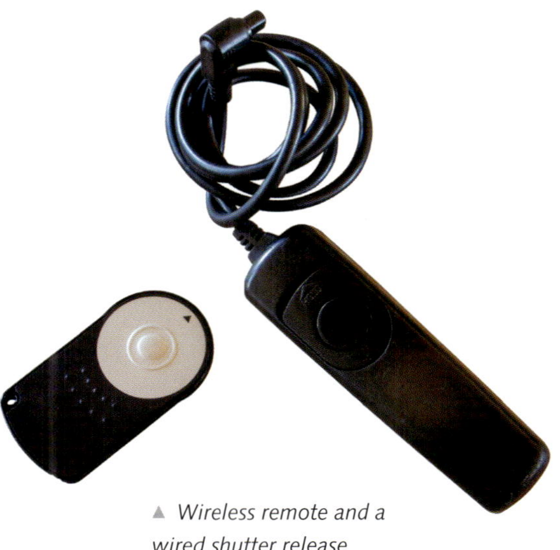

▲ *Wireless remote and a wired shutter release*

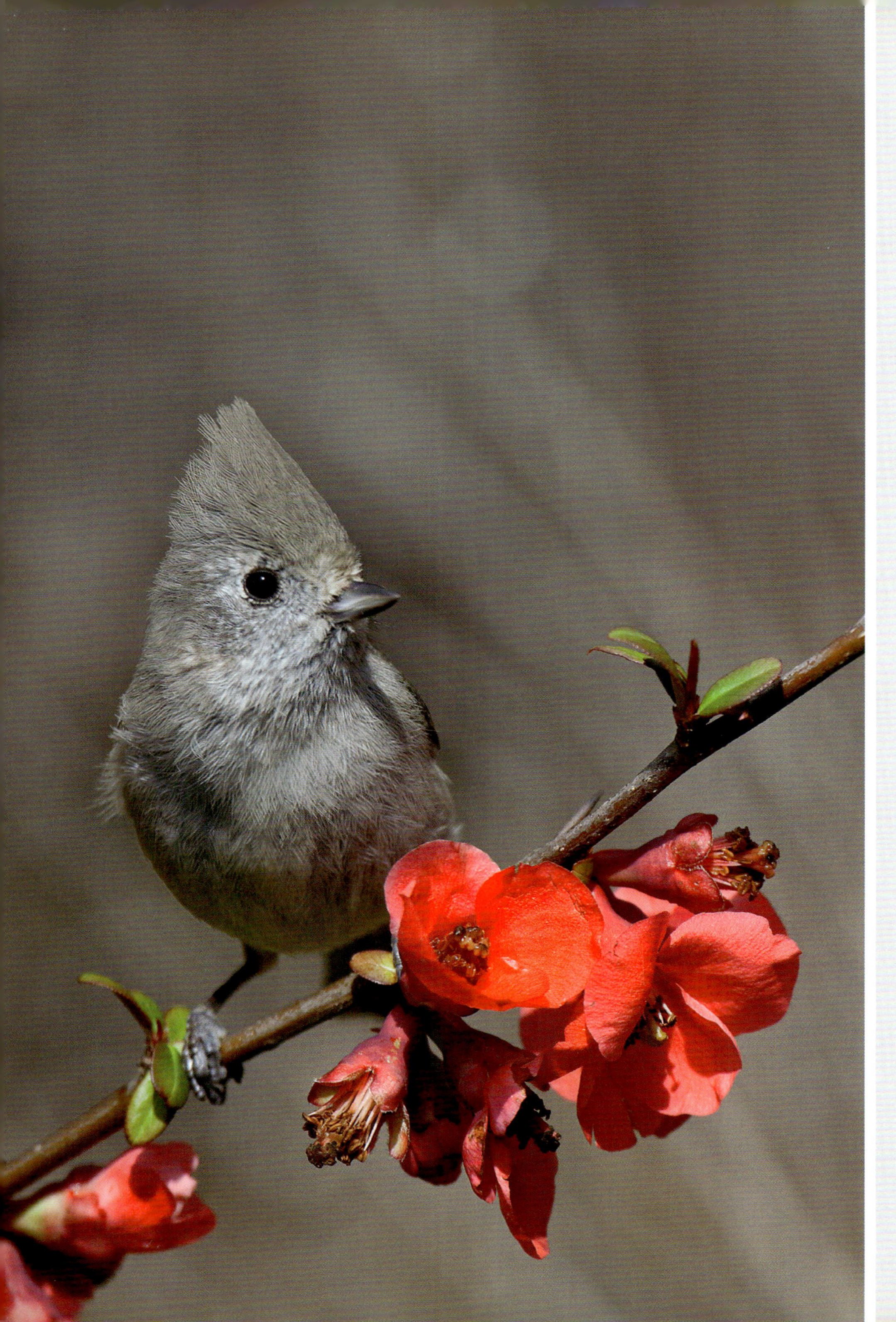

◂ *Oak titmouse on an apple blossom branch placed above a platform feeder*

CHAPTER 2

The Basics of Attracting Birds

The basic premise of backyard bird photography is to provide what the birds need to survive. Like humans, birds need food, water, and shelter. If you can provide a relatively safe perch in your backyard, along with feed and water nearby, you will most likely get a variety of birds coming to have their portraits taken. If you already feed the birds in your yard, you are already one step ahead.

Overall, you will find bird feeders to be the most successful tool for your photography. They draw the birds to your yard and concentrate them in one specific location, making them easier to photograph. There are many commercially available feeders and seeds for sale, everywhere from your local hardware store to the grocery store. The types of seeds you put out will affect what kinds of birds you will lure.

The key starting point is to provide a feeder with food on or in it. Near that feeder, place a perch for the birds to land on when they come to eat, drink, or bathe. While they are pausing to decide what to eat, you can create an image of them.

Types of Food

You can plant your yard with native seed and fruit bearing plants or you can provide a feeder stocked with goodies in a safe location in your yard. Two of the best basic birdseeds are black sunflower seed and niger seed, because they bring in a wide variety of birds. Black sunflower seed is known to attract the most species of birds. Niger seed is attractive to all types of finches and many other small birds.

Sunflower seed can be served up to your local bird population from a wide variety of feeders.

Niger seed is best served to birds from a finch or niger feeder, which is a type of tubular feeder with small holes made for such tiny seed. Niger seed has a distinct advantage—most squirrels don't like it.

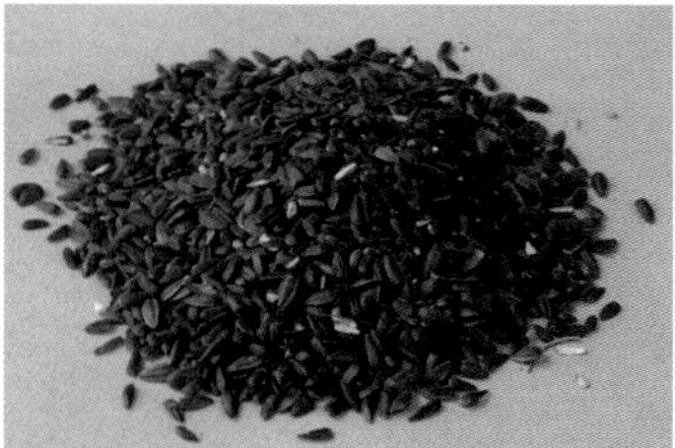

▲ *Black sunflower seed*

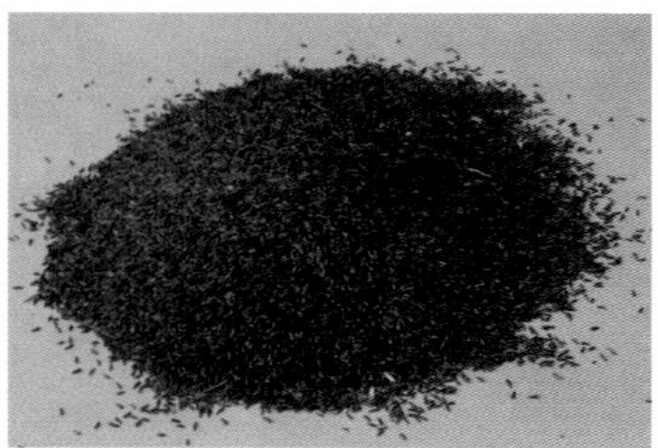

▲ *Niger Seed*

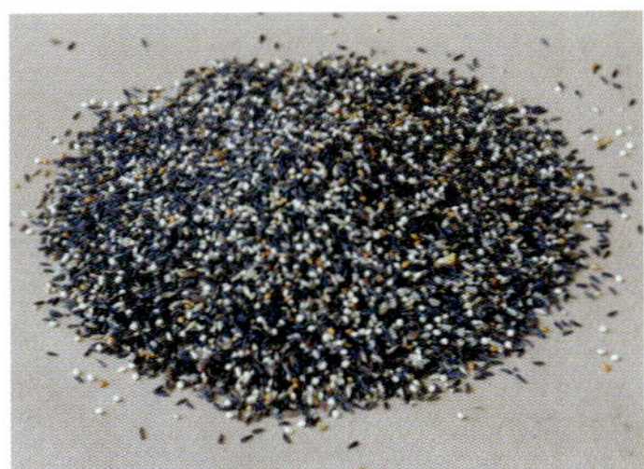

▲ *Finch Seed*

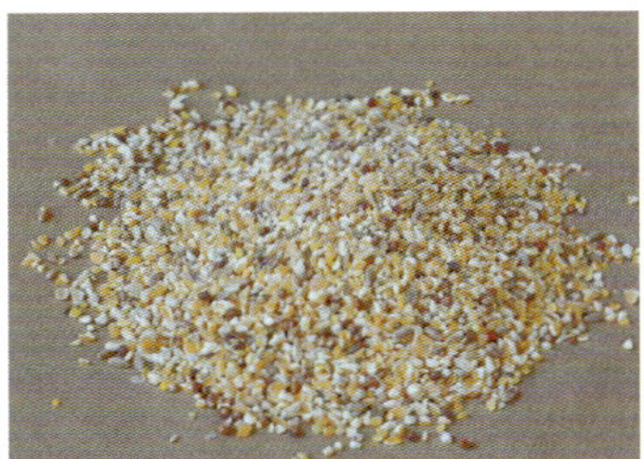

▲ *Hen scratch*

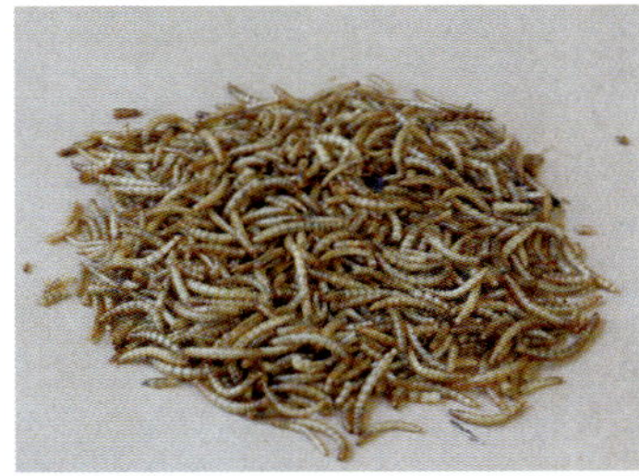

▲ *Dried Mealworms*

Other types of foods available for birds are finch feed, hen scratch, and mealworms. Finch feed is typically served to birds in a tube feeder. Hen scratch is usually placed in a platform feeder, and mealworms can be offered in a mealworm feeder.

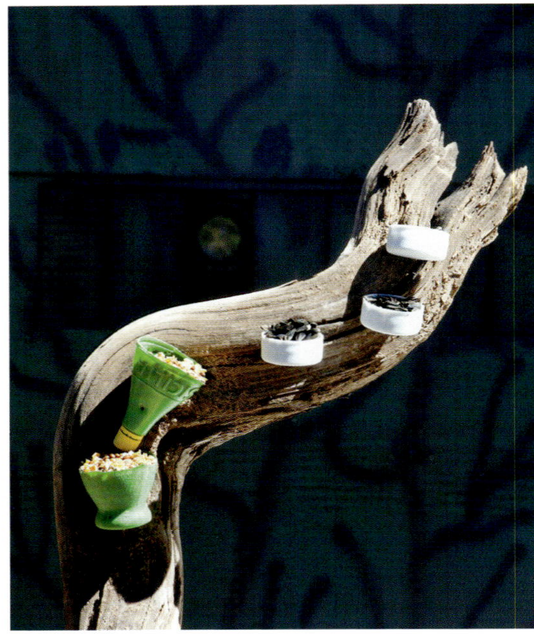

▲ *Recycled plastic containers screwed to the backside of a branch*

Types of Feeders

Platform, hopper, and tube feeders are probably the most common types of feeders available. Feeders can be fancy commercial feeders or something as simple as a two-liter plastic soda bottle with holes cut into it for the birds to feed out of, or a flat board with seed poured onto it. In addition to the commercially made models, I have used nearly everything and the kitchen sink for feeders. Almost anything can be pressed into service. This is important to consider, because many commercial feeders

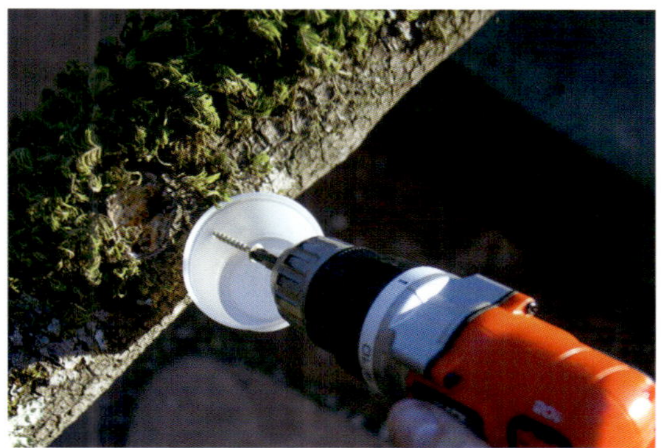

▲ *Cordless drill being used to attach feeder cups to the backside of a branch*

are much too large to be of practical use for creating some bird images. The best feeders are bottle caps and the bottoms of soda bottles, which can be hidden on the backsides of small branches or rocks to lure birds into photogenic locations.

My favorite two tools for creating and installing feeders are a cordless drill and a pair of scissors. I use the scissors to cut down plastic containers to hide them on the backsides of branches and logs. I use the cordless drill and wood screws to hold them there in place.

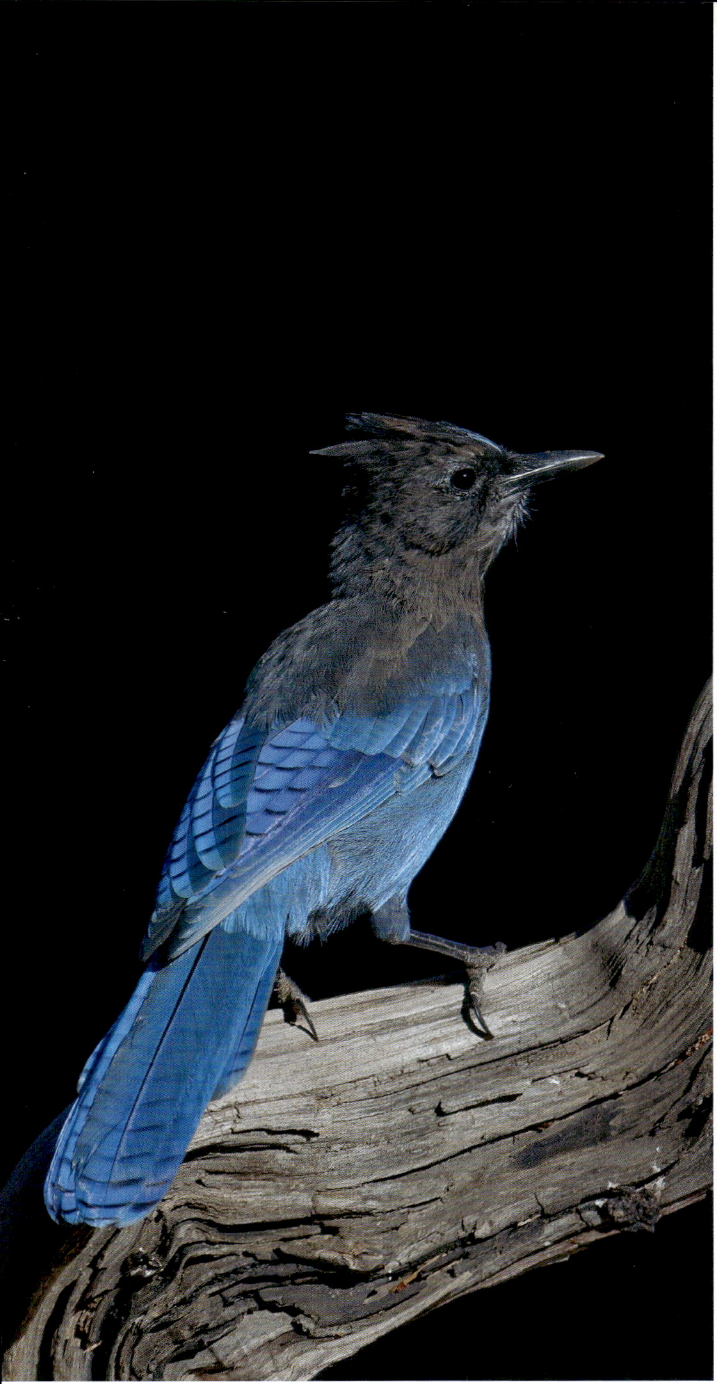

◄ *Steller's jay coming to the feeders*

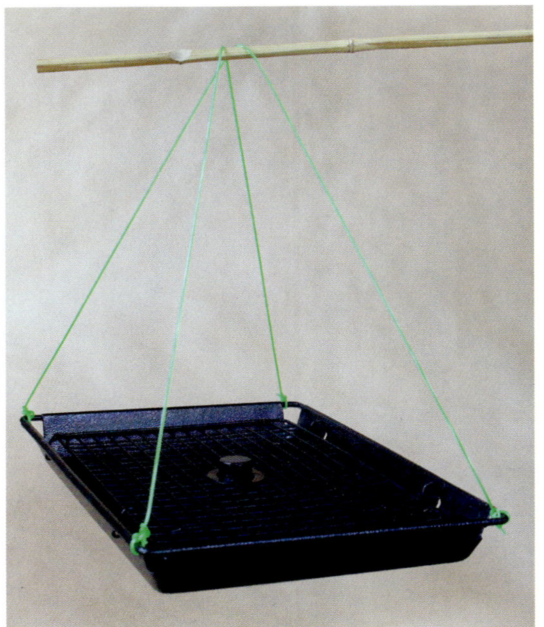
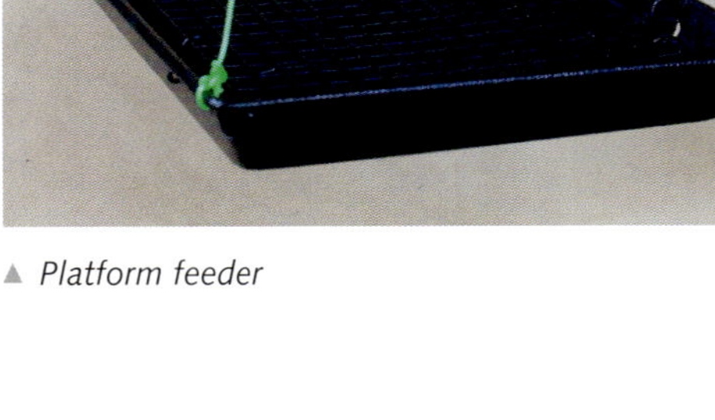

▲ *Platform feeder*

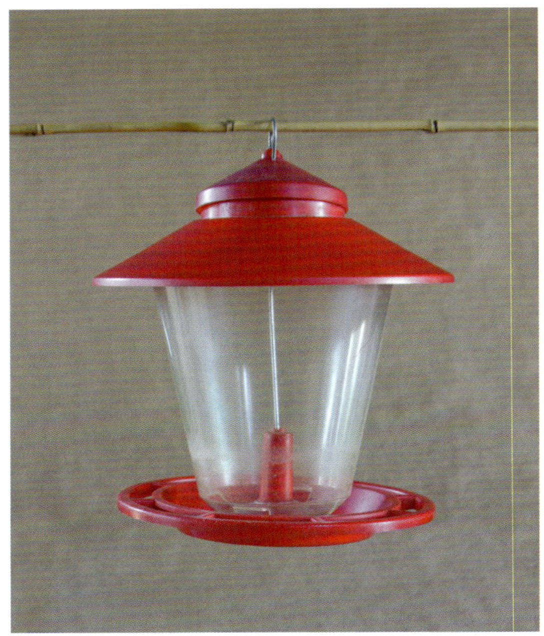

▲ *Hopper feeder*

Platform feeders are mounted on a pole or hung from something such as a tree limb or the edge of a roof. They are flat surfaces onto which seed is poured so birds can feed upon it. The advantage of platform feeders is that they draw in a wide variety of birds. Doves, jays, sparrows, finches, and many other birds like platform feeders.

A platform feeder can be made out of a small flat board: nail or screw it to the top of a post, and then pouring some seed on it. It is easy to attach perches to platform feeders, if necessary. These feeders allow the birds plenty of visibility to see predators coming. The disadvantage, though, is that they don't work as well in inclement weather because the seed gets wet.

Hopper feeders have bins or containers fitted on a narrow platform. The bins contain the seed, and have a slot at the bottom that allows the seed to fall onto the platform as the birds feed from it. Of all the types of feeders, hopper feeders attract the widest variety of species. Their advantage is that they can often hold a good supply of seed and don't need to be refilled as often as platform feeders.

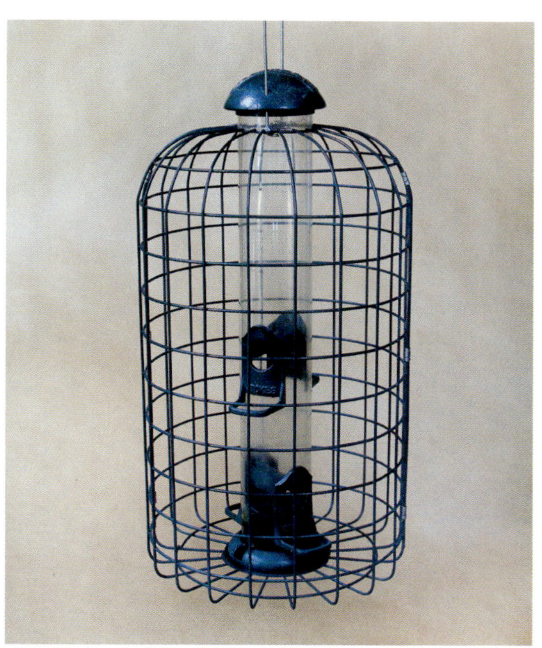

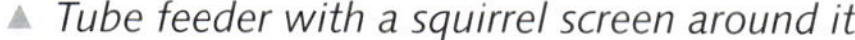

▲ *Tube feeder with a squirrel screen around it*

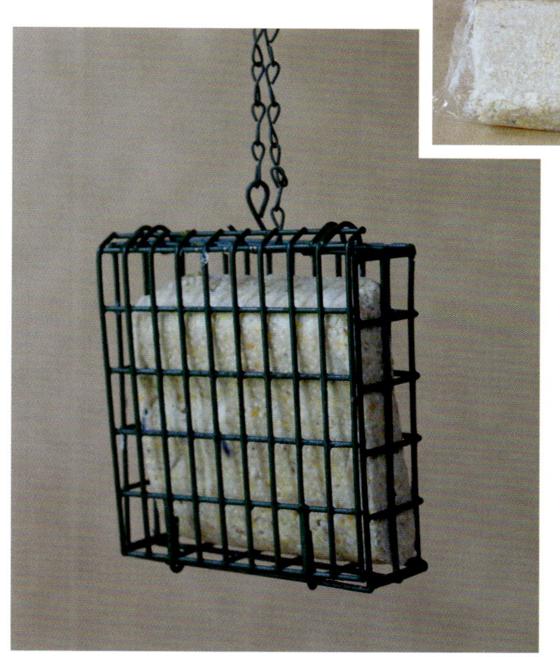

▲ *Suet feeder*

Tube feeders are usually made of a cylinder of clear plastic, with openings placed up and down the tube for the birds to feed from. Usually there is a short perch below each opening for the birds to land on. These feeders attract a lot of the smaller perching birds, such as finches, nuthatches and chickadees. Larger birds such as grackles, blackbirds, and jays have a more difficult time with this feeder if it has very short perches or no perches at all. Tube feeders are great because they can be hung almost anywhere. They are easy to attach perches to, and very transportable if you decide to move them to a new location. The biggest drawback of most tubular feeders is that they can sometimes be very difficult to clean if the seed gets wet or moldy.

Another type of feeder is the suet feeder. Suet feeders are typically open wire cages with a suet block placed inside. The feeder is then hung from a tree. Suet is fat mixed with a variety of things, including seeds. It is best served in winter or cooler regions where it won't go rancid, although many commercial types of suet are said to be heat resistant. Suet can be homemade (see Recipe section) or purchased relatively cheaply in small blocks. It is a great source of feed for bringing in woodpeckers, tufted titmouses, nuthatches, and chickadees.

A very successful feeder, especially in late spring and early summer, is the mealworm feeder. This type of feeder works well because baby birds need a lot of proteinous food—for example, insects. Mealworms can be purchased live or dried from commercial suppliers or pet stores. Dried mealworms can be rehydrated by placing them in warm water for about fifteen minutes. Bluebirds find them to be quite tasty. A mealworm feeder consists of a clear enclosure that holds the mealworms. They only have openings big enough for smaller birds, to keep out larger birds such as blackbirds and jays. In a pinch, any tray can be used as a mealworm feeder.

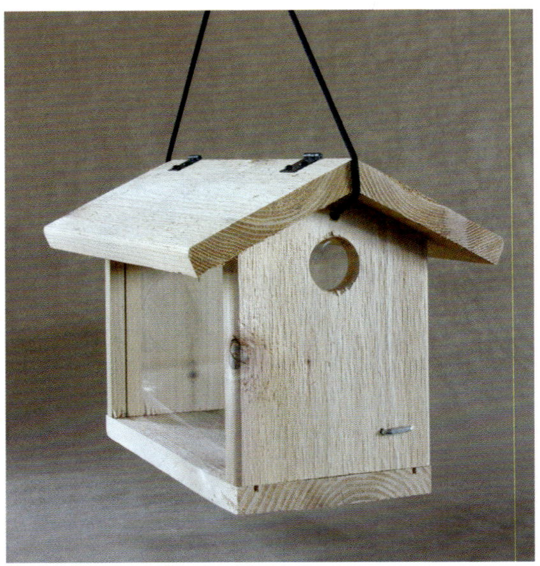

▲ *Wooden mealworm feeder*

Adding fruit and nectar feeders to your backyard can attract many fruit-eating birds that might not come to other types of feeders. Nectar feeders are available commercially and are similar to hummingbird feeders. Fruit feeders are also available, although a fruit feeder can be as simple as half an orange impaled on a nail stuck through a board, with a bowl of cut fruit beside it.

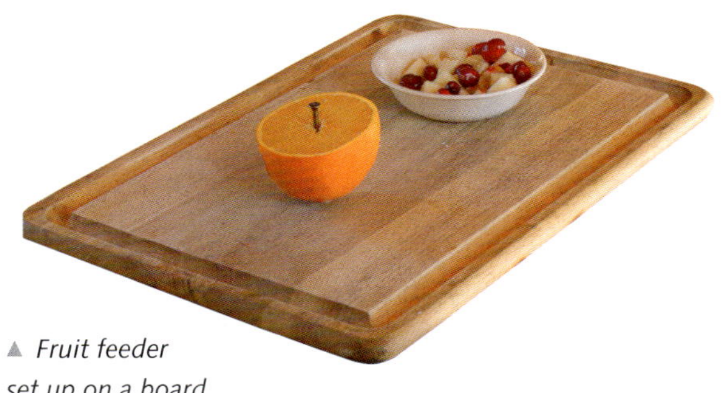

▲ *Fruit feeder set up on a board*

If you have a lot of squirrels and don't wish to feed them or photograph them, there are a variety of solutions to the squirrel problem. The first one—if you have a yard that is big enough—is to set up a diversionary feeder before you put out your primary bird feeder. Stock it with sunflower seeds, peanuts, and corn, and place it out of sight of your bird feeder. The squirrels will get used to feeding at their

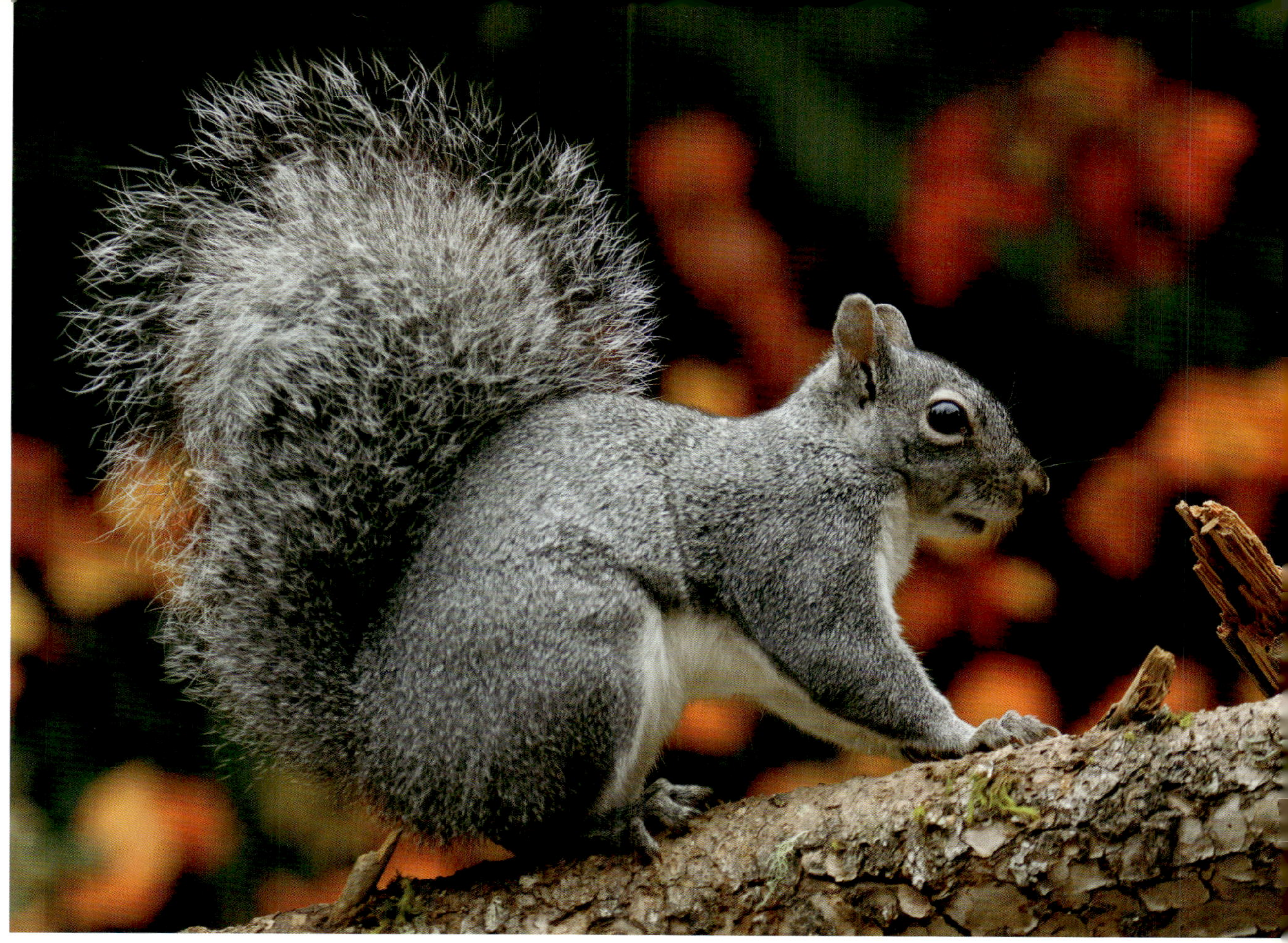

▲ *Western gray squirrel visiting feeder cups on the back side of the branch*

feeder, and will ignore your other feeder, especially if you have chased them off a few times.

A second solution is to buy squirrel-proof feeders. These come in a variety of ingenious sizes and styles designed to outsmart the squirrels. Some have cages built around them that are only big enough for small birds, thus keeping out both the jays and the squirrels. Another system uses a perch bar that will only support the weight of a bird. It will spin if too much weight is applied, throwing off the offending squirrel. Other feeders use pole baffles to prevent the squirrels from climbing them. Check the back resource section of this book for sources.

Feeder Care

All bird feeders need to be maintained on a regular basis. They should be periodically cleaned to remove old seed and shells. The type and style of the feeder will determine how often. Always remove any wet or moldy seed, since it can make birds sick or even kill them. I would suggest at least a weekly inspection at the very least.

Types of Water Sources

Providing water doesn't need to be very complicated. Just a shallow platter or bowl of water will do. One of the simplest things to use is a plant potholder that is roughly twelve inches in diameter. Just pour water in until it is a quarter to a half an inch deep and it will keep most birds happy, especially if you place it in a safe location where the birds can feel secure from predators.

Other types of water sources you can make available to the birds can be as elaborate as a backyard pond or a bird drip, which is a set-up in which water drips into a pool of water below. This can be simply done by using a water container and hanging it by its handle above a platter, and poking a small hole in the bottom of it with a small finish nail or a large pin. The flow rate can be set to a drip by tightening or loosening the cap.

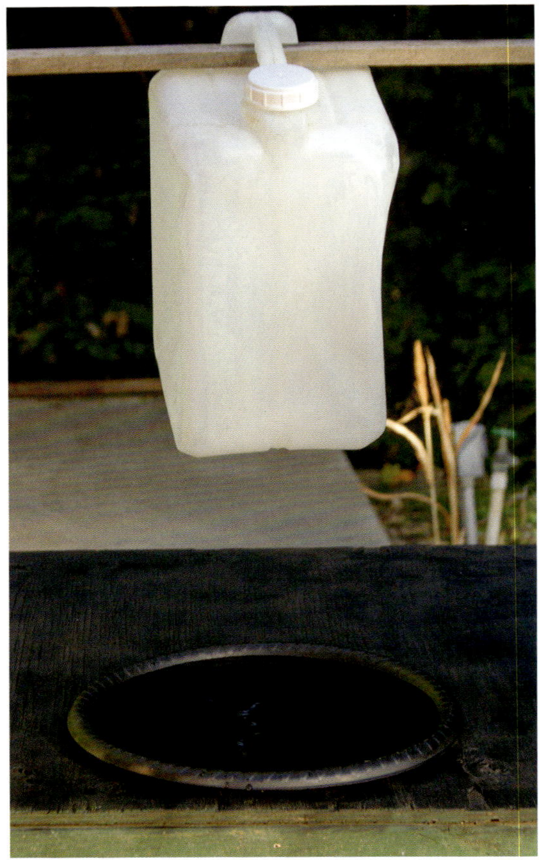

▲ *Water drip hung above a platter of water*

In winter, open, unfrozen water is a big draw for many birds. This can be accomplished by purchasing a pet water-bowl heater to keep the water from freezing over. Obviously this won't be of much use in the Virgin Islands.

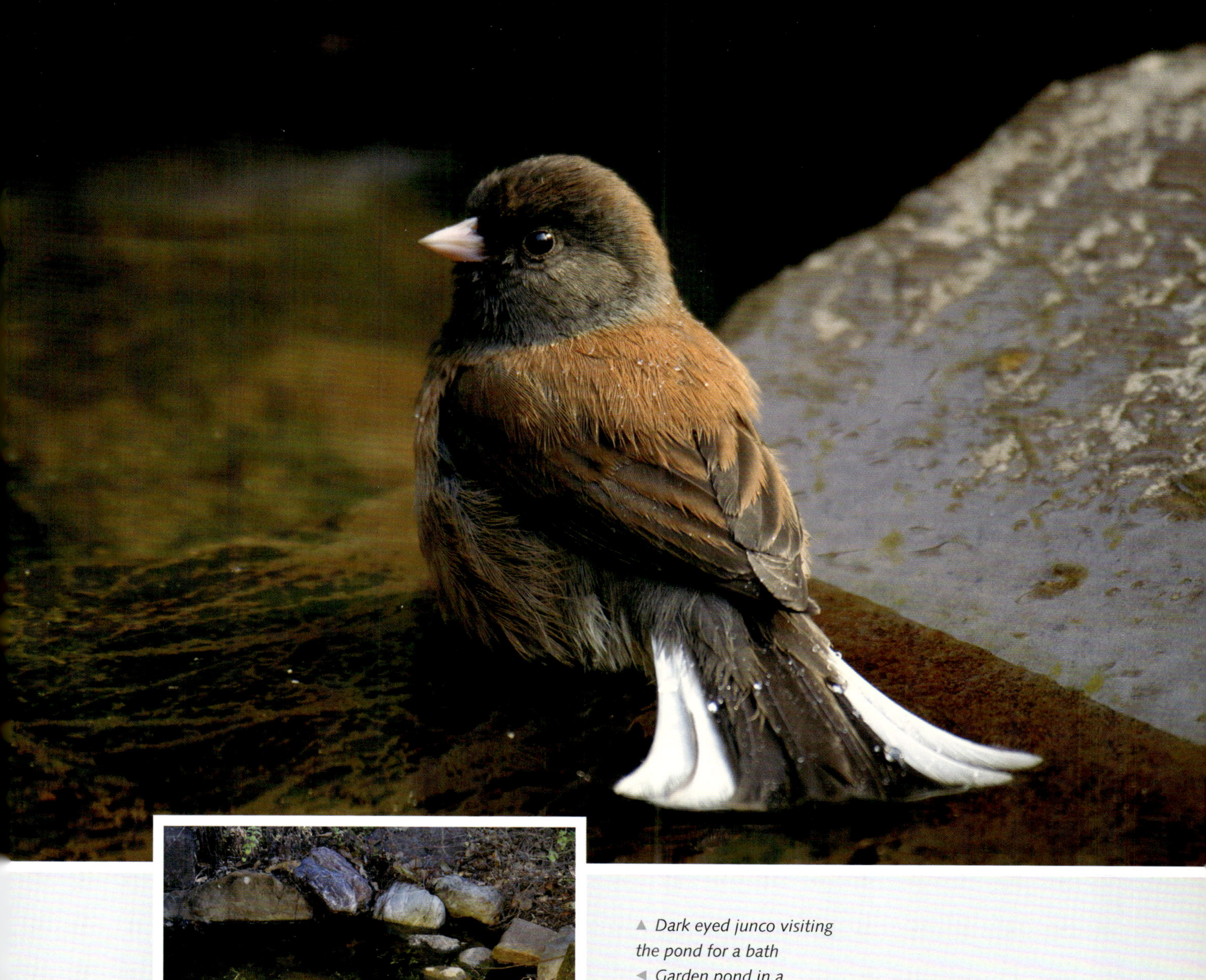

▲ *Dark eyed junco visiting the pond for a bath*
◄ *Garden pond in a backyard*

Refuge and Cover

Birds need a safe cover. You don't need to provide them with housing so much as a safe place of refuge. Birds need this in the form of bushes and trees to protect them from predators.

Just as we have our own individual comfort zones, different species of birds have theirs. Some feel vulnerable if they have to go too far out into the open to get food and water. You can cater to these species by placing your feeders and birdbaths close to sources of cover, such as the bushes and the trees in your yard. If you have a yard that is sparse in plant growth, or you live in apartment with only a balcony or small patio, you may need to buy some potted bushes or small trees in order to provide the needed cover for your birds to feel safe.

How far is too far between feeder and refuge? It varies based on the type of bird and the conditions of the environment. A general rule of thumb is to place your feeders within six feet of some type of cover. If the birds in your area are extremely habituated to people and there are few predators, you may be able to place your feeder out in the middle of the lawn, patio, or deck.

Location of Feeders

Just as realtors always espouse living in a good location, the placement of your feeders is critical to your success. We have already discussed placing your feeders close to cover, but there are a few more variables to be considered. The first and most important is light and its direction. Bird photography is best within the first three hours after sunrise and in the late afternoon.

Place your feeders with the quality and direction of light in mind. The birds should be lit up by the sun coming from behind or slightly to the side of the location you will be photographing from, so think about where you plan to locate your camera, and set the feeders based on that. Wander around in your backyard in the early morning to pick out a good location.

Usually the east is the best direction to photograph birds from in the morning, followed by the south, and then the west as a last resort—unless you are trying to create a silhouette. I prefer photographing from the south side, since it places the sun at my back and allows me to photograph from sunrise until about ten o'clock in the morning. I like the soft-colored light given by the early morning sunrise (or sunset) when photographing from the east and the west. The east is often better, since most backyard birds are more active in the morning than in the afternoon.

Another key point in feeder placement is the background behind the feeder you intend to photograph. Keep this in mind! The background can make or break a bird image. The best backgrounds are clean and fairly even in color. These can be grass, shrubbery, or hedges. Manmade backgrounds, including walls, fences, or backdrops made of canvas or other materials, can be used if they are placed far enough behind the feeder. These can be homemade or commercially purchased.

The background, whether it is a backdrop or bushes or a fence, should be a minimum of six feet behind the feeder. This helps to leave them out of focus at wider open F-stops.

Other key factors to consider are your pets, family, neighbors, and traffic. Consider where the feeders can be placed so the birds will have the least amount of disruptions from outside elements.

The height at which you place your feeders is crucial for how your bird pictures will appear. If you place the feeders too high or too low, the birds will usually look less intimate to your viewers. The best height to place feeders at is at the eye level of your camera. For example, if you are taking bird images from your bedroom windowsill, you should place your feeders at the same height as the windowsill.

The goal is to take your pictures from the same level at which the birds are feeding. This creates a more intimate feel for the viewers. You don't need a bunch of images of birds' behinds that look like they were taken from the ground looking up into a tree. It's probably not very flattering for the birds or for you.

In addition to height, you want to consider how far away the feeder should be placed from the spot you are planning to photograph from. Keep in mind that the feeder still needs to be placed close to cover so that birds feel comfortable approaching it. A typical distance from your camera to the feeder is six to ten feet, although if you are using a P&S or a 200 mm lens you may need to make that distance much shorter and be very, very quiet and still when you photograph.

A good test for distance is to go to a dollar store and buy a fake little bird about four inches tall. Set up your feeder, put the fake bird on it, and take a test picture from where you plan on photographing. If the bird doesn't cover more than a third of the frame, you will need to move the perch and your shooting location closer together. By the way, a ruler will work just as well as a fake bird if you mark it with tape at the height of the type of birds you plan on photographing.

▲ *Fake stand-in bird*

Providing a Perch

Now that you've got the feeder and food prepared, the next step is to look at the choice of perches you can use for the birds to land on when they come to visit your gourmet shooting spot.

Perches can vary in size from a small twig to a whole branch. The most important thing to consider here is the aesthetics. You will want to use a perch that is appropriate to the size of the bird. Generally speaking, the smaller the bird, the smaller the perch size can be. Picture if you will a sparrow on a tree trunk. In the image, the tree trunk would overwhelm the sparrow—unless, of course, the log is covered in delicate moss or lichen. However, if you were to create an image of a sparrow on a tiny branch, the perch would appear to be more balanced with the size of the sparrow.

Where do you get perches? The best and easiest place is your own backyard. Take a pair of rose clippers and snip off a small cutting from the backside of one of your plants. Ask neighbors for clippings when they are trimming their roses or bushes. After storms, look for branches on the side of the street that were blown off by the wind. Don't overlook buying what you need. For that special look, go to the local nursery and buy a beautiful flower to stick next to your feeder.

Choose a perch that is pleasing to the eye. Interesting weeds or cuttings from bushes and trees of your yard that are budding, in bloom, or yielding berries will look fantastic. Look for small branches that are covered in moss or have an interesting wood grain pattern to them. Be sure to choose a perch that can be easily attached to the feeder, or that can be placed close enough to the bird feeder that the birds will land on it.

In addition to using plants and cuttings from your yard as perches, consider the use of interesting sections of small logs, old mossy stumps, or volcanic rocks placed on a platform feeder. Quail and other ground perching birds can look fantastic on perches like these.

▶ *Some methods of attaching perches to feeders: Top l-r: wired, clamped, and screwed on. Bottom l-r: drilled, placed in feeder hole, and bread wire tied.*

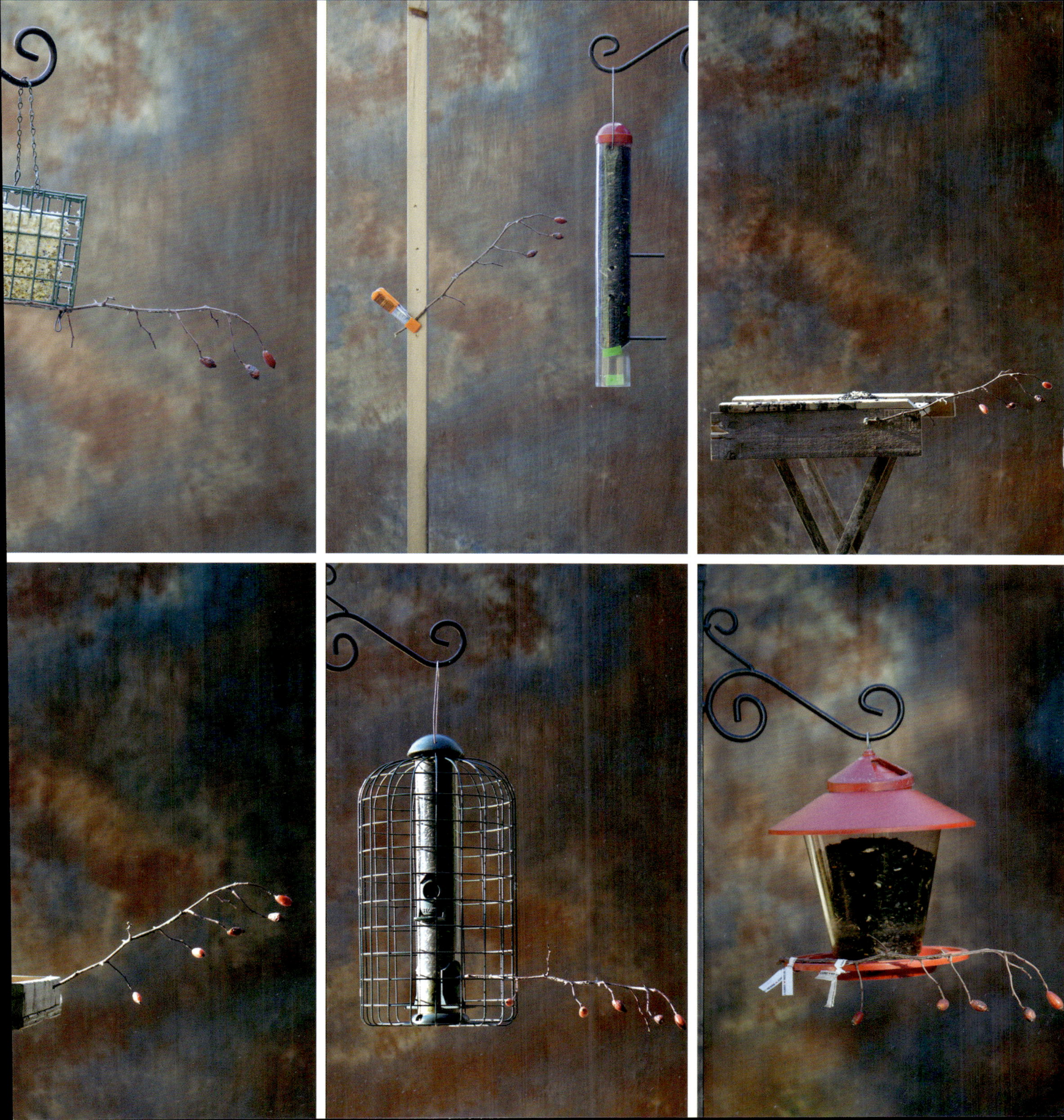

Whatever perches you use, be sure to change them often so that your images don't become repetitious to your viewers. I like to change my perches after every session to something new so my images don't look like they were taken in the same location each time.

How do you attach perches to your feeders? A lot depends upon which style of feeder you decide to use. The goal here is to get the bird to land upon the perch before feeding. This means that it needs to be placed in a position that is just slightly above or off to the side of the feeder. Perches can be attached to feeders in a wide variety of ways. They can be tied onto the feeder with string, wire, bailing wire, or ties for bread bags. My favorite tools for attaching perches are a cordless drill and wood screws. Other possibilities are to use duct tape, wood clamps, spring clamps, or even strips of Velcro. A hammer and nails will work as well, although I recommend the use of duplex nails so they can be pulled out more easily when you decide you want to change or reposition perches.

Placement of Perches

Placement of perches is critical in terms of light and other factors. It is very important that you place the perch in a location that is evenly front-lit with no shadows being cast upon it. The perch should be placed within six feet or less of cover so that birds will feel comfortable using it. Height-wise, the perch should be placed above the feeder so that birds will alight on it before they drop down to the feeder. Usually a distance of six inches to a foot will work. Larger birds and smaller birds will use different distances depending upon their comfort level. A lot of experimentation will be needed to find out what height will work best. Don't forget you want the feeder to be at the eye level of your camera, so raising or lowering the feeder may be required.

How many perches should you use? It's best to start with one, and typically try not to use more than three. The primary reason for this is that you want to prevent the birds from landing on perches out of your frame. If you provide too many perches, birds will land where you aren't focused. Start out by limiting yourself and the birds to one perch at your feeder. This will help you practice focusing and composing images in one location without the added complexity of having to move your camera.

If you decide to use more than one perch, I would limit it to three. Beware of "Perch Envy." You know the old adage, "the grass is greener on the other side of the fence"? This can apply to situations in which you are using more than one perch. When you are focused and composed on one perch, stick with it. Avoid chasing the birds from perch to perch with your lens. Stick with your original vision. Perch envy may get you to start looking from perch to perch with your camera and lens, trying to capture all the birds as they land. This can be distracting to both you and the birds; the movement may make them nervous, and they might fly away.

After I have created at least one great image on a perch, I will focus my attention on another perch, or reset the perch if it isn't working and try to figure out why birds aren't using it.

When using more than one perch, it's important to try and set each perch at roughly the same distance from the location you are photographing from. This will limit the time you spend refocusing and recomposing when you change your focus to a different perch. If you decide to switch to a different view, very, very carefully and slowly move your lens to focus on another perch.

With a little bit of creativity, you can nudge the birds into using the perches you want them to use. Some commercial feeders give you the option to block off one or more of the various feeding ports. If you are using a feeder like this, you can direct the birds to your perch by temporarily blocking off all feeder ports other than the one closest to your perch. Use electrical tape or masking tape that can be easily removed later. If you are using more than one feeder, you can take down or cover up the feeders you do not plan to photograph in order to push more birds to the feeder you are using. When using platform feeders, you can cover part of the platform with cardboard to limit the birds to the side of the feeder where your perch is attached.

At what direction do perches need to be placed in relation to your camera? Perches should usually be placed so that they are parallel to the front of the lens element and ninety degrees to the feeder opening. In other words, they should be placed like a crossing gate at a railroad crossing. The purpose of this is that the whole perch will be in focus and you can photograph the front or back of the bird when they land. This makes for a very pleasing image.

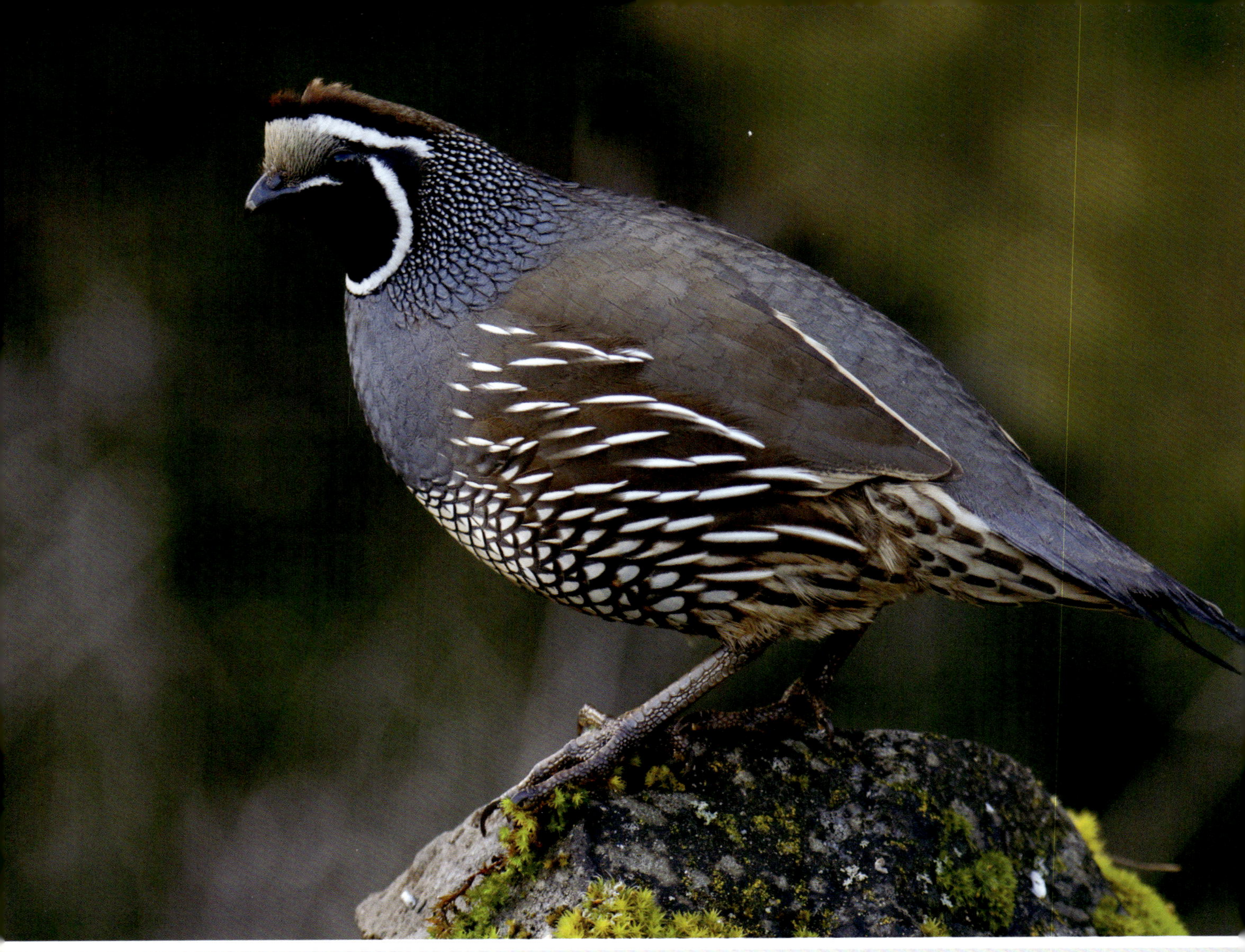

▲ *Quail on a mossy rock placed next to a bowl of food on a TV tray*

CHAPTER 3 A Few Tricks of the Trade

I often use temporary mini-feeders on the back side of medium and large perches. I fill a plastic salsa container or the cut-off bottom of a soda bottle, and use some wood screws to drill it onto the back side of a branch where it can't be seen in the image of the bird. It's important to check your set-ups through your camera before attempting any photography. From experience, there has been too many times where I have looked through the lens to spy the corner of a feeder cup sticking up into the image.

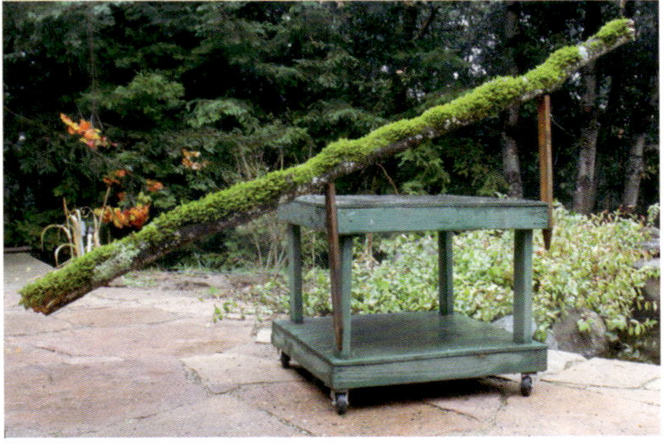

▲ *Mossy branch with feeder cups*

▼ *Steller's jay on mossy branch*

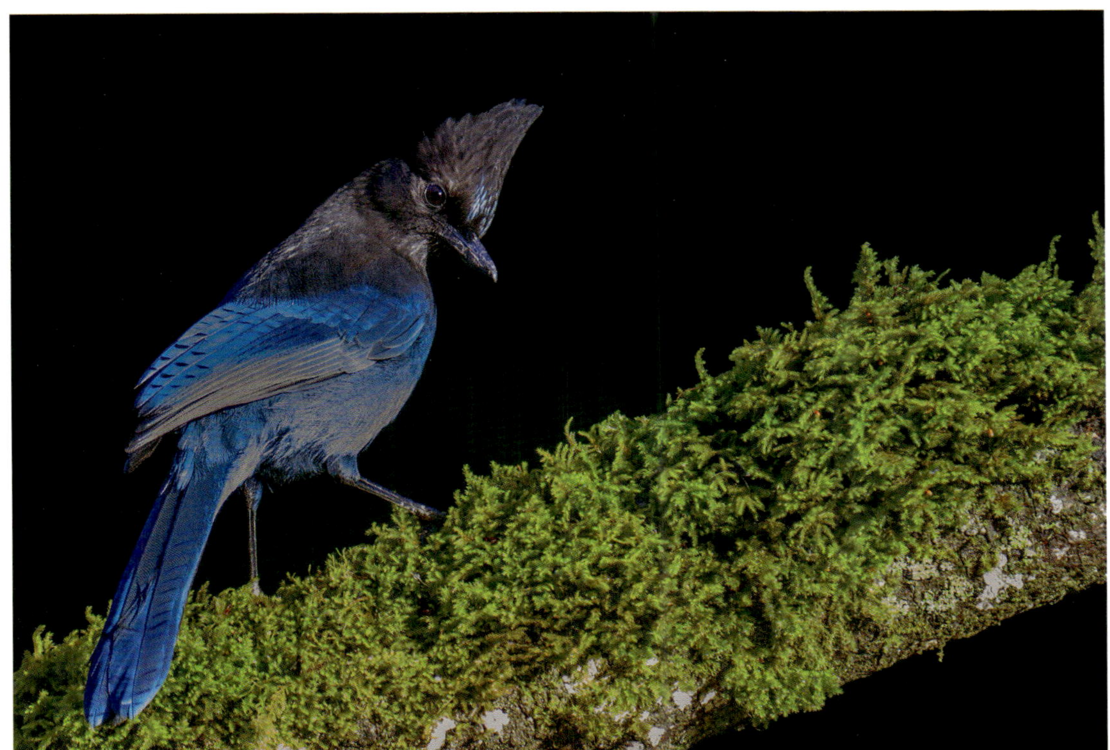

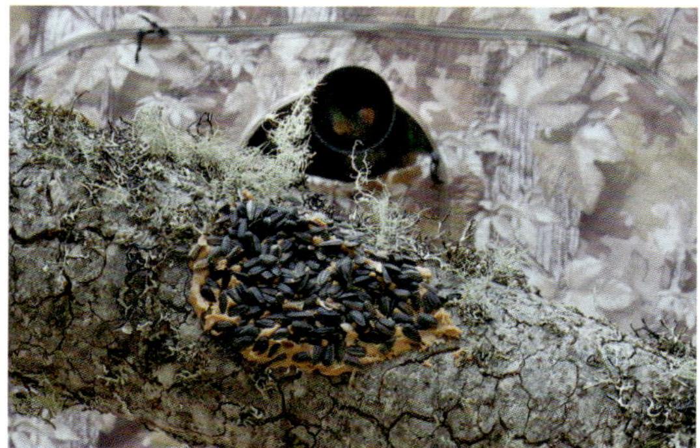

▲ *Peanut butter with sunflower seed smeared on the back of a log*

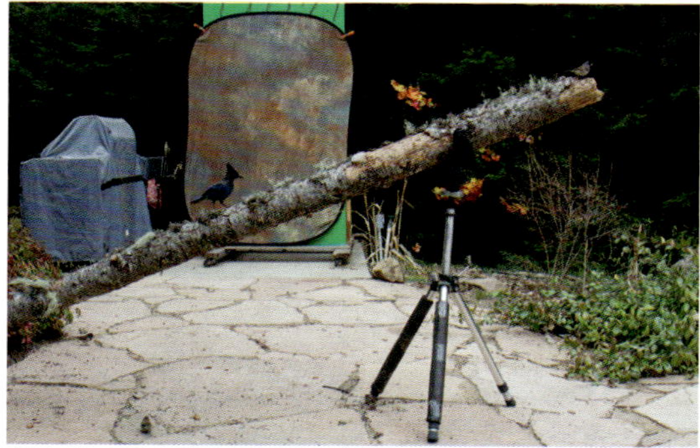

▲ *View of set-up from the photo blind*

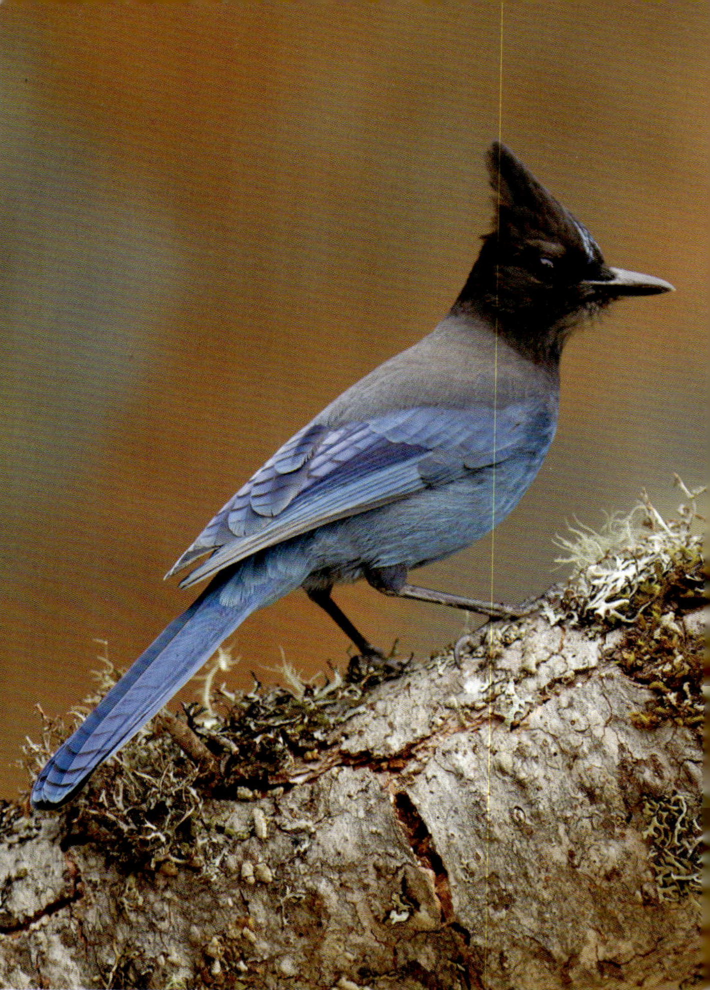

▲ *Final image of a Steller's jay*

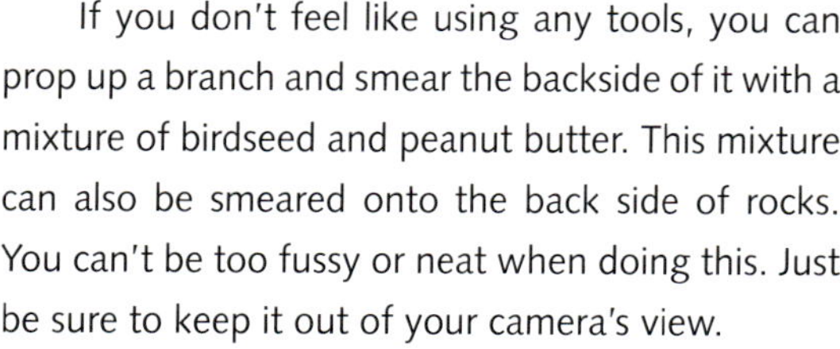

If you don't feel like using any tools, you can prop up a branch and smear the backside of it with a mixture of birdseed and peanut butter. This mixture can also be smeared onto the back side of rocks. You can't be too fussy or neat when doing this. Just be sure to keep it out of your camera's view.

When using tube feeders, it is quite easy to just insert a small branch into one of the feeder holes and let the weight of the seed hold the perch in place. This works with really small perches like twigs or very small branches. It is the perfect set-up for very small birds like nuthatches and finches, since they prefer these types of feeders.

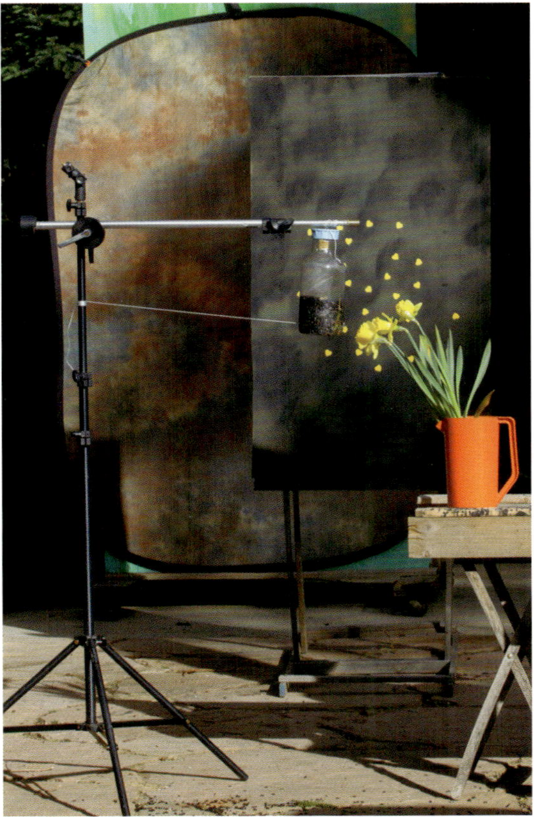
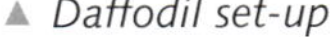

▲ *Daffodil set-up*

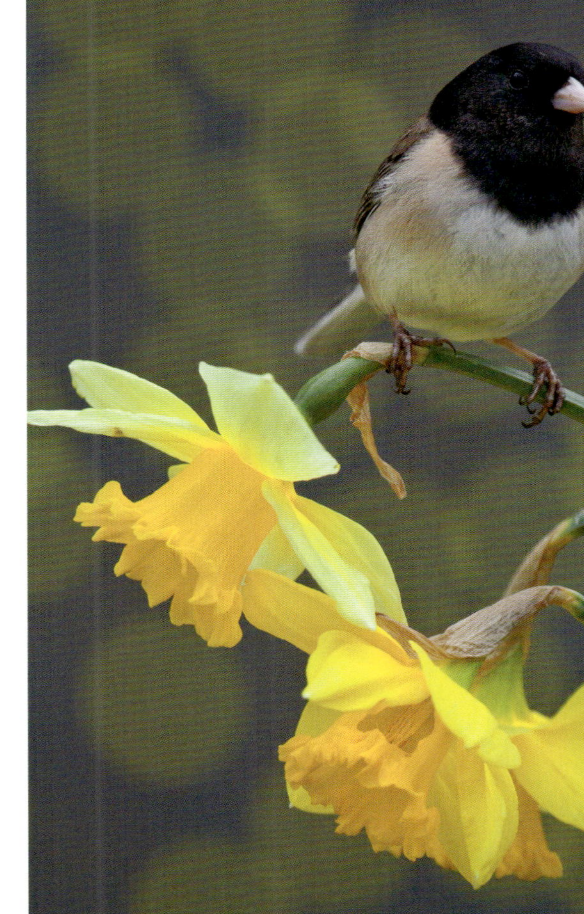

▲ *Resulting image of a junco on daffodils*

By using flowers, such as daffodils or zinnias, as perches, you can add a beautiful splash of color to your bird photos. Just stick them into a block of floral foam or lean them out of a vase weighted to keep it from toppling over. One of the really neat tricks I use is to insert a stiff wire into the stalk of the flower to give it more rigidity when a bird lands on it.

There is an incredible variety of perch set-ups that can be used to attract birds, including rocks, sections of logs, branches and twigs, and flowers. One great idea for a perch-and-feeder set-up is to

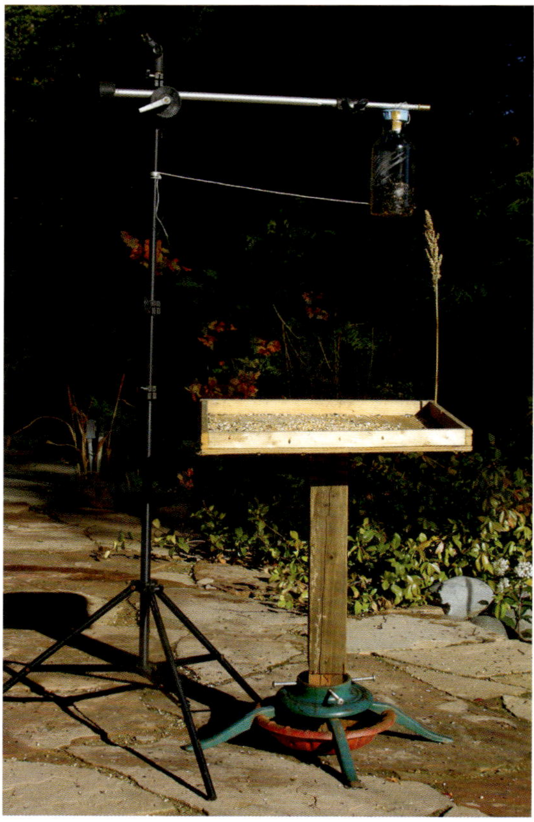

▲ *Platform feeder on a Christmas tree stand*

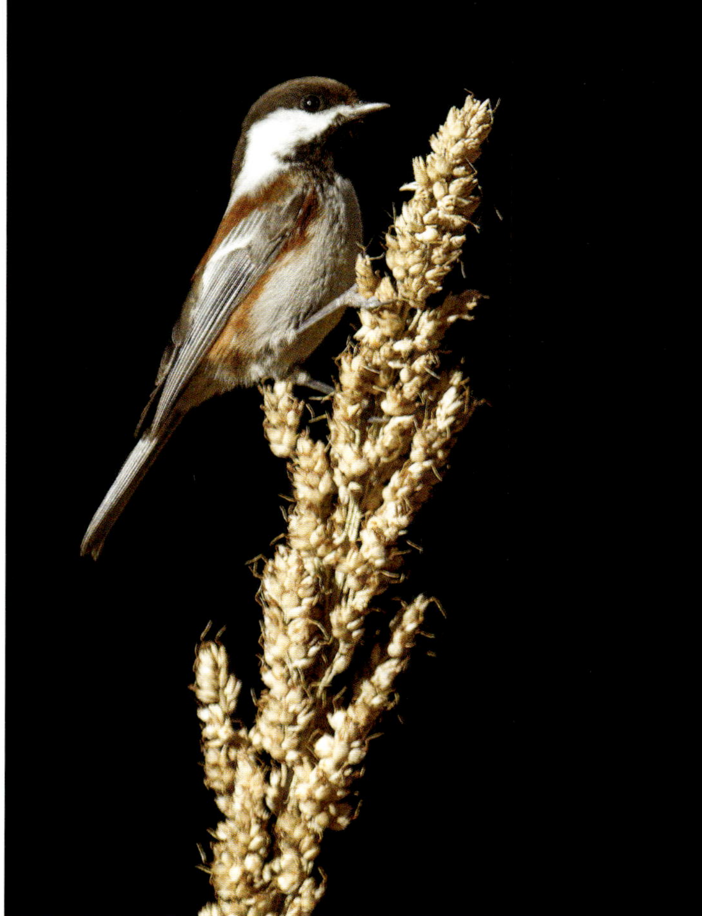

▲ *Chestnut backed chickadee on a Sorghum stem drilled into the feeder*

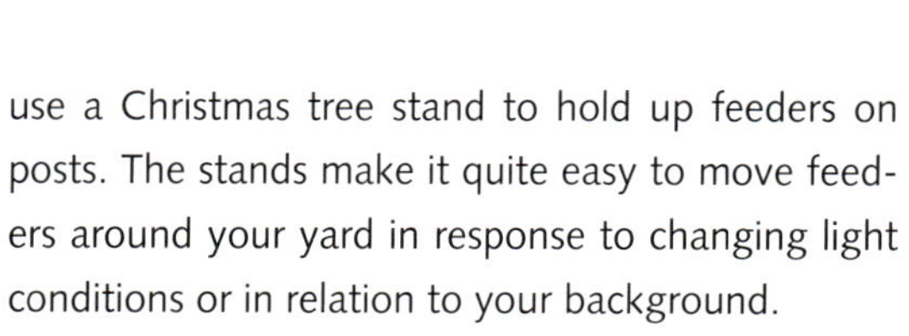

use a Christmas tree stand to hold up feeders on posts. The stands make it quite easy to move feeders around your yard in response to changing light conditions or in relation to your background.

Flowering branches are an incredible and beautiful source for perches. Early springtime, when trees are just coming into bloom, can be the perfect time to cut some branches to use for perches. Tape or wire one perch to a pole, just barely in reach of a tube feeder. One or two inches away is just about right for smaller birds. Cut several more branches to be placed six to eight feet behind the feeder to provide color and an out-of-focus background at a wide open F-stop of F-5.6 or larger. Check the

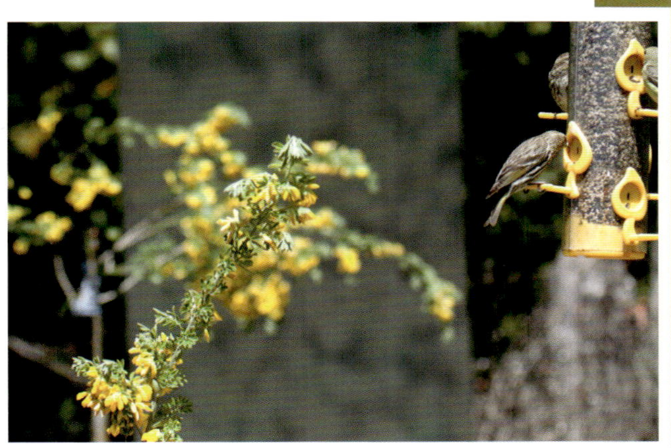

▲ *Flowering branch next to tube feeder*

set-up with your camera to make sure no poles (or the feeder) are in the image. Some adjustment of the branch by the feeder may be needed once birds start using it.

Plastic feeder cups work great as a short-term feeder. They do, however, have a couple of problems. One is that they are easily dislodged or broken by bigger birds and squirrels. The other is that

► *Resulting image of a pine siskin coming to feed*

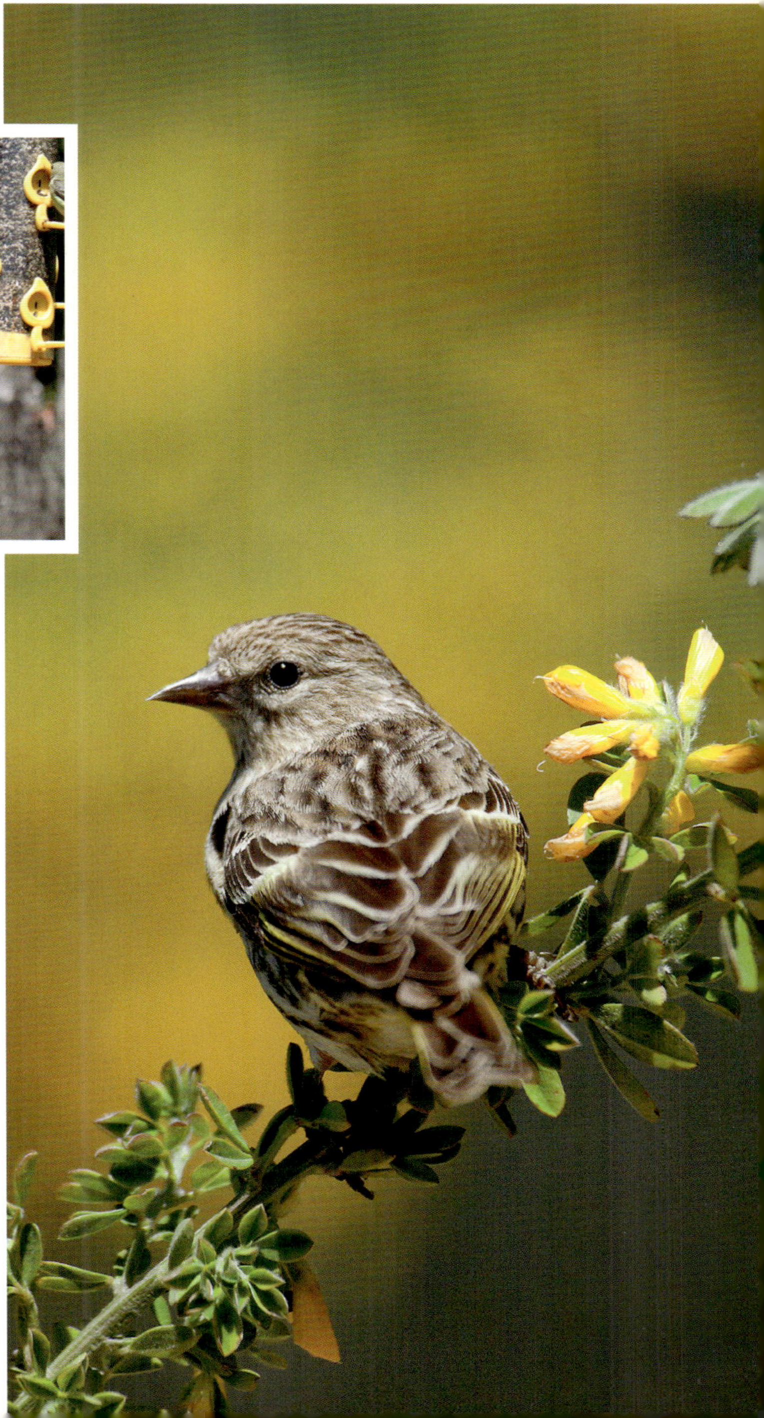

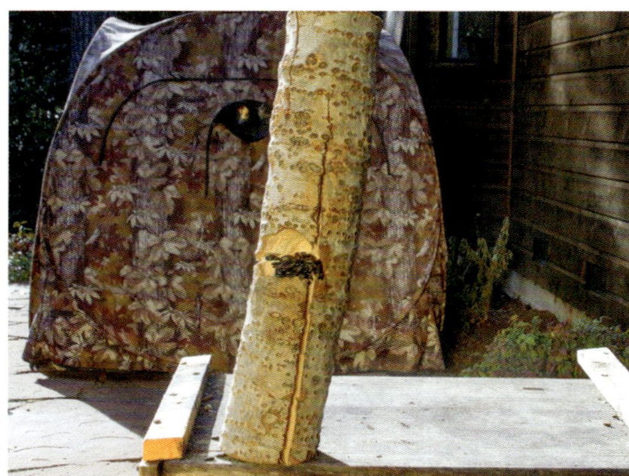

▲ *Hole (drilled with a spade bit) with seed, in the side of a section of branch*

they can't be placed on the sides of vertical perches because they will be visible to the camera and appear in the image. For larger perches, the solution to this problem is to use a spade bit on your drill to drill a hole into the side or back of the perch. Then fill the hole full of seed.

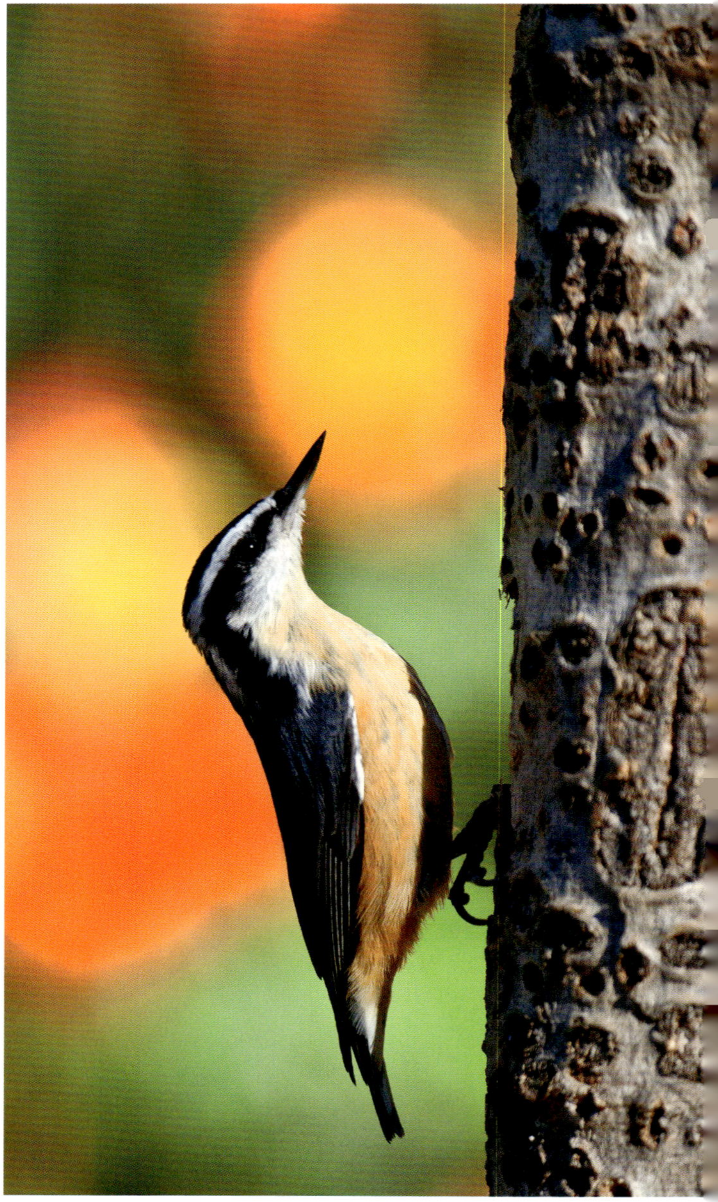

► *Red-breasted nuthatch coming for some seed*

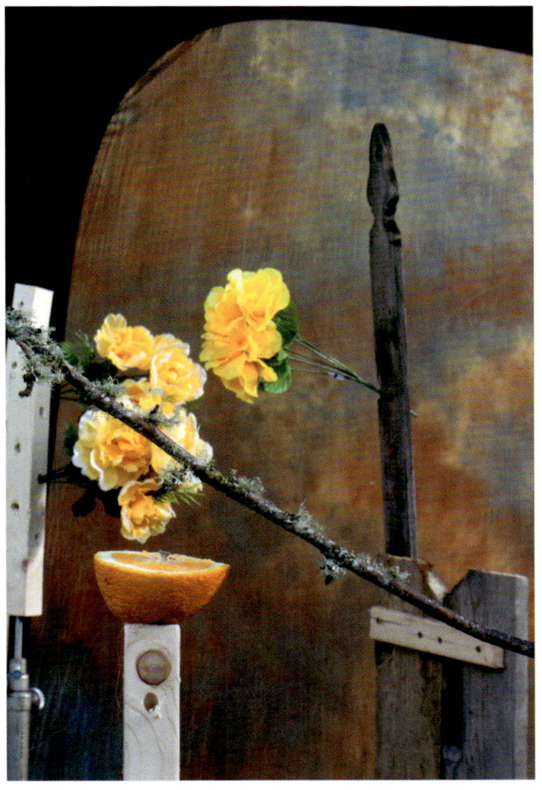

▲ *Perch set above an orange half on a pole with bouquets of fake flowers behind.*

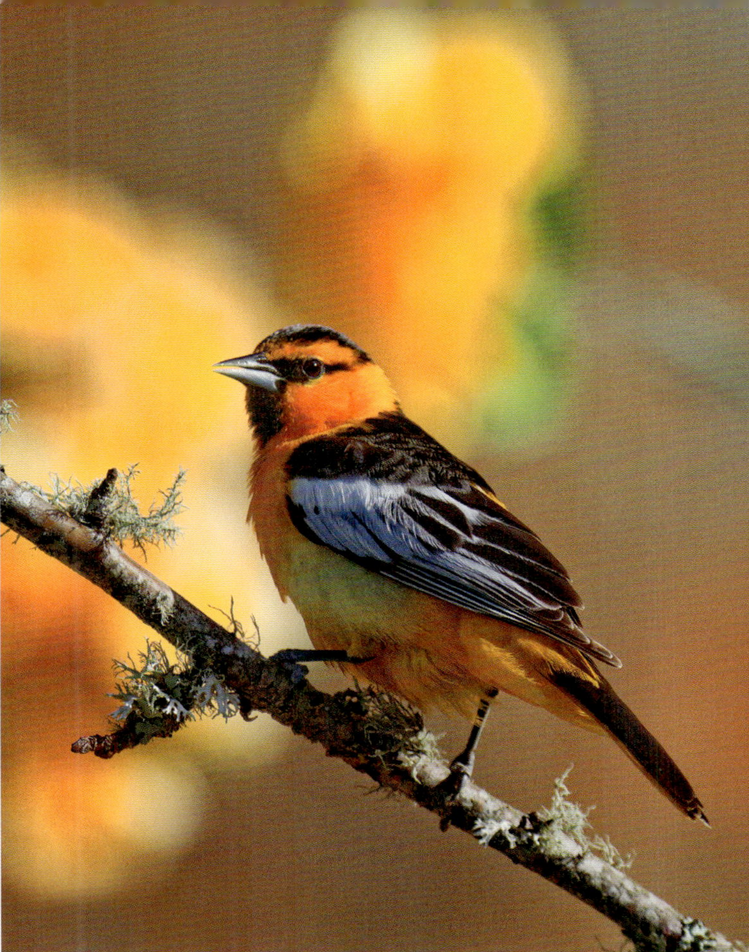

▲ *Bullock's oriole coming for some orange*

Sometimes a simple perch can be enhanced with the placement of bunches of brightly colored fake flowers. Yes, fake flowers! Silk flowers, when placed out of focus behind the perch, can really set an image apart—especially if you use flowers with the same or complementary colors to the plumage of your subject.

Here is a set-up composed entirely of artificial flowers. Keep in mind that if you are using artificial materials for your perches, you may be able to tell—especially when the photos are zoomed in, or when the print in enlarged. To avoid this, replace your artificial perches with natural ones for those really tight shots.

Top View of Perch Set-up

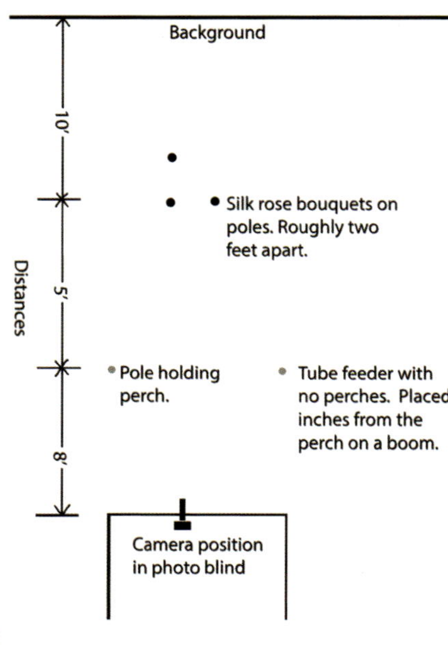

Front View

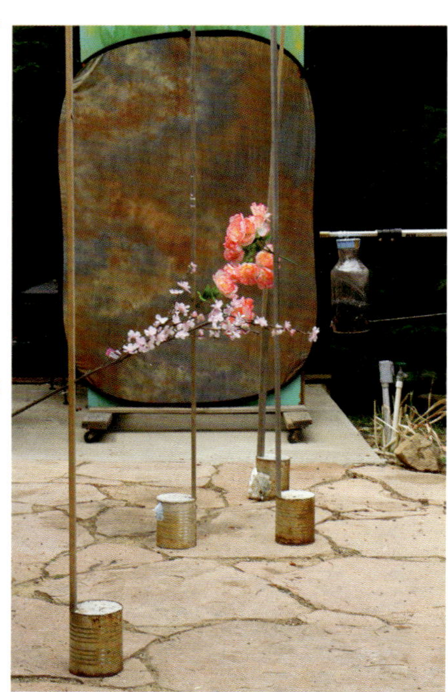

Sample Image From Set-up

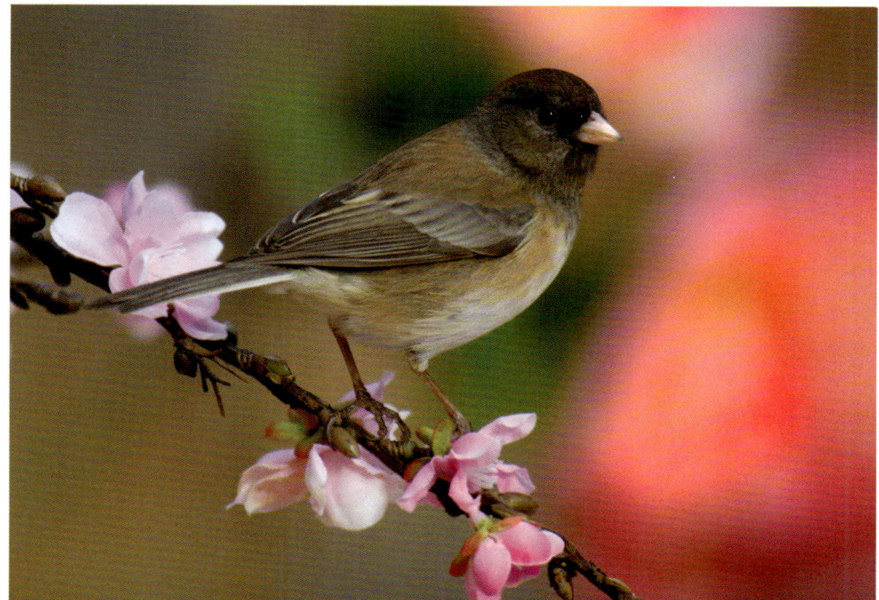

◄ *Dark eyed junco coming for seed at an artificial set-up*

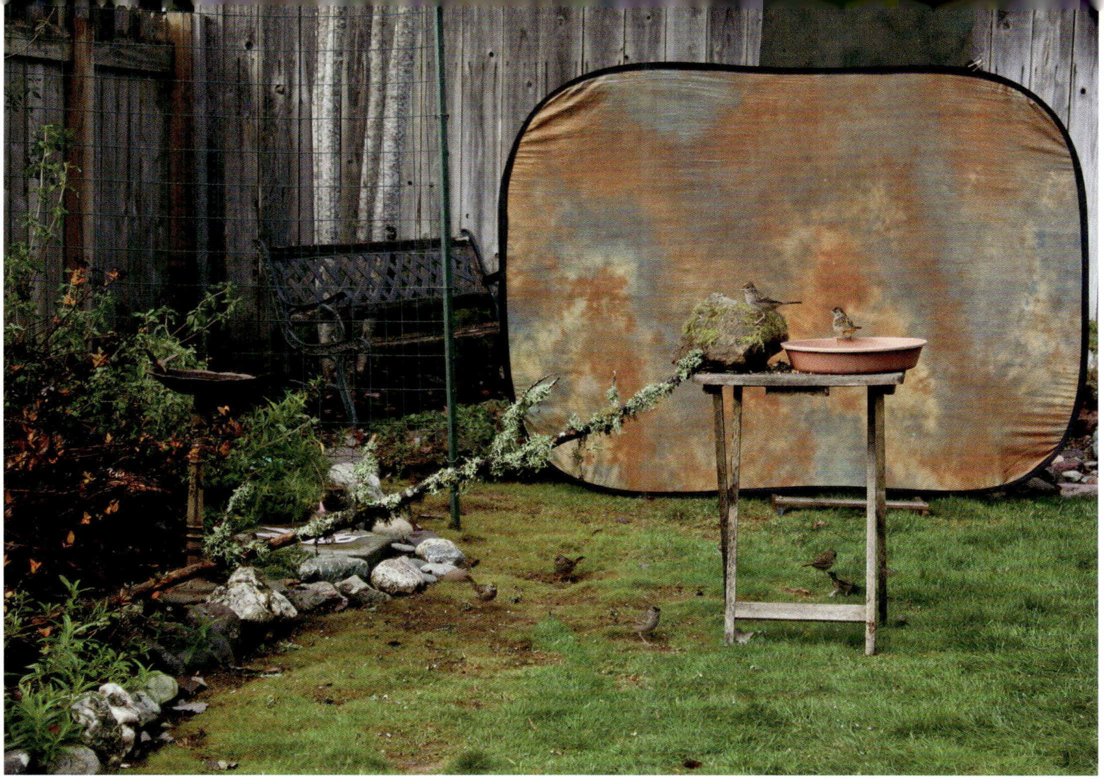

▲ *Branch used for ramping up to the rock next to the feeder*

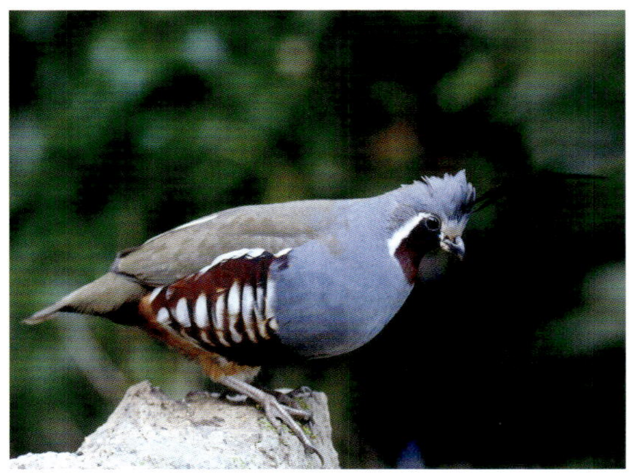

▲ *Mountain quail coming for some seed*

Ramping Up and Laddering Down

Certain ground birds, such as quail, pigeons, and doves, prefer to use ground-level feeders. They will sometimes use platform feeders, but it is not their favorite. So how do you get them onto a perch? One really effective technique for luring hard-to-photograph birds onto a perch is called ramping up. This process involves creating a ramp of rocks, boards, and branches to entice the birds to walk up to a platform feeder. Place attractive perches along the way for birds to stop on as they make their way toward the feeder.

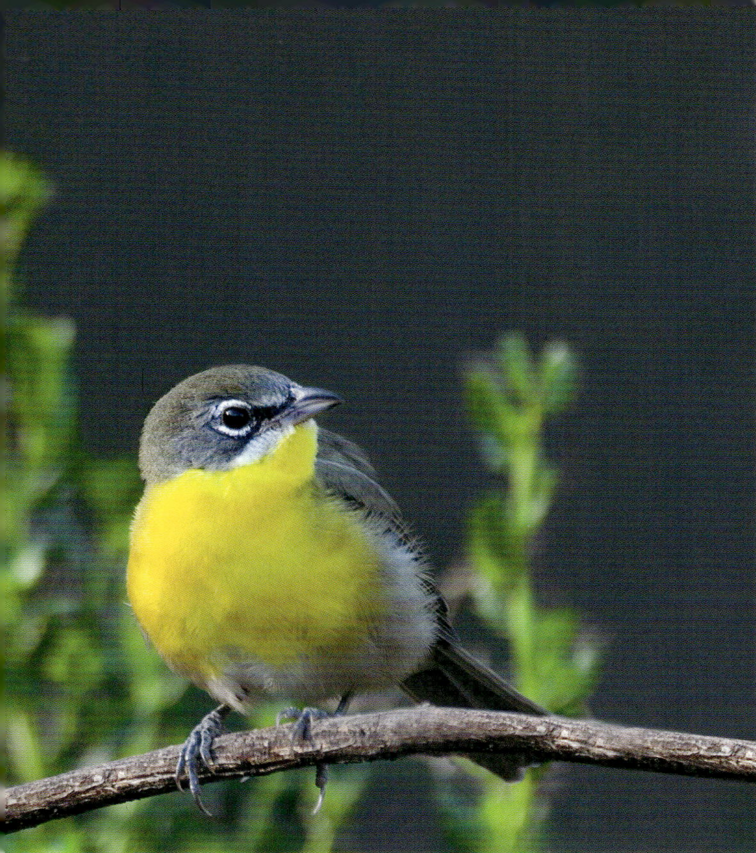

▲ *Warbler on perch coming for water*

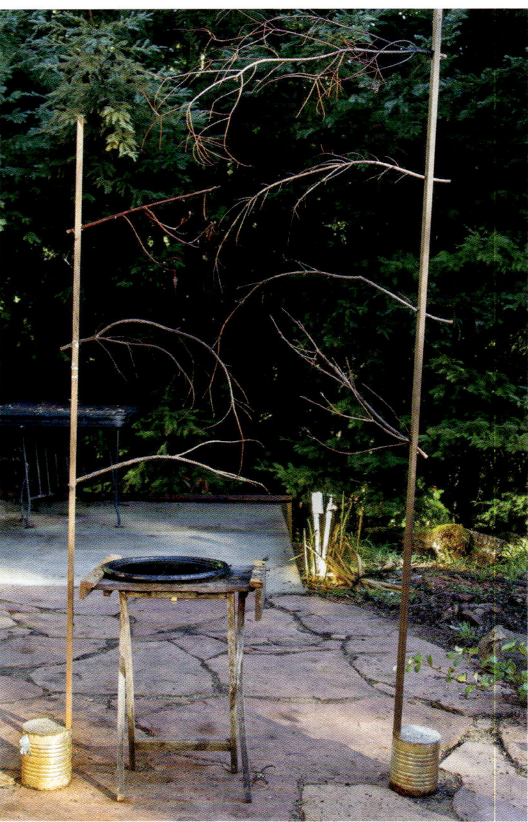

▲ *Laddering perches coming down to water*

Laddering Down

Many birds, such as warblers, don't often come to bird feeders. They will, however, come in for water. Laddering down is the technique used here. Provide plenty of perches starting about six feet up, and place them alternating, going back and forth about a foot apart, down to a water source. When birds are laddering down they will often pause on the last perch just above the water. The last perch should be placed about three inches above the level of the water.

Backgrounds

Another concern of note is backgrounds. I can't emphasize the importance of backgrounds enough. Make sure the area behind the feeder is evenly colored and free from bright spots. The perch should be six feet or farther from the background. This will help you create a nice backdrop for your bird images.

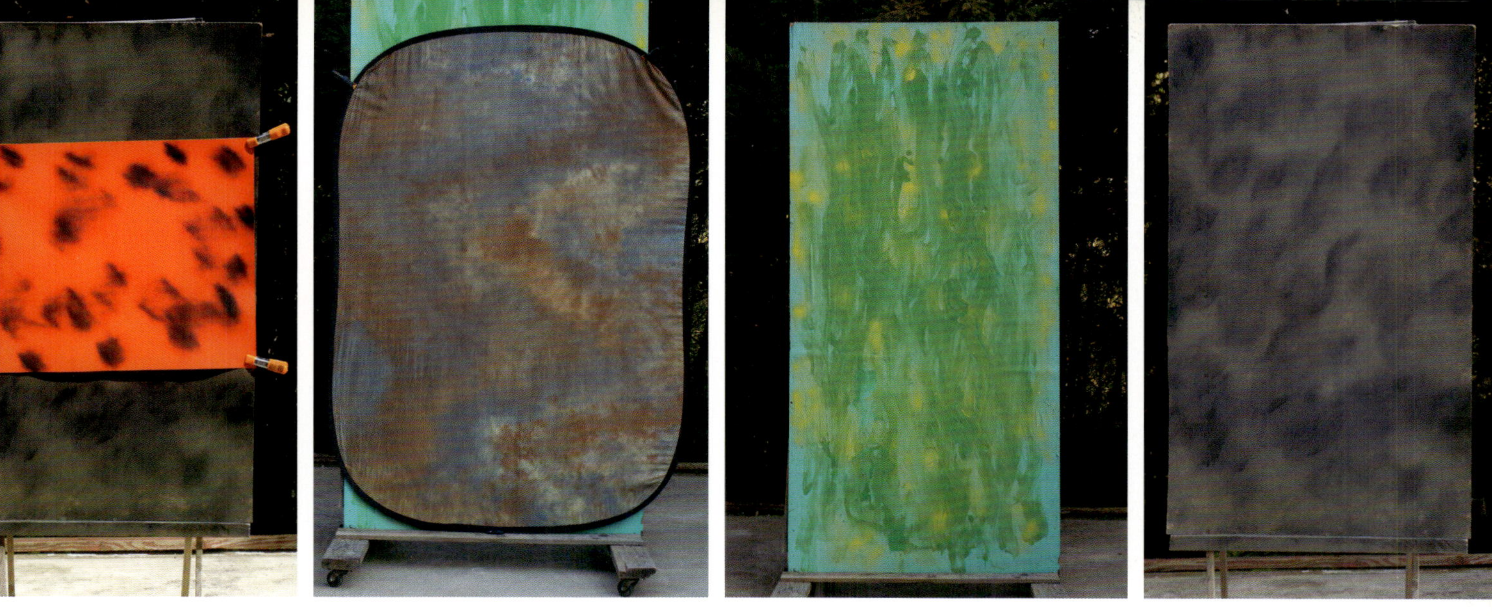

▲ *Backdrops l-r: posterboard, commercial pop-up, painted plywood, and painted hardboard*

The Use of Artificial Backgrounds

What if you don't have a nice even backdrop or you want to create an image with a colored background different from what is already there? The answer is as close as your nearest office supply or art store. There is a bountiful supply of tag board and presentation boards in a wide range of colors. Just be sure to choose ones that have a matte surface so they won't be too reflective and create bright spots in your images.

It is also better to stick to a color palette that is earth toned unless you are trying to create some special image that is bright and unnatural.

One other handy choice for artificial backgrounds is to use pop-up studio backgrounds. These have become a favorite choice of mine because they are easy to store and come in a range of earthy colors. They fold down into an easy-to-store flat case and they can be assembled with a pop just by taking them out of their case. A cautionary note here is to unfold these backgrounds carefully; the pop can come with some force that can be quite painful. They are typically available in two sizes: 5 × 6 feet or 6 × 7 feet. These are the best artificial backgrounds I have ever used for bird photography. The only disadvantage that I have experienced with them is that they can be difficult to use in the wind.

The other possibility is to paint your own backdrop on watercolor paper. You can create a washed look and add blotches of color to resemble out-of-focus flowers.

Yet another possibility is to use photographic posters or prints, including your own images. Just print your own interesting 16″ × 20″ print with a matte finish. A background like this is placed

2–3 feet back from your perch. Other possibilities include putting up fabric screens or other material on frames. Regardless of what you use, just make sure the material is large enough to cover the background behind your perch. Usually 16″ × 20″ is large enough.

When using artificial backgrounds, be aware of shadows and bright spots being cast upon your backdrop. I sometimes solve these problems by attaching a piece of cardboard above or to the side of the backdrop to keep it in permanent shade while I am photographing. Also remember that it is usually best to use the widest F-stop your lens has in order to keep the background out of focus—unless it is your intent to have the background in focus. I tend to prefer the softer, out-of-focus backgrounds that place the viewer's attention on the main subject: the bird.

The Use of Reflectors

Often times you will want to photograph in an area that is lacking in light. Whether it is too dark to photograph or it just needs a little bit more light to makes things pop or stand out, using reflectors can help. Sometimes I place a reflector under the perch to bounce more light onto the breast of the bird so it doesn't fall into shadow when I'm photographing it. There are commercially available reflectors

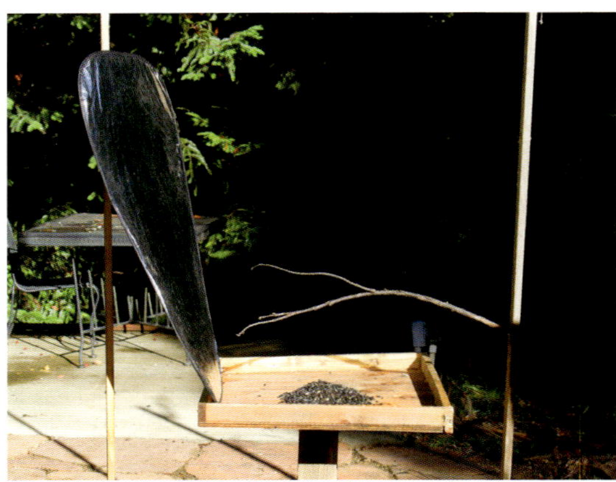

▲ *Car windshield shade used as a reflector to bounce light onto the perch*

in gold, silver, and white. The larger and closer a reflector is, the more even the light it will cast. You can also make your own reflector by using a piece of white cardboard or covering a piece of cardboard with crumpled aluminum foil. I find mirrors to be too direct for my taste. Another possibility is to use a sunshade for a car's windshield, like in the case shown above.

Using Interesting Items to Enhance the Scene

Don't overlook the possibility of using interesting items from your home or backyard. Many manmade objects, such as shovel handles, garden utensils, and old antiques can be used for perches as well. Natural materials also work very well. Fungi, for example, can be impaled upon a needle or a sharpened finish nail that has been driven into the wood.

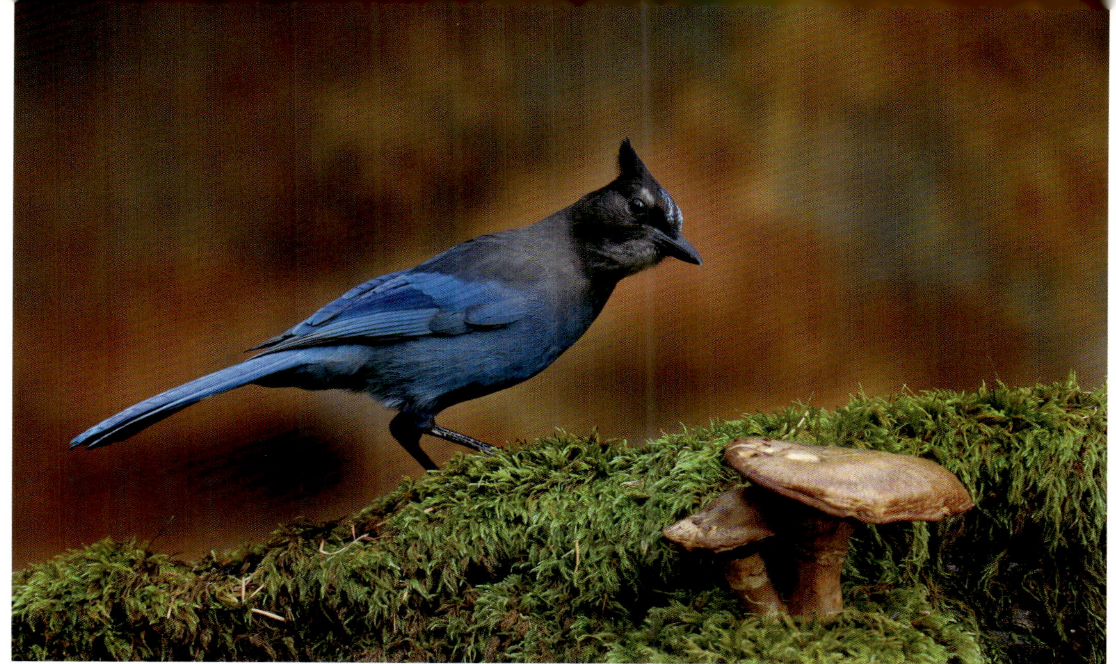

▲ *Steller's jay looking for seed by a mushroom impaled on a sewing needle*

Inclement Weather

Rain, snow, and cloudy weather can be used to produce some beautiful images. When other feed sources start being covered with snow, birds are drawn to backyard bird feeders like a magnet. Foggy or cloudy weather helps produce a very even, soft light that can be quite appealing on the plumage of birds. Rain is a bit harder to photograph in, but with the proper precautions, such as wrapping up your camera with a camera raincoat and using a permanent blind, you can produce some very appealing bird images. Keeping your camera warm and dry is the key to success. Either photograph from inside your home or, if you are in an outside photo blind, be sure to dress for the conditions.

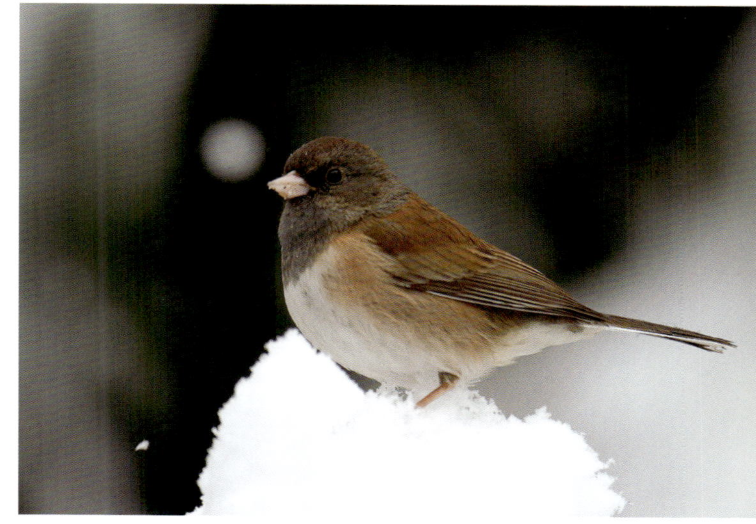

▲ *Dark eyed junco on a perch in the snow*

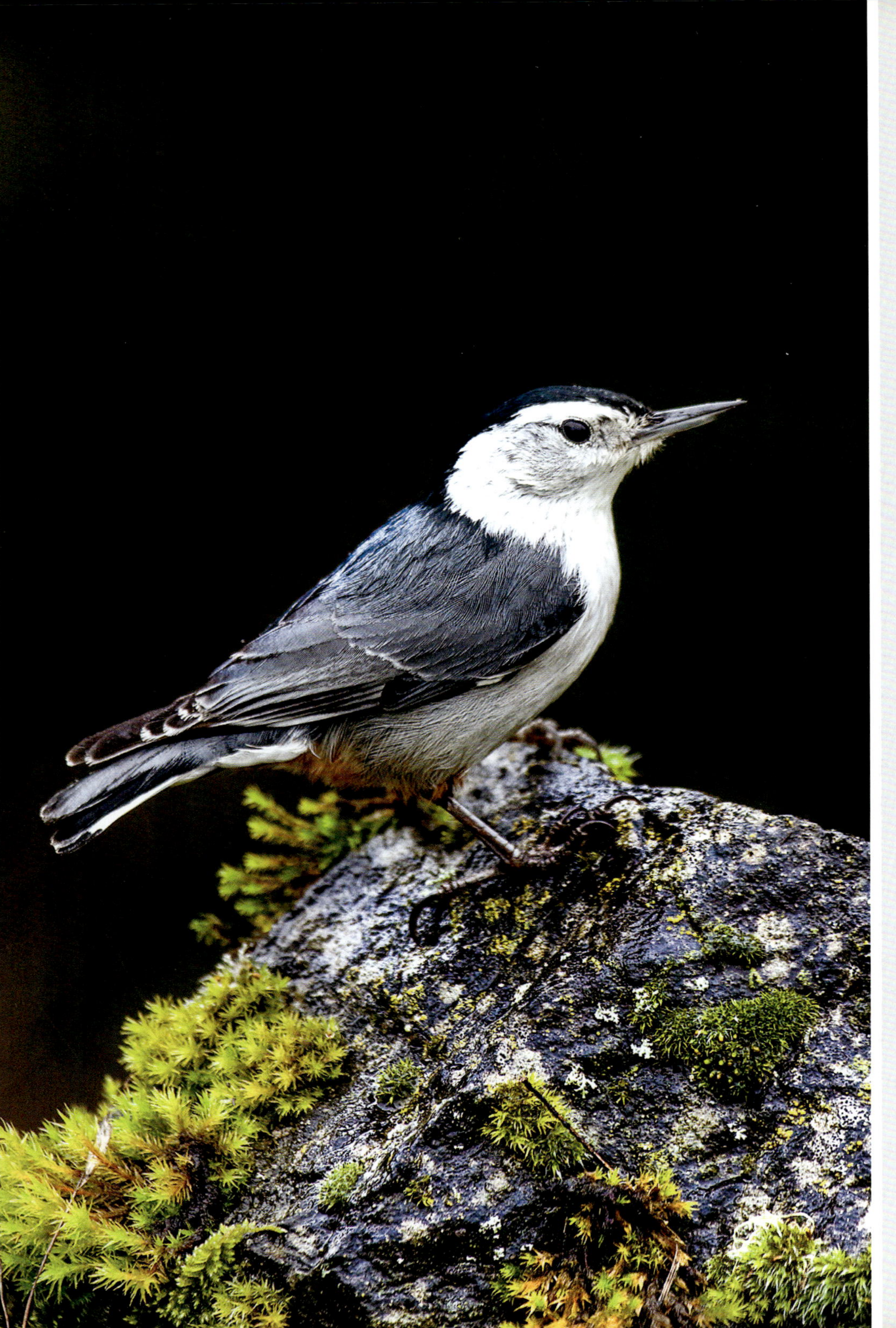

◄ *White-breasted nuthatch coming to a rock placed on a platform feeder*

CHAPTER 4 The Use of Blinds

A "blind" (as it pertains to photography) is a concealment device used to camouflage the photographer from the subject of the photograph. When photographing birds, you can either sit in plain view of the birds, or use a blind to remain hidden from them. Personally I prefer to use a blind whenever possible. It typically allows for a closeness that is difficult to get with many species of birds that are wary of humans. Working from a blind can be comfortable; it allows you to move, have a drink or a snack, or reposition yourself as needed without startling the birds you are trying to photograph.

A blind is anything that can be used to block the birds' view of you, but still have some sort of opening for the camera—the purpose is to have a clear view of the birds without the birds having a clear view of you. Simple blinds can be made by using objects at hand, such as the latticework of a deck or a wooden fence. Cut a small viewing hole to look and photograph through. Other good examples of simple blinds are a sheet hung over a piece of rope, or a large cardboard box from a new appliance like a washer or dryer.

One of the best blinds of all is often equipped with heating and air conditioning, a phone, TV, computer, and a bathroom. You guessed it—the inside of your house. Just set a comfortable chair near an open window from which to photograph. Cover the window with an old sheet or some leftover wrapping paper. Set up your camera and cut a small opening in your blind for a viewing port at the height of your camera. Now you're in business!

The advantage of using your home as a blind is that you can take short breaks to accomplish other tasks around the house. Just be sure to use earphones or shut the window so as to not scare the birds. The main disadvantage is that you may miss the crucial moment to photograph that special bird you've been waiting for.

More permanent or semi-permanent window blinds can be made from thin plywood or heavy cardboard. The edges can be wrapped and taped

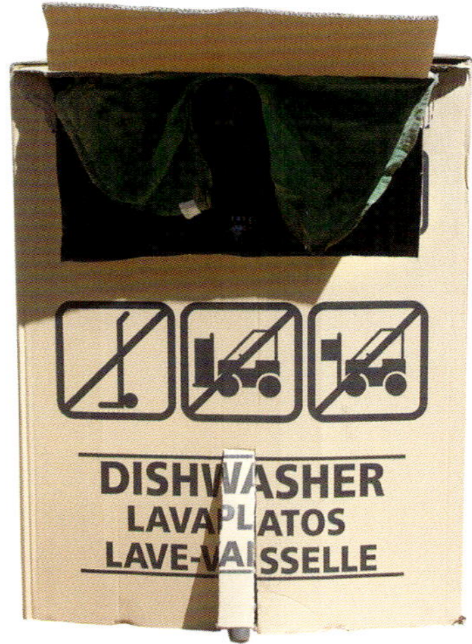

◄ *Cardboard dryer box photo blind*

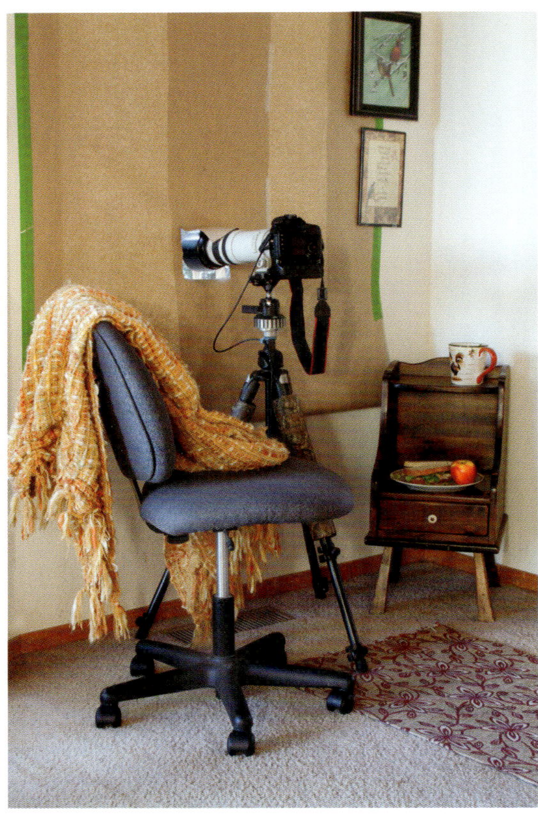

▲ *Wrapping paper covering a window for a photo blind*

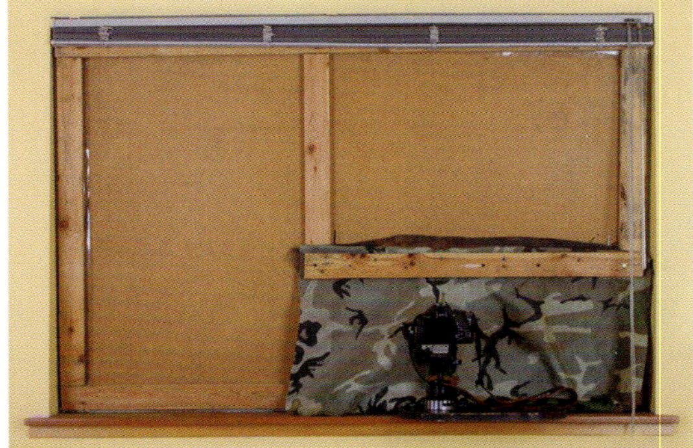

▲ *Wooden window blind in a bedroom*

to prevent scratches to the windowsill. They can be stored easily behind the couch or other furniture, or against the wall, ready for when you want to use them. Measure the inside dimensions of your window, and then transfer those measurements onto a piece of cardboard or plywood and cut out your blind. Then cut an opening for the camera. If the opening is rather large, you might consider covering it with a dark piece of fabric to help conceal your movements while still allowing the hole to be accessed by your camera lens.

The disadvantage of using a room in your house is the potential for interruptions and distractions within your home that will ruin prime moments of photographic opportunity. Make it clear to other household members that you wish to be left undisturbed while you are photographing.

Other blinds that can be used out in your yard are hunting blinds. These can be purchased commercially from sporting goods stores and other suppliers. Many of them are quite simple to use and can be set up or taken down in a matter of minutes. The other possibility is to go the DIY route and make a blind by either sewing one yourself or building one out of wood or plywood, or making frames and covering them with material. There is an incredible amount

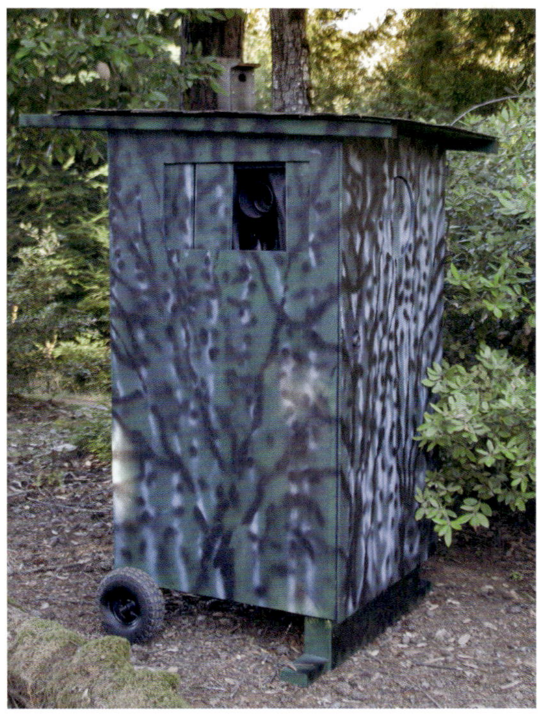

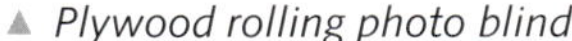
▲ *Plywood rolling photo blind*

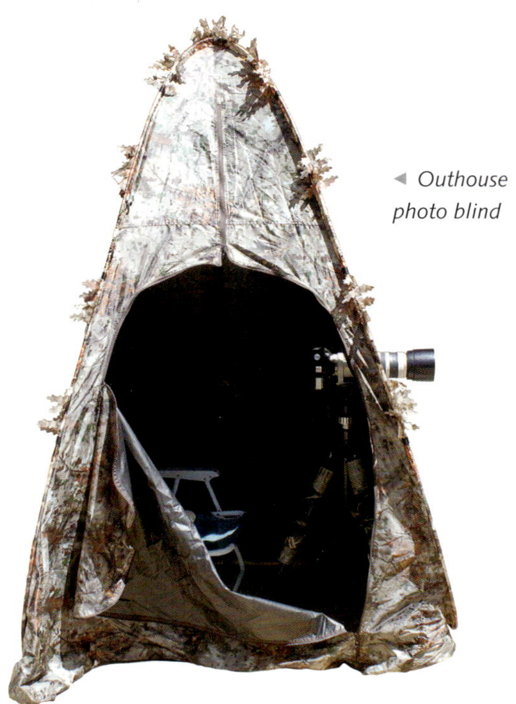
◄ *Outhouse photo blind*

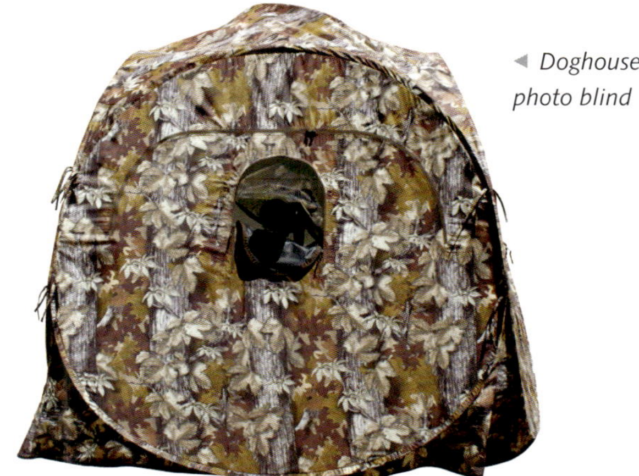
◄ *Doghouse photo blind*

of options. If you live in the far north you can make a blind out of an ice fishing shack. The main advantage these types of blinds have is that they are not limited to use in your yard. They are usually small and portable enough that you can take them with you on photo excursions in other places in the world!

Should you decide to build a more permanent blind in your yard, be very sure of its location, since it will be difficult to move. Make careful note of the backgrounds and direction of the sun.

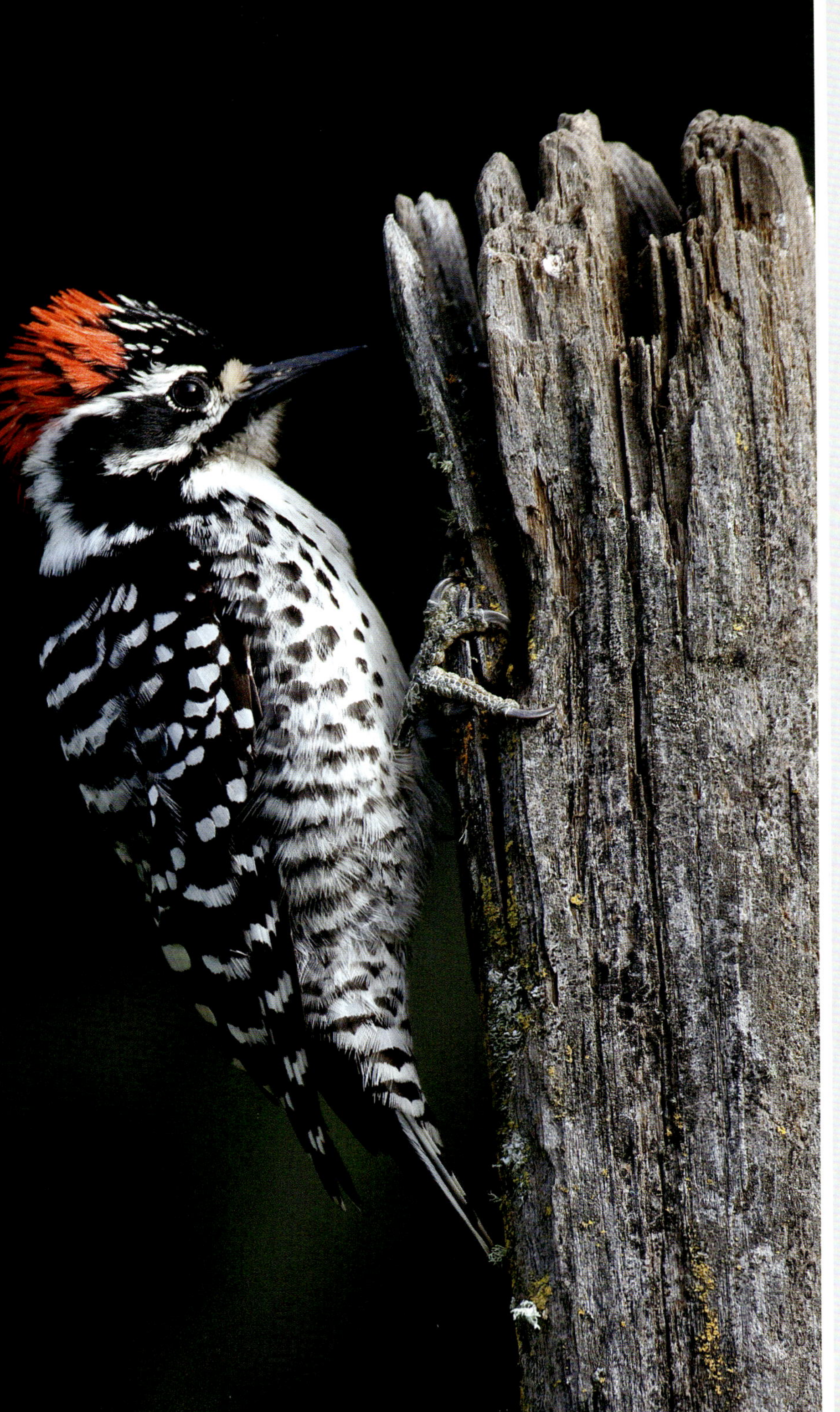

◄ *Nuttall's woodpecker on an old wooden fence post with seed cups on the back side*

CHAPTER 5 How to Capture the Best Bird Images

When photographing birds, you will learn that patience is a virtue. This means keeping your activities in the blind to a minimum. No loud noises or waving your lens around through the lens opening. Birds aren't always predictable and it may take some time for them to come and start using the feeders that you have set up. It is important to let them get used to visiting your feeders so they will consider your yard a safe location. Your job is to quietly observe them to learn where they land when they come to feed. Watch for patterns in bird behavior. You will notice that birds each have their own particular way of approaching the feeder.

The vast majority of birds do one thing that is really critical to your success as a bird photographer. They almost always pause for a second or two after they have landed on the perch to look around for predators. This spot on the perch is where you want to focus your camera to capture these moments—they make for some great bird images. Make note of the background behind this spot in the frame because it is very important to have a clean, uncluttered background. Be sure it is clear of bright spots and has a nice even color to it.

Once you have learned the birds' behavior and patterns and are satisfied with your set-up, you can start taking some images. I would suggest checking your images after every sequence to see if there are any changes that need to be made. Take the time to carefully review your images. Check for exposure, composition, and lighting. There should be no harsh or distracting shadows on the bird. If you are not familiar with composition, see "Composition: The Rule of Thirds."

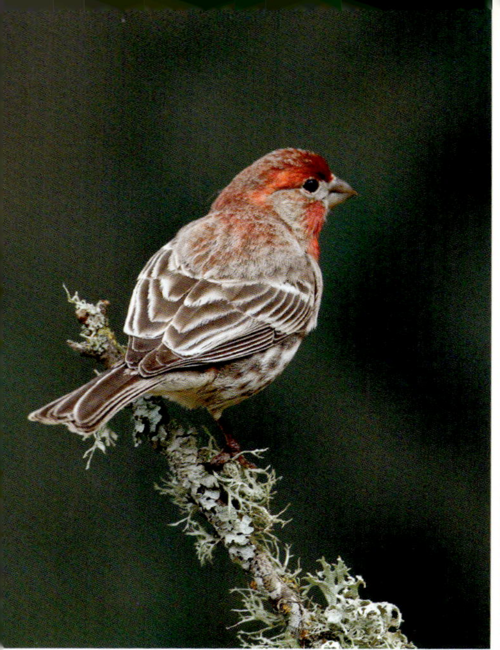
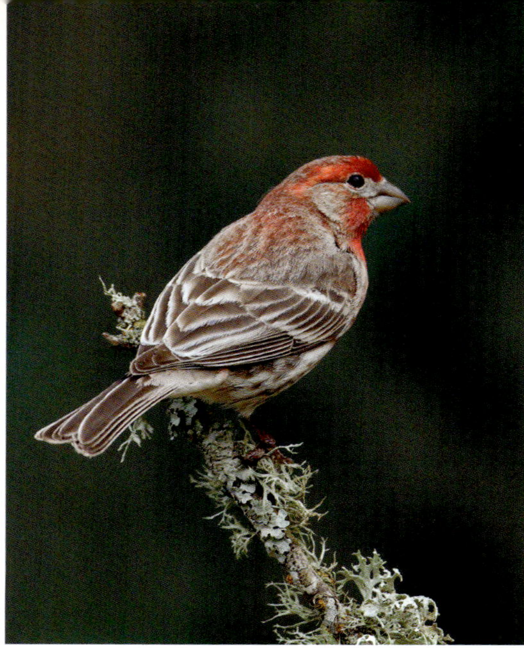
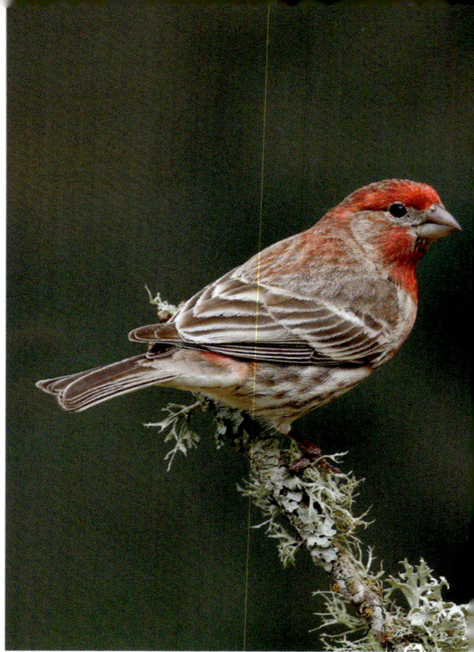

▲ *Sample head angles: the one on the far right is the most pleasing*

Head Angle

Head angle refers to the angle of the bird's head in your image. A bird that is looking away versus one that is looking ever so slightly towards you can mean the difference between a mediocre image and a fantastic one.

Catch Light

The "catch light" is a bright spot of specular light in the eye of the bird. Images with a catch light in the eye make a huge difference to the quality of your bird photograph. In photographs without the catch light, the birds' eyes appear lifeless and flat. Always look for it when you are photographing your birds and when you are editing your images. Birds with a catch light look much more alive in images than birds without one.

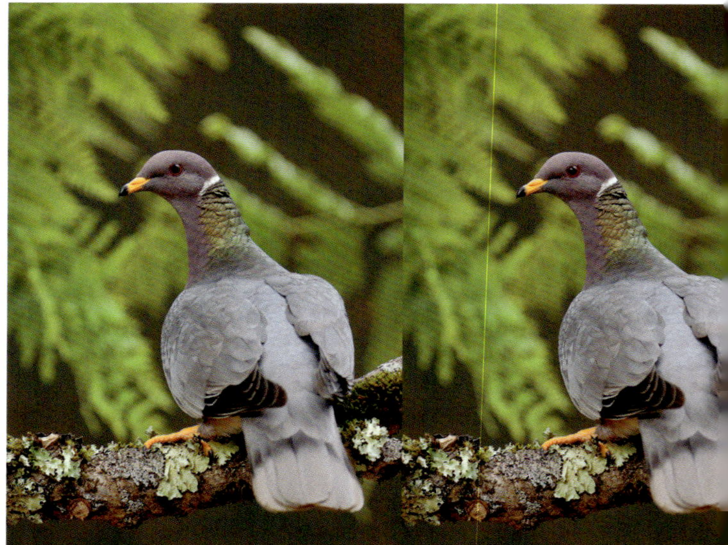

▲ *Band-tailed pigeon without and with a catch light in the eye*

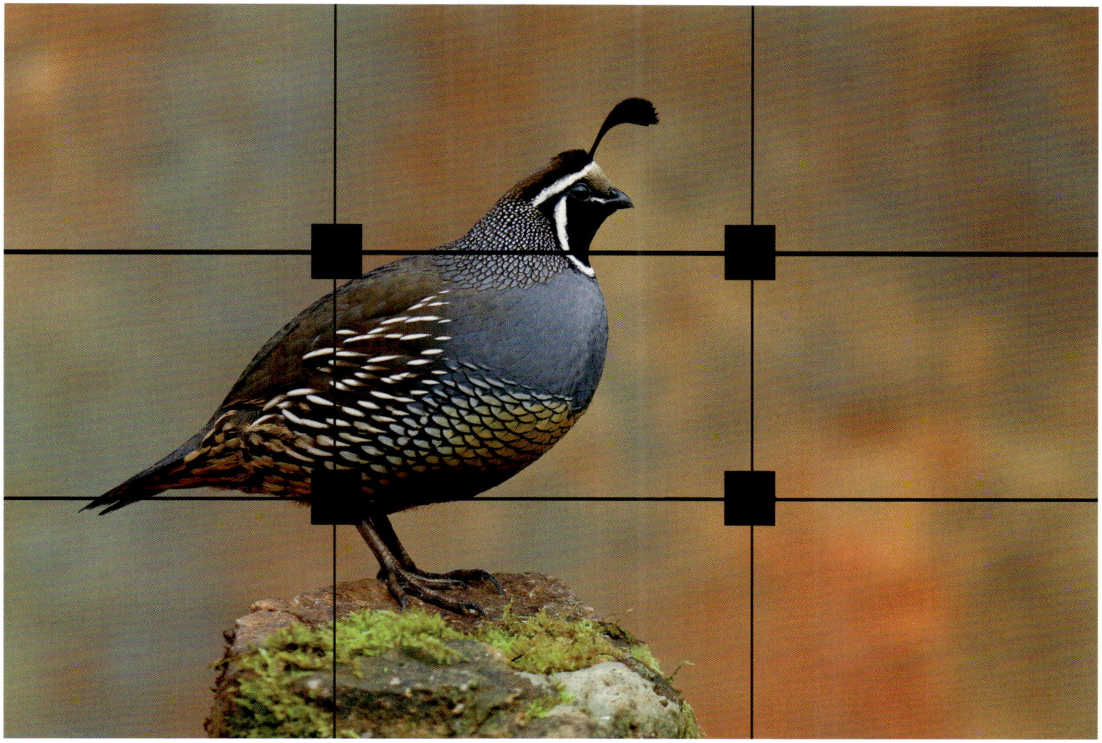

▲ California valley quail illustrating the rule of thirds

Composition: The Rule of Thirds

When composing an image in bird photography, it is a good idea to apply the rule of thirds. The rule of thirds is a **guideline** of where to place the focal point or the main center of interest in the image. In bird photography, usually the center of interest is the center of the body of the bird.

So what is the rule of thirds? First divide the frame or image into equal, vertical thirds. Next divide the image horizontally into thirds. What you

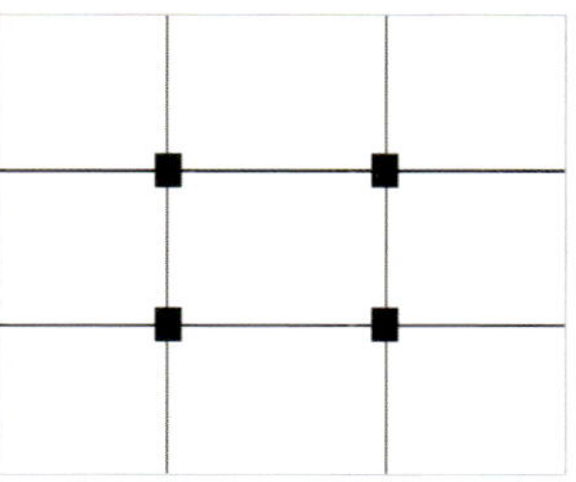

▲ *Blank white image showing the rule of thirds with power points shown by black squares*

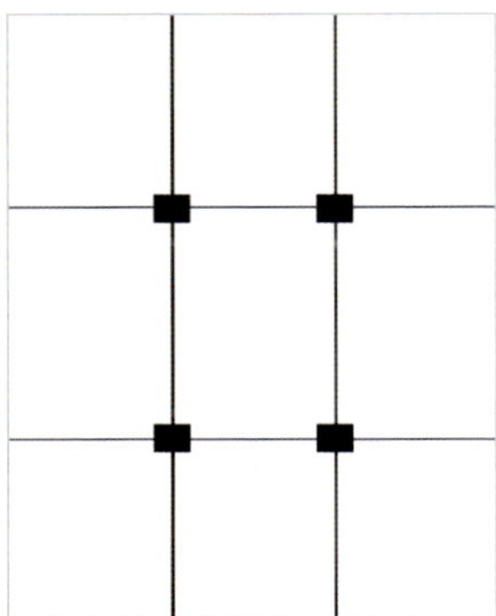

▲ *Vertical blank white image showing the rule of thirds with power points shown by black squares*

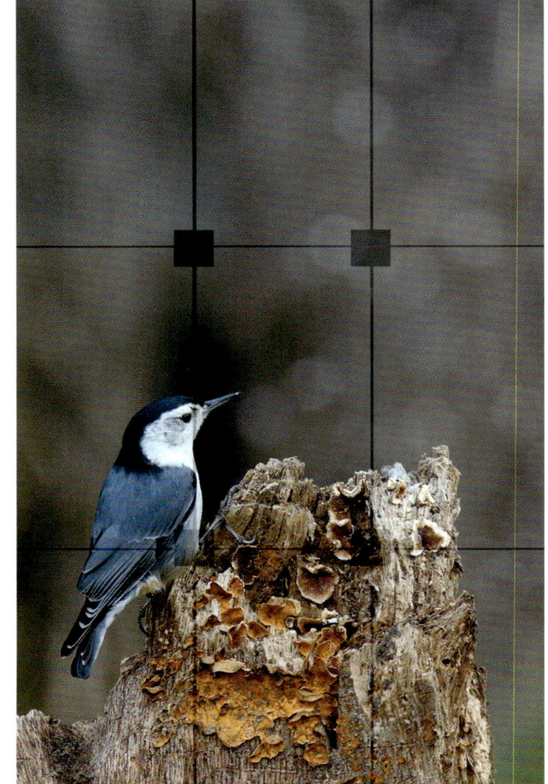

▶ *White-breasted nuthatch—illustrating the rule of thirds*

end up with is a pattern that looks like a tic-tac-toe diagram placed over the top of your image. The locations where the lines intersect on the four corners of the central rectangle are sometimes called power points. These power points are the locations where you should try to place your bird within the frame of the picture. Try to compose the image with the bird facing into the frame. Provide space for the bird to look into. A bird facing the edge of the frame looks like it's trying to leave or escape, which creates a feeling of unease.

When photographing birds, I simplify things by setting up and prefocusing my camera, and pre-composing the image. I visualize where the bird will be on the perch using the rule of thirds. This way, when a bird does come and land I'm prepared to press the shutter release and not cause a lot of motion that may scare it off.

Where to Focus

When focusing on a bird, the most important focus point is the center of the eye. If your camera has adjustable focus points you should set them so they will be at the approximate point of where the bird's eye will be (assuming the bird's body will be centered on a power point). If your camera does not have adjustable focus points, you should prefocus on that area instead, and lock in the focus.

The Preferable F-Stop

Because birds are almost always moving, you'll want to use the largest lens opening possible. To do this you should set your camera to Aperture Priority and set the F-stop to the largest available lens opening. The camera will automatically choose the highest shutter speed to match it, which is desirable because high shutter speeds help prevent camera shake and minimize any movement by your subject. Wide-open F-stops are also preferable because they allow the background behind your subject to appear out of focus, which makes the bird stand out.

The Best ISO Setting

It is preferable to set your ISO to 400 at the very least. Birds move quickly and you are going to need all the speed you can get. On dark or cloudy days, moving up to ISO 800 is a good idea.

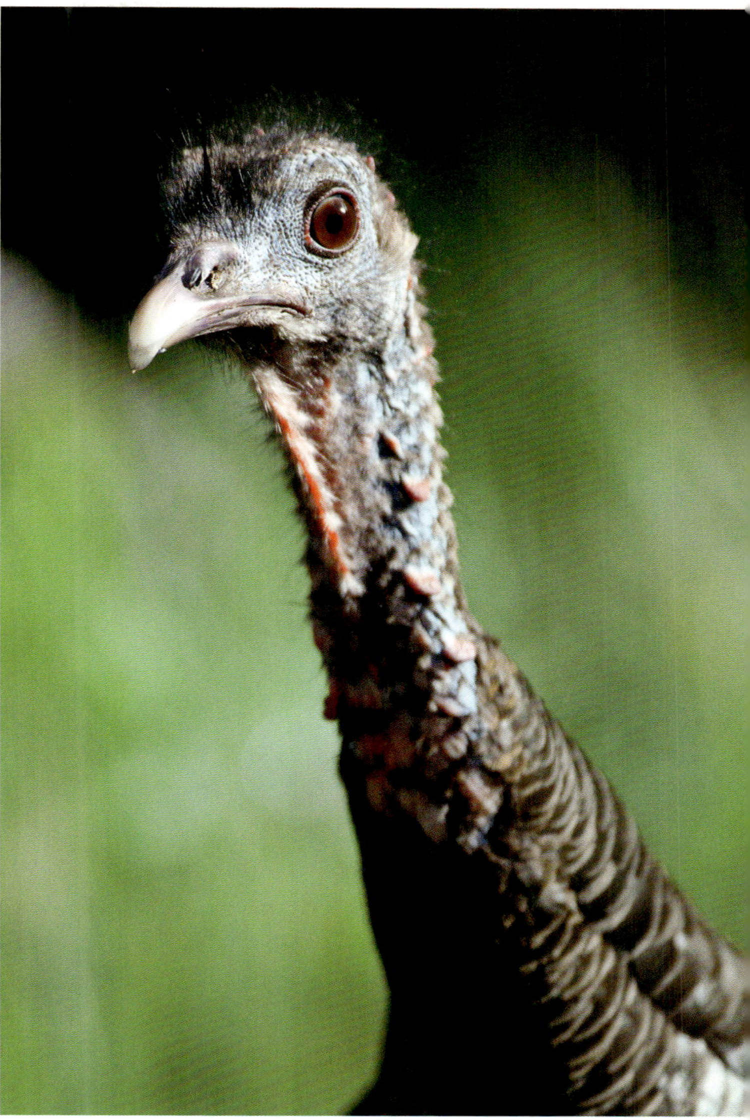

▲ *The focus point is on the eye of this wild turkey at a ground feeder*

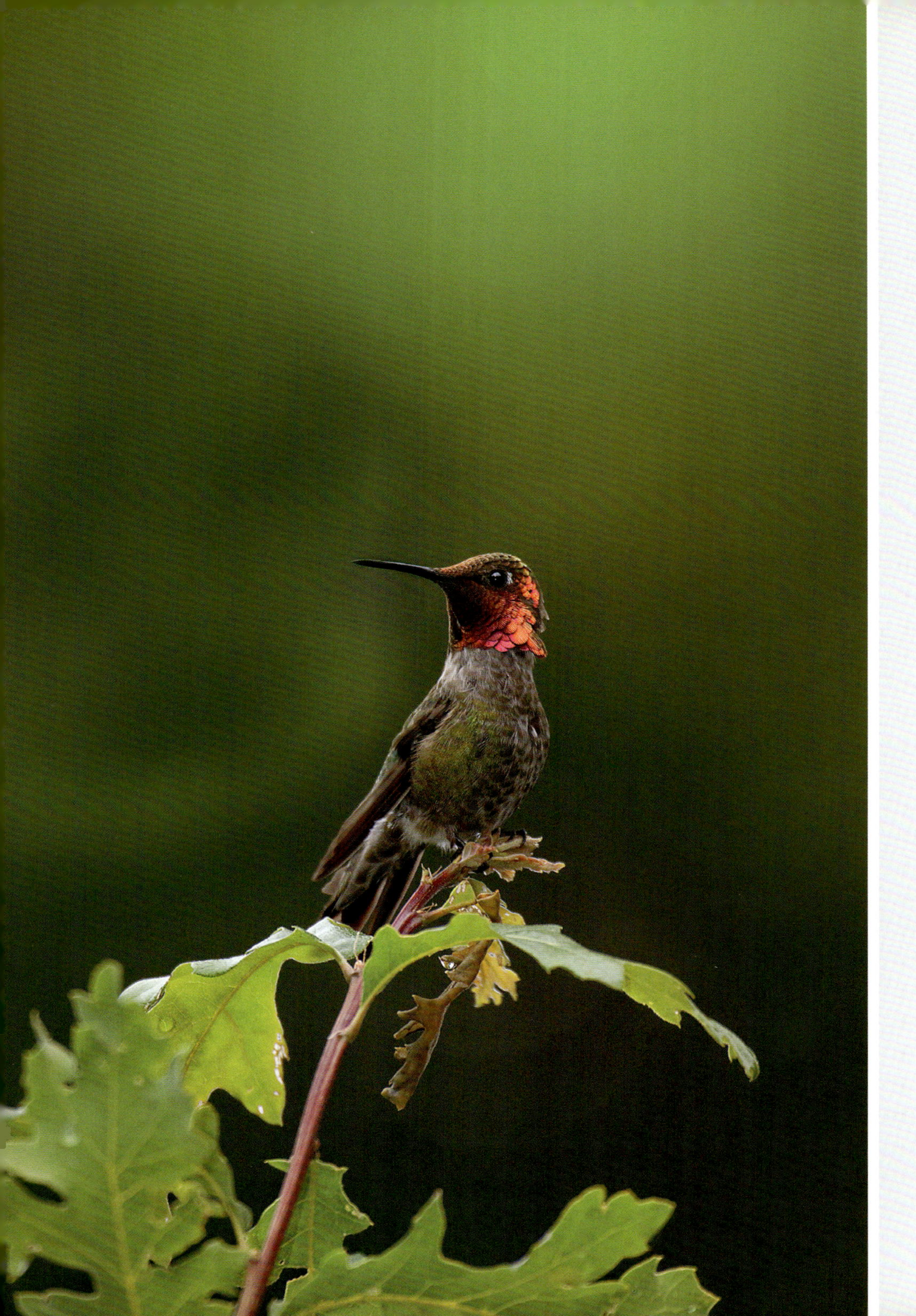

◄ *Anna's hummingbird resting after eating*

CHAPTER 6

Photographing Hummingbirds

Are you up for a challenge? Photographing hummingbirds is incredibly challenging, but also quite addictive and a lot of fun. It takes more of an investment in equipment than other types of backyard bird photography, but the results are well worth the effort when you capture a sharp image of one of these dazzling birds in flight.

So you need a really, really fast shutter camera or shutter speed for photographing hummingbirds in flight, right? No! What you actually need is a hummingbird feeder and a really, really fast flash, or better yet, several flashes. The vast majority of the incredible hummingbird images you've seen in magazines were done with a hummingbird feeder and a flash set-up.

A basic flash set-up for photographing hummingbirds consists of four flashes. More complicated set-ups can use six or more, but for now we will just stick to the basics. The best flashes for hummingbird photography are hot shoe flashes that have a manual setting for power reduction (1/16 power or less is ideal). Some hot shoe flashes have the unique ability to shorten their flash duration as the power is manually lowered. Most hot shoe flashes working at 1/16 power have a flash duration of less than 1/5000 of a second or faster, depending upon the model. This incredibly fast flash duration is what freezes the action of hummingbird wings in flight—not a fast shutter speed on the camera. Typically studio flashes won't work as well for images of hummingbirds in flight, because the flash duration is too long to effectively freeze motion. One exception to this is the Einstein E640 studio flash, which is designed for stopping action. However, these are a bit pricey.

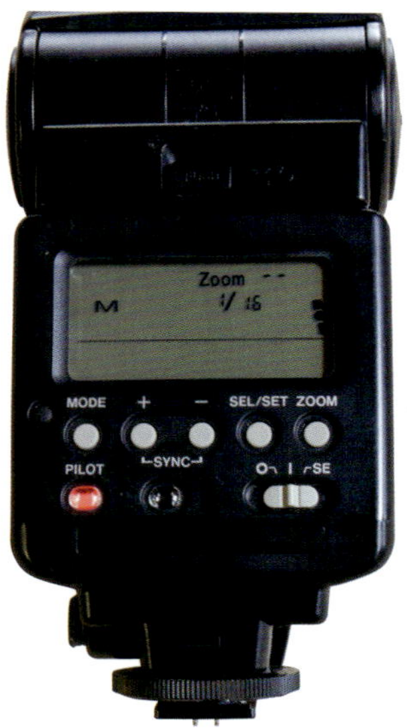

▲ *Control panel of a Canon 540EZ flash set on manual at 1/16 power*

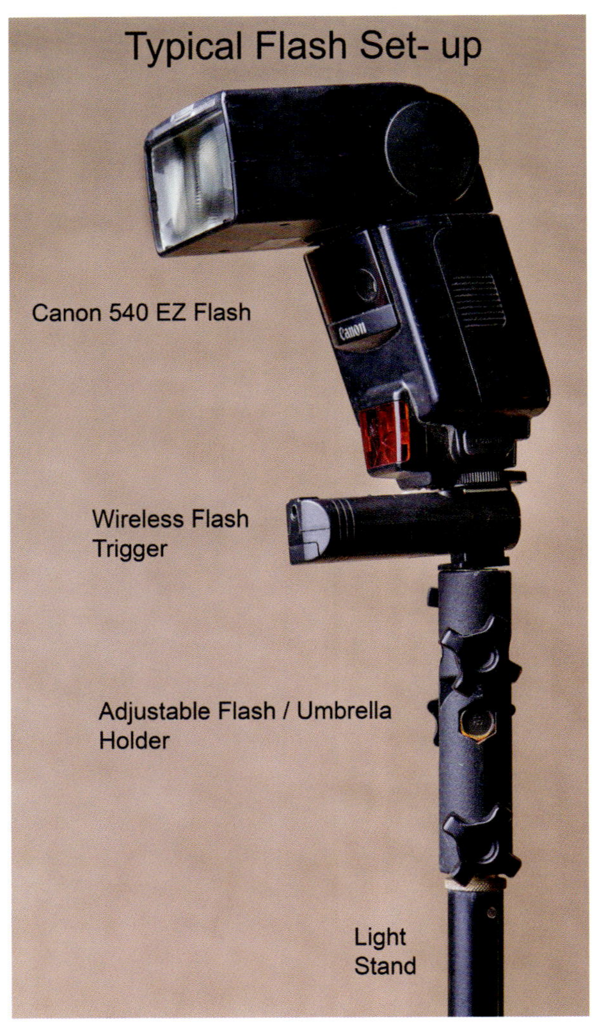

▲ *Typical hummingbird flash set-up*

Flashes that work well for hummers include the Canon 430EZ, 430EX, 550EX, and 580EX. Also, Nikon Speedlites SB-26, SB-600, SB-700, and SB-800 work well, as does the Metz 48 and the Vivitar 283 with a VP-1 module. Again, the key feature required is the ability of the flash to be manually dialed down to 1/16 power to achieve that short flash duration. There is a trade off, however. In reducing the power of the flash you also reduce its effective range. At such a low power, the flashes need to be placed two feet or less from the hummingbird.

There are many older flashes that can be manually used off-camera, but should never be used on-camera or with a pc/sync cord because the high trigger voltage can damage modern DSLR cameras. However, when they are used with a wireless flash triggering system, this isn't a problem because they aren't connected directly to the camera.

So what do I mount these flashes on? One of the best supports for flashes are light stands with an umbrella/flash holder. These can be raised and lowered to a variety of heights, and the flash holder allows the flash to be tilted or angled in almost any direction. I highly recommend anchoring down your flash stands with sand bags, cinder blocks, or water bags to prevent them from being knocked over. You could also use old tripods to hold your flashes. My personal set-up is a mix of tripods and light stands.

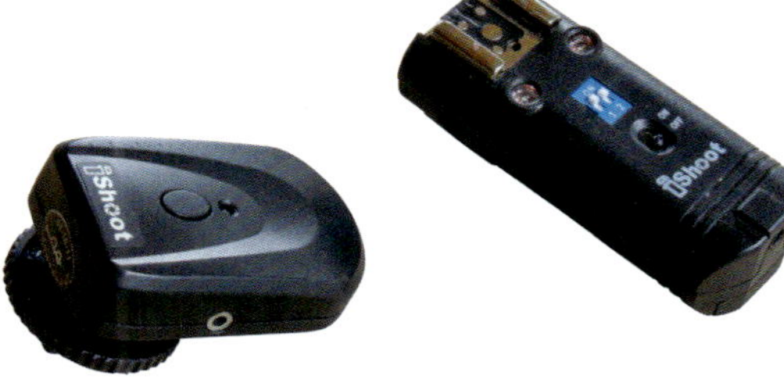

▲ *Wireless radio flash trigger. On the left is the sending unit for the camera, and the receiving unit for the flash is on the right.*

The camera best suited for photographing hummers is a DSLR that can be set to manual mode and has a hot shoe. Point-and-Shoot cameras, for the most part, are unsuited for this type of photography unless they are equipped with a hot shoe. Cameras with a PC connection port may be used, but this involves the connection of wires to each flash and is a bit of a hassle.

So if I don't use a PC or sync cord, how do I trigger my flashes? The vast majority of hummingbird photographers now use wireless flash triggers. They are quite reliable and don't require a direct line of sight like optical slaves (I used to use optical slaves; they were a pain to set up and not always reliable). There is a wide variety of triggering systems out there. I use Ishoot Snipers and they work well.

Wireless flash triggers use a transmitter that slides into the hot shoe on top of the camera. Each flash unit has a receiver mounted to the underside of the flash foot. The flash foot then fits onto a ¼-inch stud on the top of each flash holder on a light stand. When the shutter button or release is pushed on the camera, the transmitter in the hot shoe sends a radio signal simultaneously to the flashes to fire them at the same time. Flash triggers are available from many major camera manufacturers or they can be purchased at many auction sites on the web.

In a basic hummingbird set-up, two flashes are placed roughly two feet from the feeder spout of a hummingbird feeder at a 45-degree angle. They are aimed at a point about 7 inches away from the feeder to catch the hummingbird when it backs up to take a break from feeding. The other two flashes are used to light up the backdrop. They are placed at the same height as the feeder at 45-degree angles facing the background. The key here is to use the light of the flashes to expose your subject, and to use as little ambient light as possible.

In order to minimize ambient light, it's best to photograph hummingbirds in the shade. One simple solution is to photograph under an awning or porch, or to use an instant shade pop-up that is 8 feet × 8 feet or larger. That way most of the light is coming from the flashes. A shady spot is also a pleasant place to photograph on a hot, sunny day. When photographing using a pop-up, be aware that flashes will pick up a slight color cast of the

Basic Set-up

Backdrop set back 4–8 feet from the feeder.

Background flashes set at 45-degree angles to the background about two feet away at feeder height.

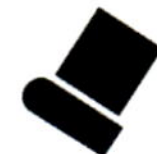

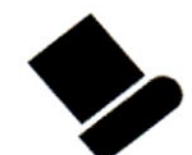

Single spout hummingbird feeder

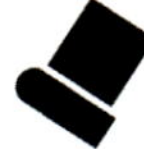

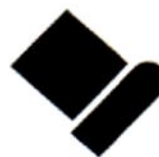

Front flashes set two feet away at 45-degree angles to the hummingbird feeder. They are placed level with the feeder height.

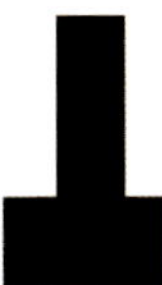

Camera position roughly 4–6 feet from the hummingbird feeder.

◄ *Diagram showing the top view of a basic hummingbird set-up*

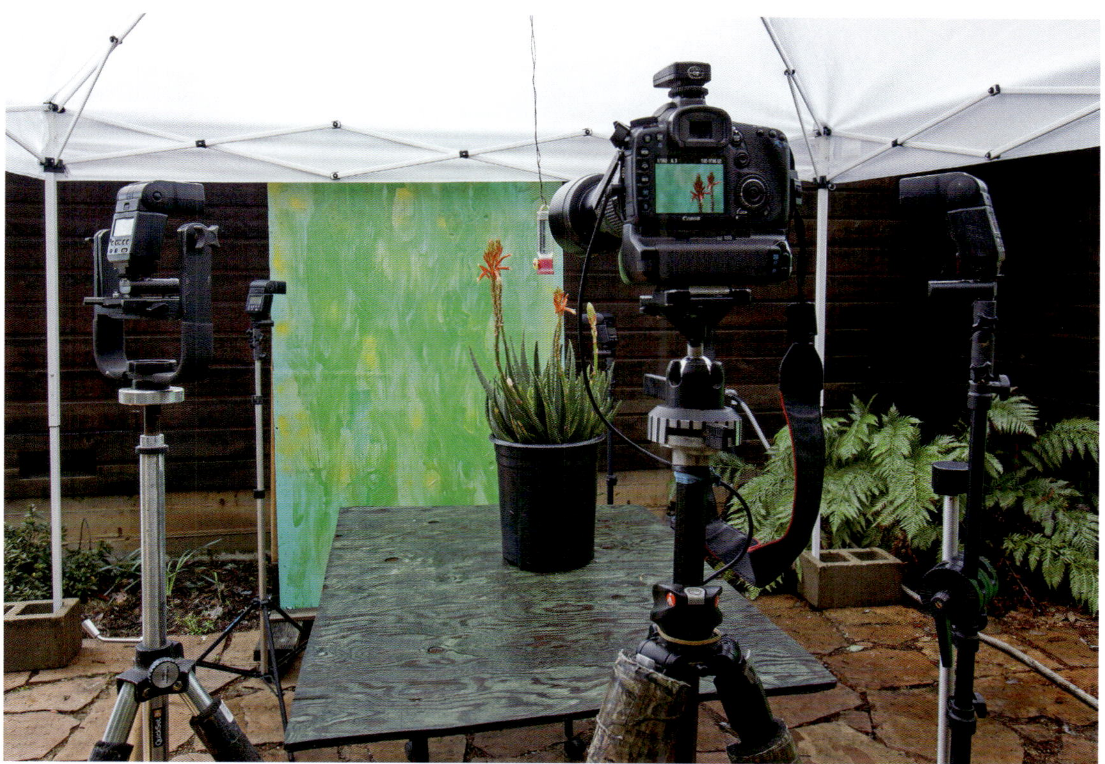

▲ *Image of a basic set-up*

fabric that will be apparent in the image. White pop-ups are the best because they have no color cast and act as a giant reflector. However, they have the disadvantage of being able to cut less ambient light. This issue can be solved by throwing a dark tarp over the top of the pop-up before beginning to photograph. Take down your pop-up before it rains or snows, and be sure to have it properly anchored to keep it from blowing over in the wind. I speak from experience when I say that they have a tendency to self-destruct under these conditions.

Once you have all of your equipment organized, it is time to work on the set-up. The premise of hummingbird photography is quite simple: hide the feeder with flowers or use the flowers themselves for hummingbirds to feed from. A typical set-up uses flowers placed close to or in front of the hummingbird feeder spout in order to cover it from view. It's good to include flowers just behind the feeder as well. Many photographers will include the feeder spout in the initial creation of the image and then remove it later in Photoshop.

The other option is to feed the hummingbirds at one location using a single-spout hummingbird feeder. Replace the feeder spout with a tubular flower, like a honeysuckle or a trumpet vine. Then use an eyedropper to load up the flower with sugar water, and the hummingbirds will use the flower instead of the feeder spout. It really works well! If an eyedropper is unavailable, sugar water can be placed in a flower blossom by using a drinking straw. Just dip the straw in sugar water, and then press your finger over the top of the straw to seal off the opening. Still holding your finger tightly over the hole, place the bottom of the straw inside the flower blossom and lift your finger to release the liquid. Now you've got your flowers. What's next?

Backgrounds of a wide variety of colors and designs can be used for photographing hummers, and are extremely important. If a backdrop isn't used, the hummingbirds will look like they were photographed at night with a black background. The backdrops used for other backyard birds work perfectly well. They should be placed about 4–8 feet behind the feeder.

A few shots of green, black, or colored spray paint on a piece of tag board can create an amazing backdrop. Some photographers use a blow-up of an image of out-of-focus flowers as a backdrop. Whatever backdrop is used, make sure it is large enough to cover the image area behind the feeder. Set it up and check it out by looking through the camera before attempting to use it.

Exposure is dependent upon the flashes and the camera's sync speed. It's typical to use a shutter speed of 1/200 of a second at F-stops ranging from of F-13 to F-18. Stopping down helps to keep the hummingbird's eye in focus. The camera's white balance should be set to flash. Check the lighting set-up before starting to photograph hummingbirds. Take a test shot, and then check the camera's histogram for proper exposure. You will save yourself a ton of time by doing this before starting to photograph.

For focusing manually, prefocus on the tip of the hummingbird feeder with the camera on a tripod. Then turn the camera so that it is pointed to an area with the feeder spout just out of the frame before changing the camera back to autofocus. A typical camera position is about six feet away from the feeder.

The best lenses for photographing hummingbirds are in the telephoto range of 200 to 500

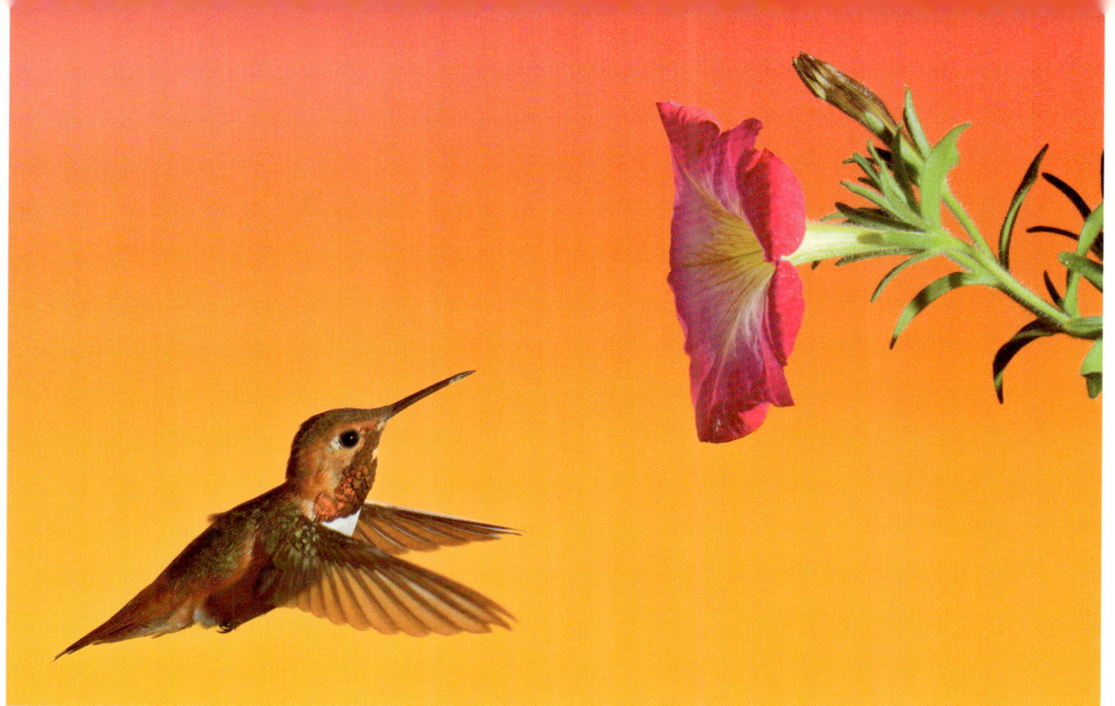

▲ *Hummingbird with a sunset gradient tagboard purchased at an office supply store*

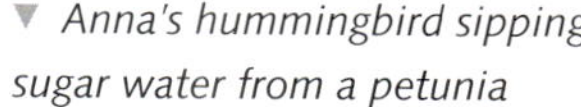

▼ *Anna's hummingbird sipping sugar water from a petunia*

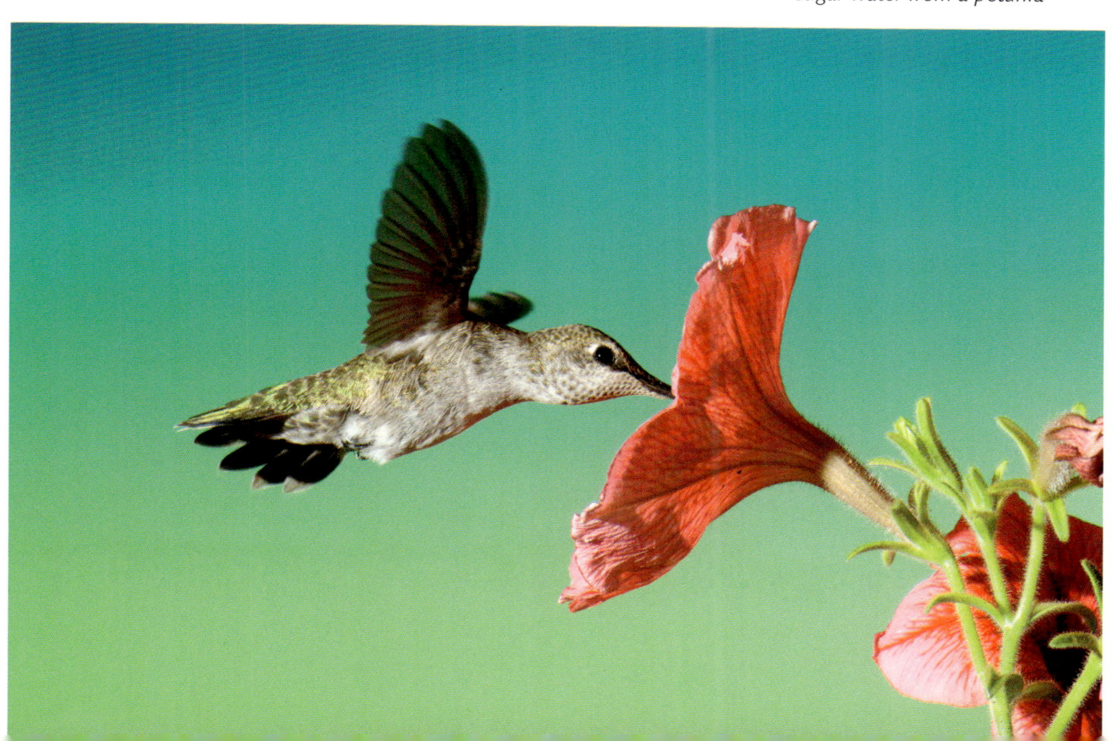

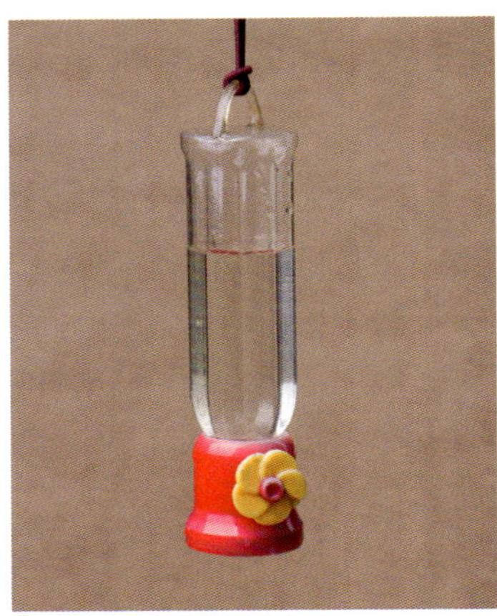

▲ *Small inverted-style hummingbird feeder*

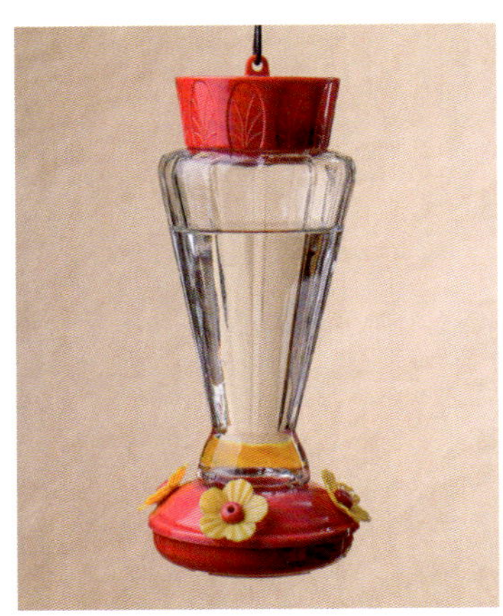

▲ *Saucer-style hummingbird feeder*

millimeters. My personal choices are 100-300mm zooms and 100-400mm zooms with an extension tube added for close focusing. Zoom lenses have the added advantage over fixed lenses because you can design your image without having to change your position to alter the composition of the shot.

A hummingbird feeder is a critical item to have when photographing hummingbirds. Unless you live in a climate where you have hummingbirds year-round, it's best to put up feeders in early spring. Fill your feeders with a mixture of plain white sugar mixed at a ratio of one part sugar to four parts tap water. Hang out multiple feeders to attract the hummers, and then reduce to one when it comes time to take some pictures. A single-spout feeder is the best for photography. A multi-spout feeder can be used by blocking off all but one feeder spout with tape.

There is a wide variety of hummingbird feeders out there. For the most part they fall into a couple of basic styles: the inverted and the saucer. Inverted feeders store the sugar water above the feeding port and the birds feed from the side or bottom. Saucer feeders have feeding ports above a simple dish filled with sugar water.

Hummingbirds typically approach inverted feeders from below and saucer feeders from above. Because of this, you can get different looks depending upon the type of feeder being used. Inverted feeders work really well when using hanging tubular flowers like honeysuckle, fuchsia, and salvia. Saucer feeders work best with flower blossoms that point upward, like zinnias and petunias. Matching the flower blossom and the style of feeder can make your hummingbird photography much easier and more visually pleasing. Regardless of which style of

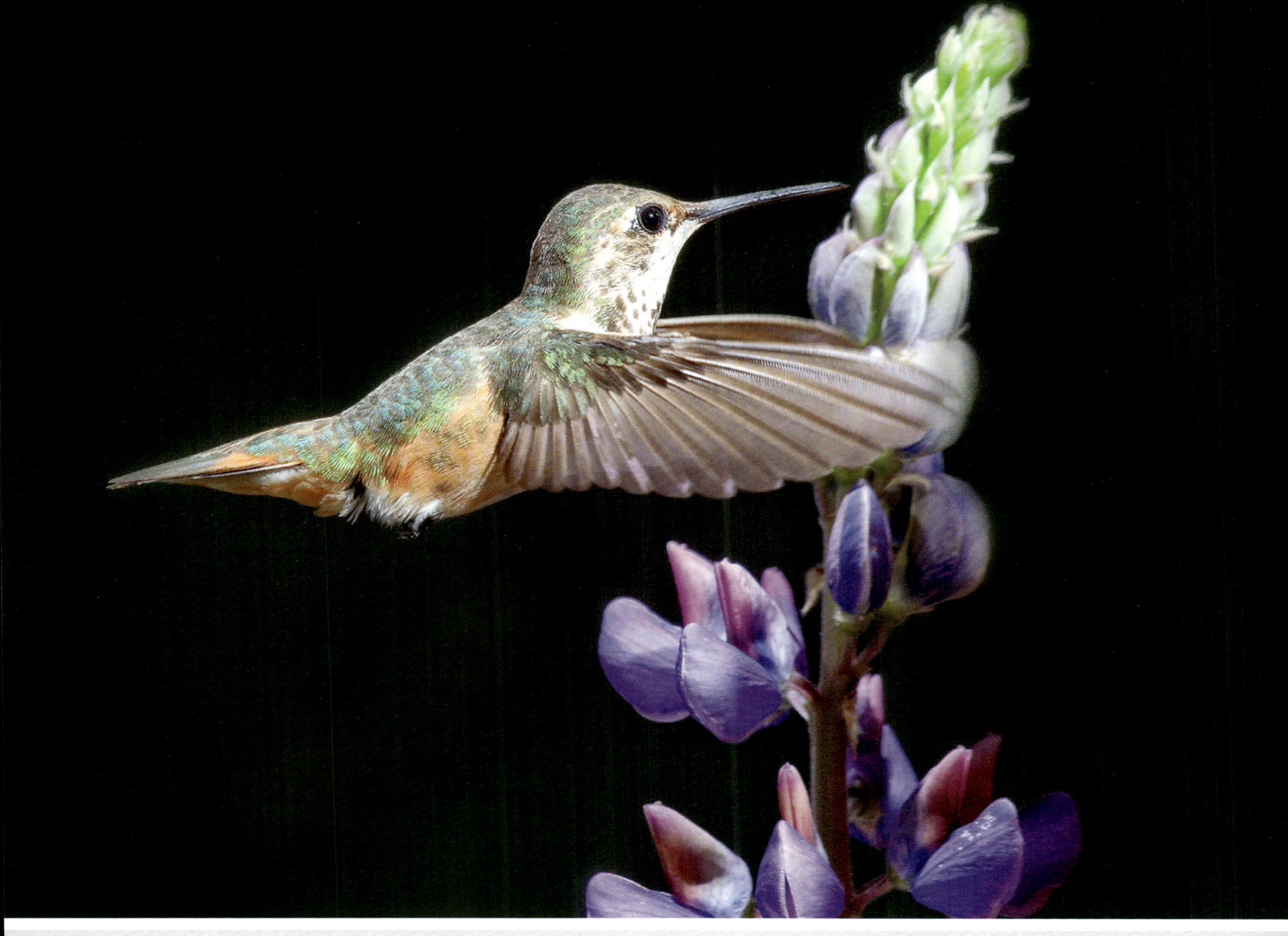

▲ *Hummingbird coming up to an inverted feeder*

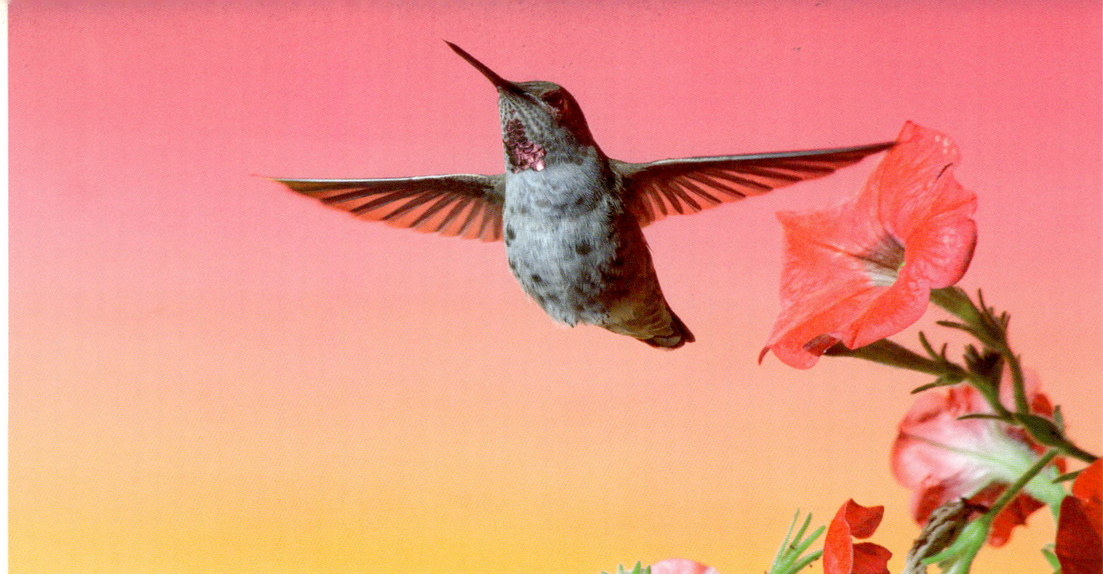

▲ *Hummingbird turning away from an inverted feeder*

feeder you choose, the best ones are those that don't use a perch—otherwise you'll only get photographs of hummingbirds on plastic perches instead of hovering in mid-air!

With hummingbirds it is a bit of a waiting game. If you don't use a blind you must sit as motionless as possible with your finger on the shutter release. Wait for the hummingbird to begin feeding before blasting away with the flashes. Start off slowly, and eventually they will get used to the flash. Usually the best time to click the shutter is when they back off from the feeder to take a break from feeding. They will move forward to feed, then back off 4–8 inches or so and hover for several seconds before moving forward to feed again.

I have photographed hummers both with and without a photo blind. I have discovered that I get a lot more hummingbirds coming to the feeders when I use a blind, and as result, I have more successful images. Keep in mind that your home can be used as a comfortable photo blind. It's quite easy to tack up some fabric or cardboard over an open window, and then cut a small opening in it to photograph from.

Don't neglect photographing perching hummingbirds. If you carefully observe hummingbirds you will find that many are very territorial. After feeding, they will invariably go back to the same perch to rest and guard the feeder until they feed again. You can capture some beautiful hummingbird images by setting up a portable blind or using a very slow approach to their perching spot.

Regardless of whether you photograph them flying or perched, you will find that hummingbirds are exciting and beautiful birds. They are like flying jewels. So put some gear together and go photograph some hummingbirds!

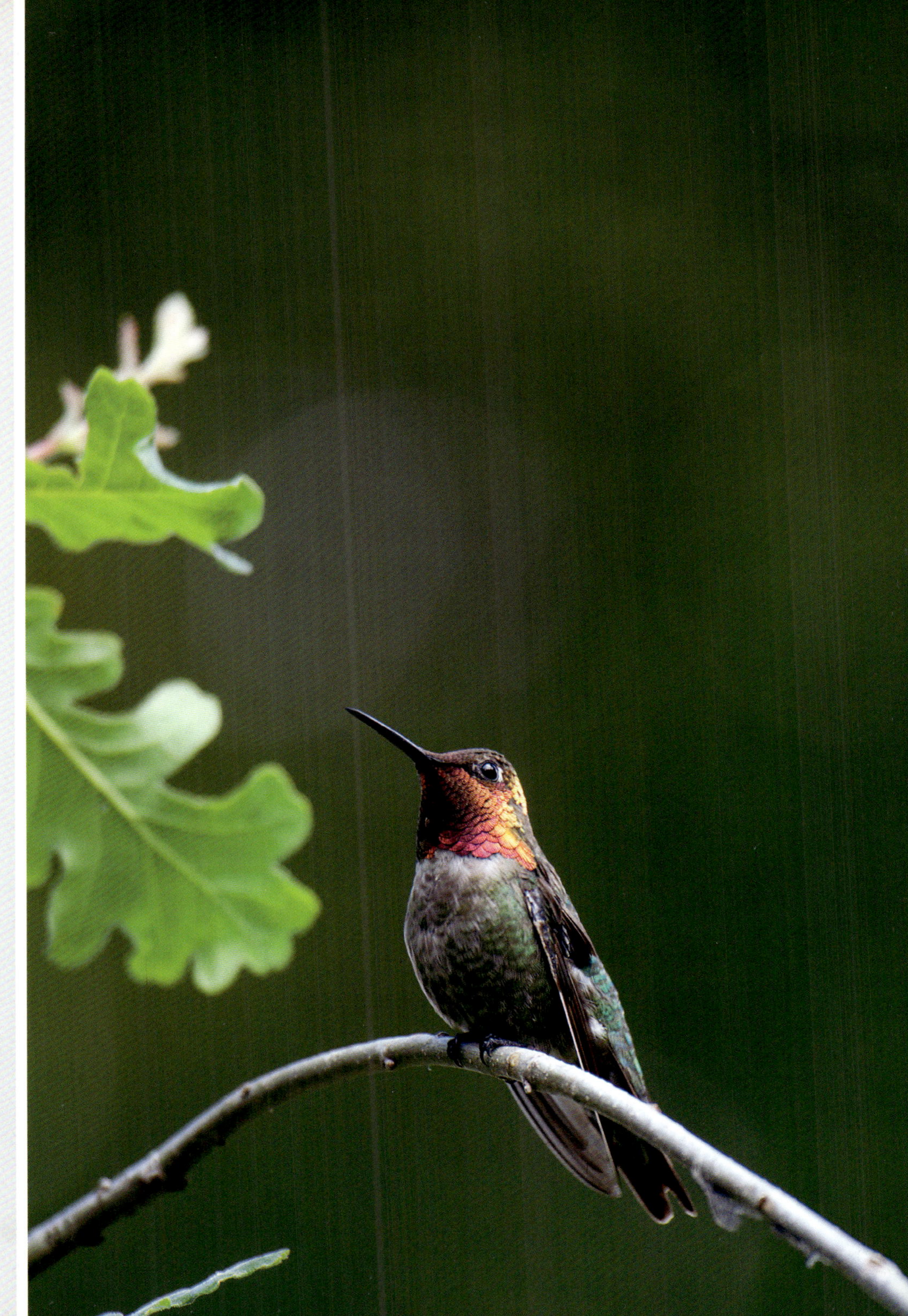

► *Male Anna's hummingbird guarding the feeder*

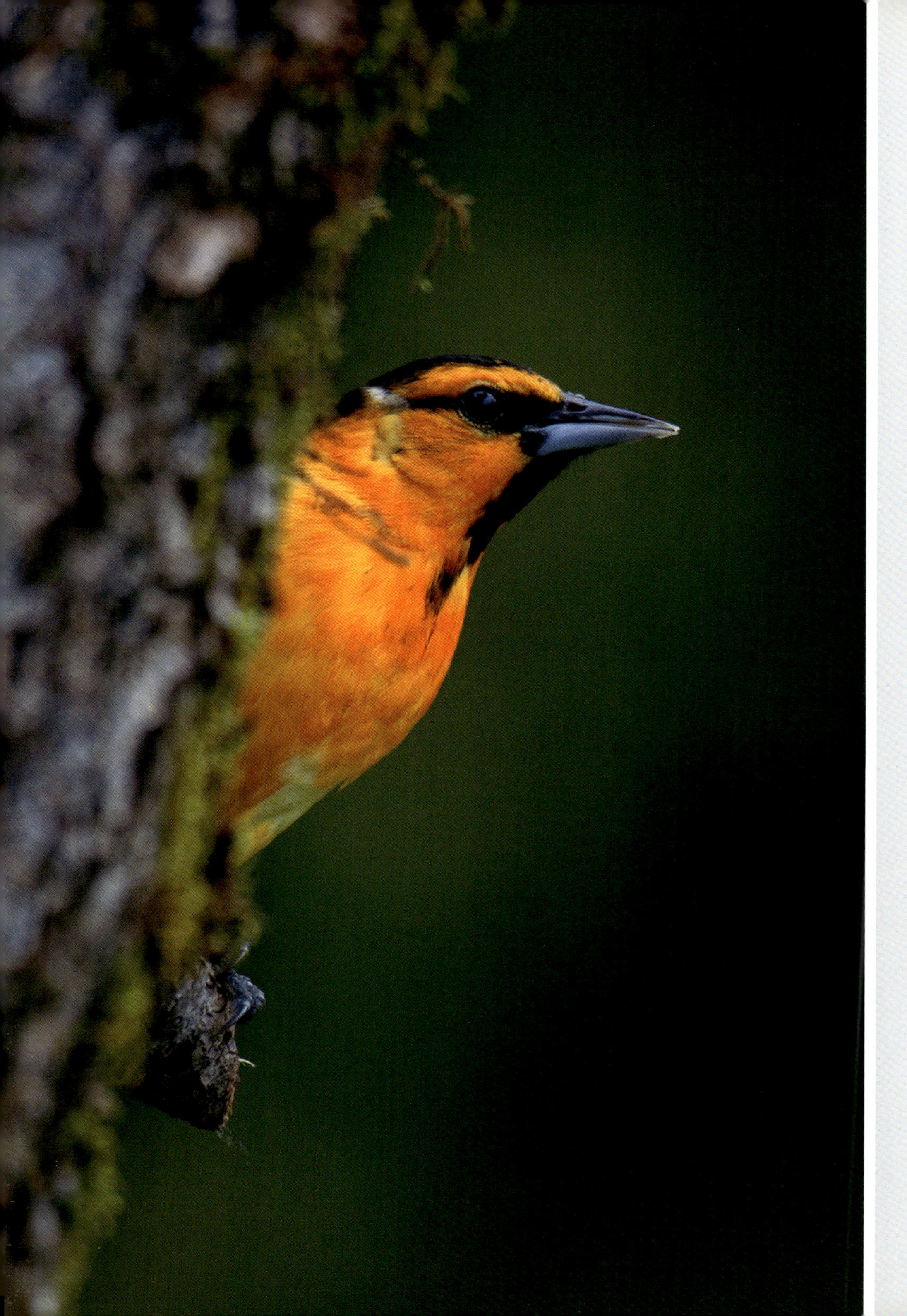

◄ *Bullock's oriole on a perch above a fruit feeder*

CHAPTER 7 Beyond the Backyard

What can you do when you have exhausted all the bird species in your backyard? Branch out! Think of all the people you know that have birds in their yards. The home of friends, relatives, and coworkers are all possible places where you may be able to photograph, if you ask politely and explain what you would like to do. Show them samples of your work and possibly even show them your set-up in your backyard.

If you do get permission, just be sure to keep things simple and neat. Try to have the least amount of impact that you can on their lives and property. It always helps to give them prints or cards of your work in appreciation for being able to use their property to photograph birds.

Other than the homes of friends and relatives, think about open space areas. National forests are a really good example, as are parks and other natural areas nearby your home or work. Some of these areas may work well for photography. Please check local laws and ordinances about setting up a blind or feeders. Sometimes talking to the local ranger or manager can open the door into places where you can photograph. It can help to carry around a three-ring binder or a small portfolio of some of your best bird images. Often times you can work out a trade of donating prints to their organization in exchange for a permit to photograph there.

In the past I have used a cardboard appliance or refrigerator box as a blind when photographing in public places where I want to leave my blind set up overnight. One time I returned to find my box blind vandalized—I'm glad it was only a cardboard box instead of one of my portable commercial photo blinds!

Many of the techniques discussed in the previous chapter can be used when you are traveling. But how do I carry all those feeders and seed? I've found that it's easier to buy cheap plastic feeders

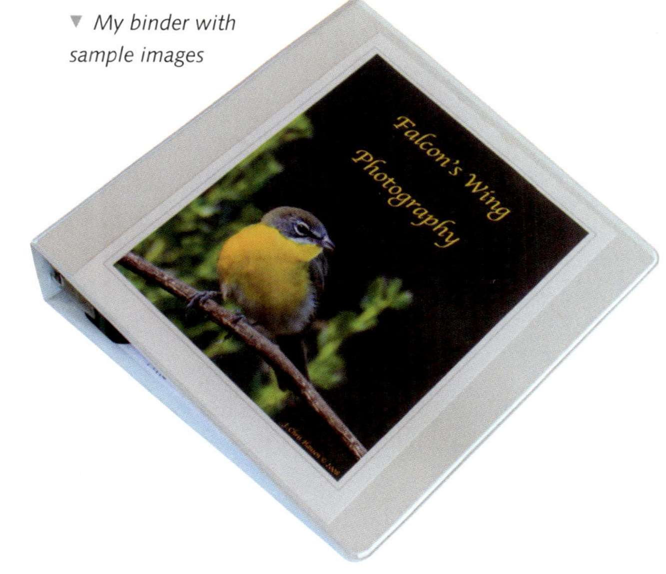

▼ *My binder with sample images*

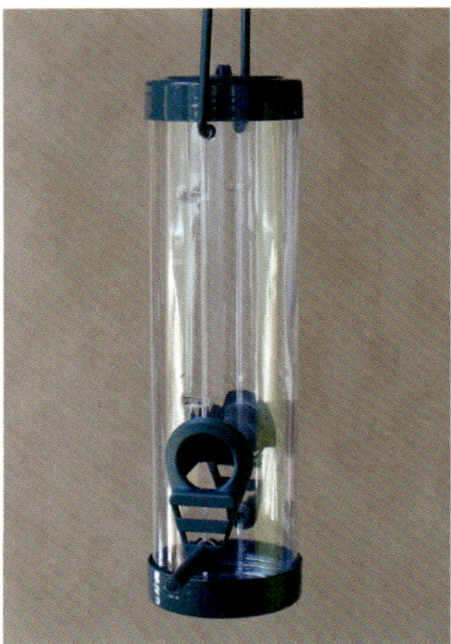

▲ *Dollar store bird feeder*

and small bags of seed at the arrival point. When I am done photographing I can give away my feeder and seed, or donate it to a nearby nature center.

What about perches and supports to hold up the feeders? Some good equipment is easy to acquire in the garden supply center of the nearest major box store. Buy some duct or electrical tape, some electrical ties, and most important of all—some plant stakes. Plant stakes are made of either plastic or bamboo and come in lengths of 18 inches to eight feet. They are perfect for holding up your feeders and perches when used in combination with electrical ties and tape. For perches, walk down the garden aisle and pick out some good plants to use.

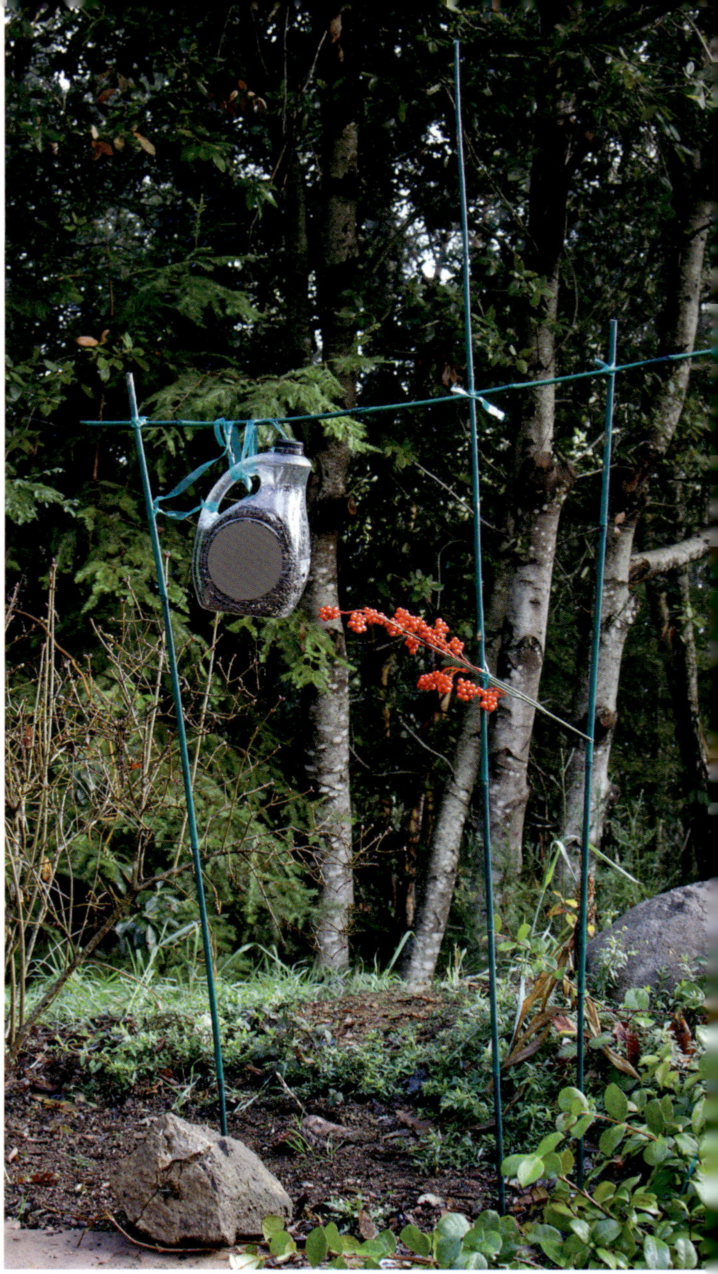

▲ *Feeder set-up with plant stakes from a garden center and a discarded plastic container*

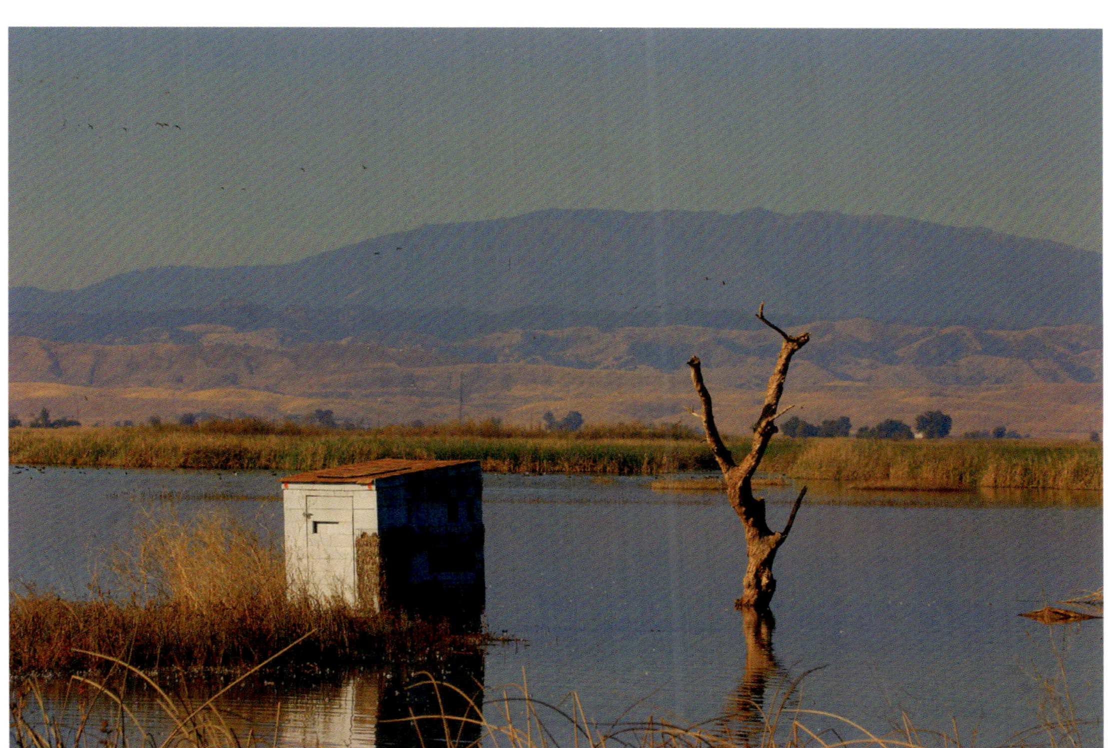

▲ *Photo blind on a National Wildlife Refuge*

You can always give the plants away when you are done with them.

What if you want to avoid the hassle of setting up feeders or blinds? There are many places around the world that cater to bird photographers by providing blinds and set-ups. The majority of them can be rented for a daily fee, although some of them require that you also pay for a guide. A few of these places are included in the resource section at the back of this book.

Think out of the box. Don't forget that many of the techniques that work for small birds also work

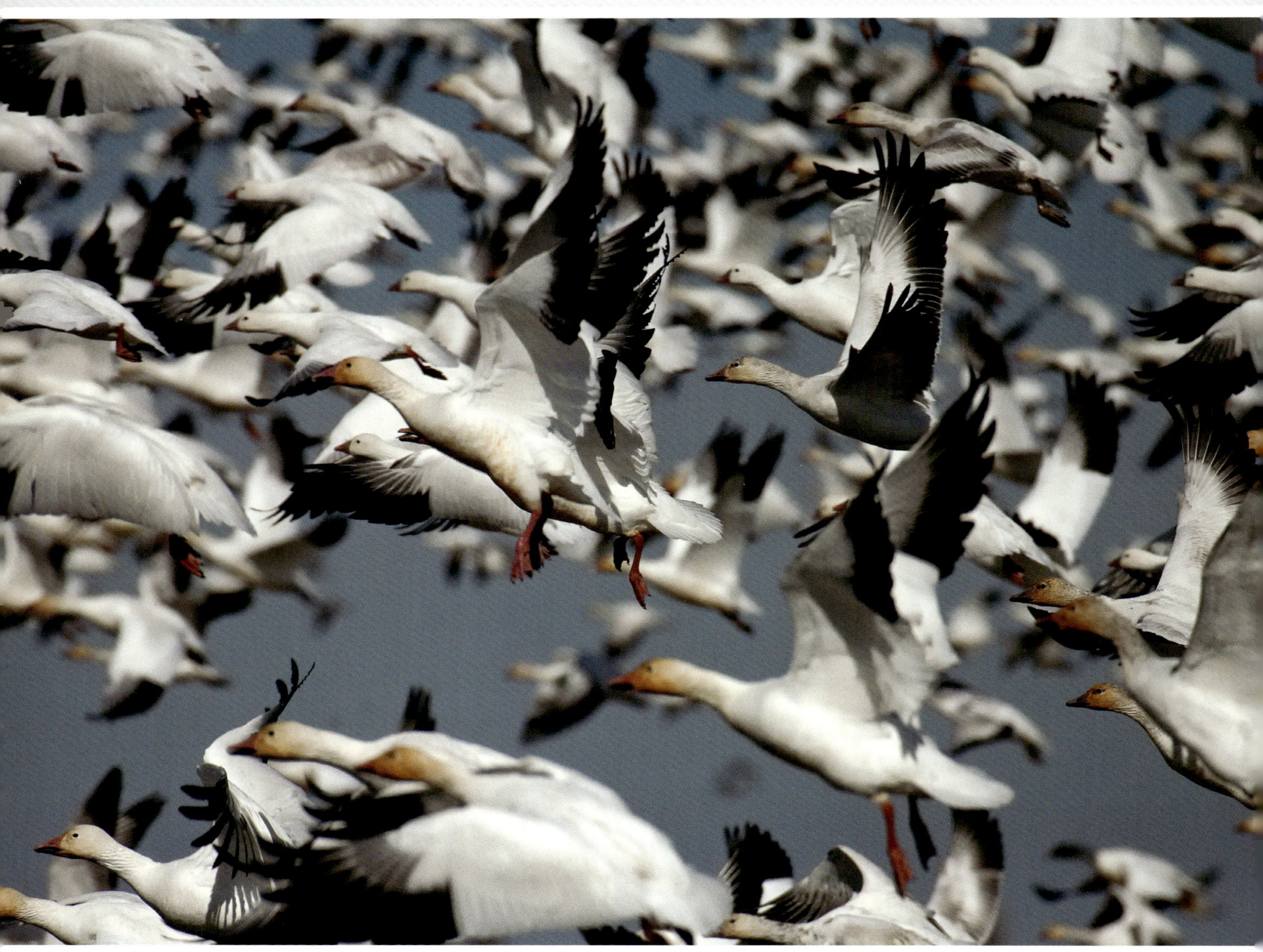

▲ *Snow geese lifting off next to the photo blind*

for larger birds, including birds of prey. They will all use a perch if it is properly positioned near a food source. This image of a vulture was created by wiring a wooden perch to a metal fence post. The Turkey Vultures were feeding on a dead deer beside the road. Cars make a great photo blind—most birds are comfortable around cars, as long as they don't move.

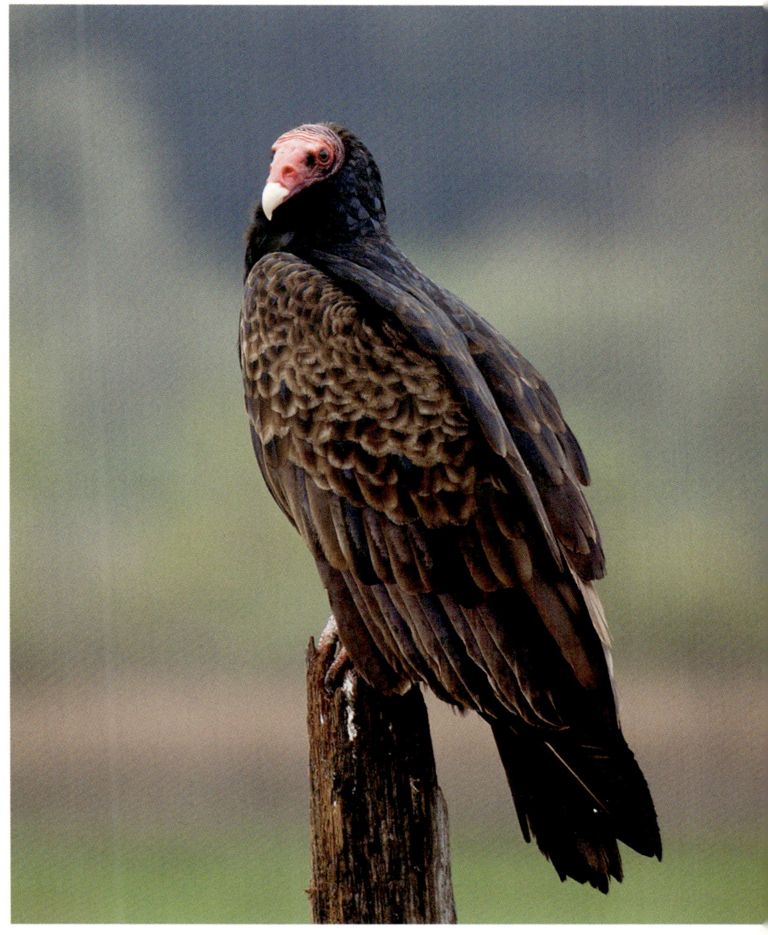

▲ *Turkey vulture on a wooden perch*

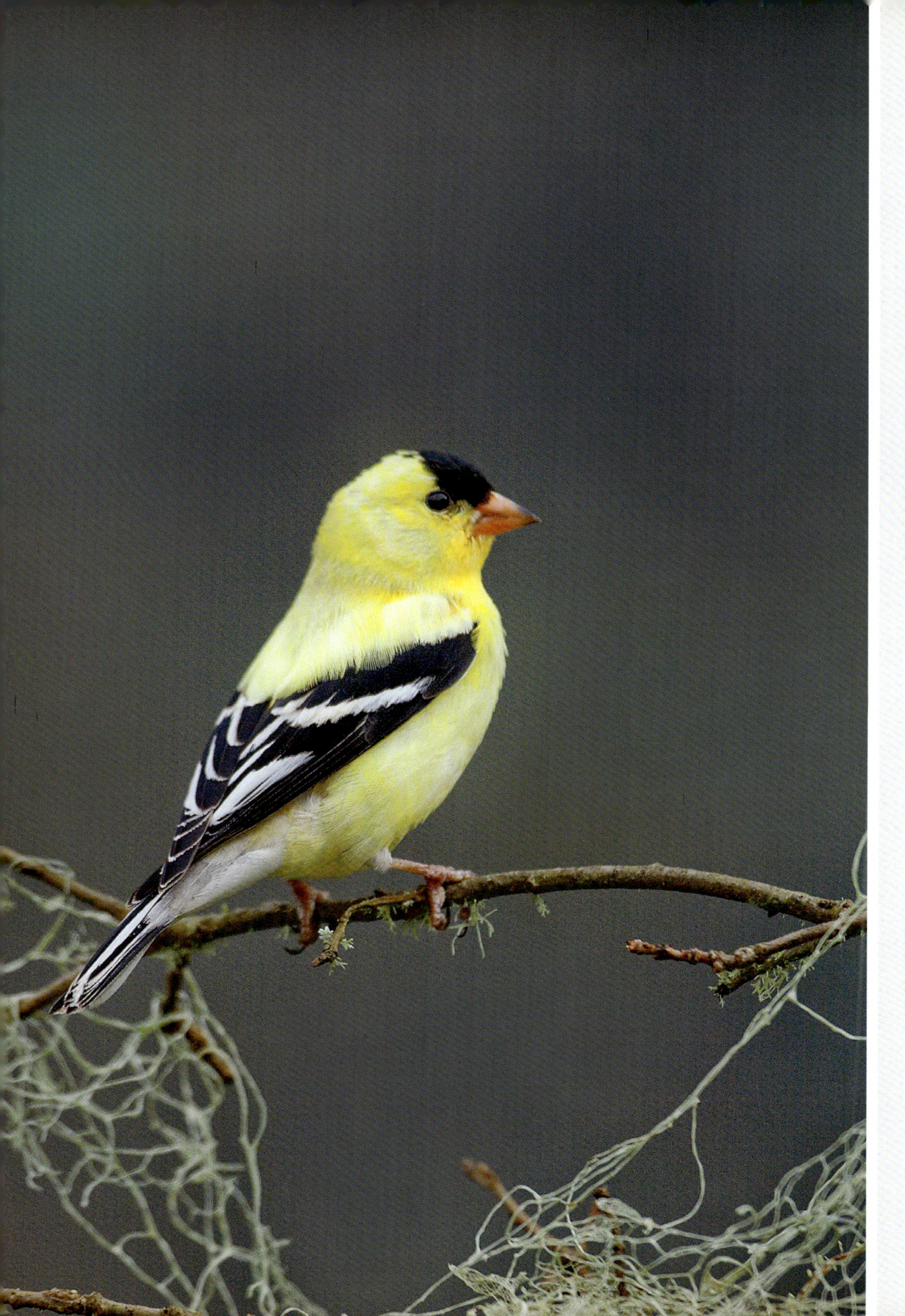

◄ *American goldfinch on a perch above a platform feeder*

CHAPTER 8 Showing Your Bird Photography

With a little practice you may end up creating some images that you are really proud of and want to share with others. There are so many ways to show off your photographs. The most common way to show your work is to have a print made, and then mount and frame it. You can also have it enlarged and printed onto a canvas. Alternatively, you can have a canvas wrap made.

You can also make or have made blank note cards or greeting cards from your images. Send your friends a note card or give them a boxed set of cards.

For personal use, a simple thing to do is to create stationary with your image. You can use this in all your correspondence to help spread the word of your great bird photography skills.

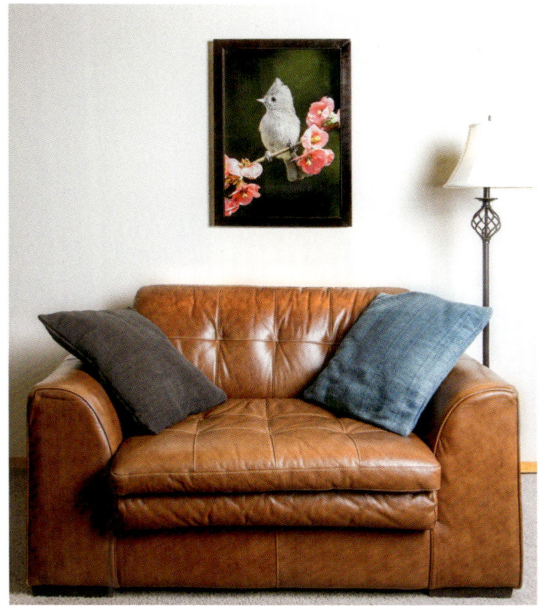

▲ *Framed poster of an oak titmouse above a living room couch*

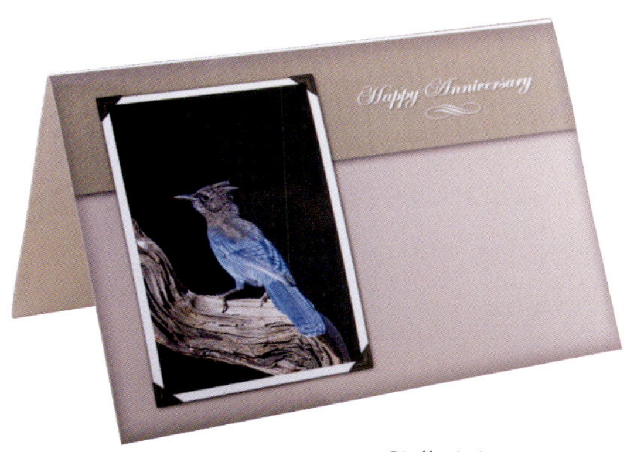

▲ *Steller's jay on an anniversary card*

Posters are a wonderful option. There is an incredible amount of online services that are available to make them for you. Frame the photograph yourself or have it professionally framed and provide some wall space for it in your home or give it as a gift to a bird lover that you know.

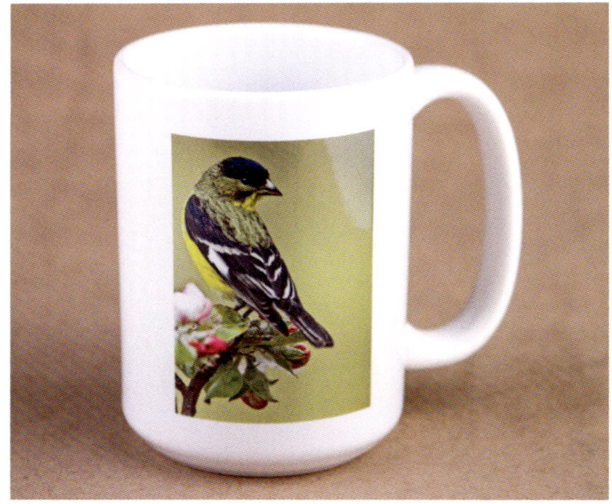

▲ *Lesser goldfinch image on a coffee mug*

Postcards are a wonderful and simple option. They can be created on your own ink jet printer or by an online service. They too are another great way to spread the word of your photography. Another possibility is to make yourself a coffee mug that you can use to sip your coffee while you're sorting your bird images. You could have a set of mugs made with six of your images.

When you have a dozen great images, you can have a calendar created. You can gift these calendars to your family and friends, or donate calendars to sell at a fundraiser for a local conservation group.

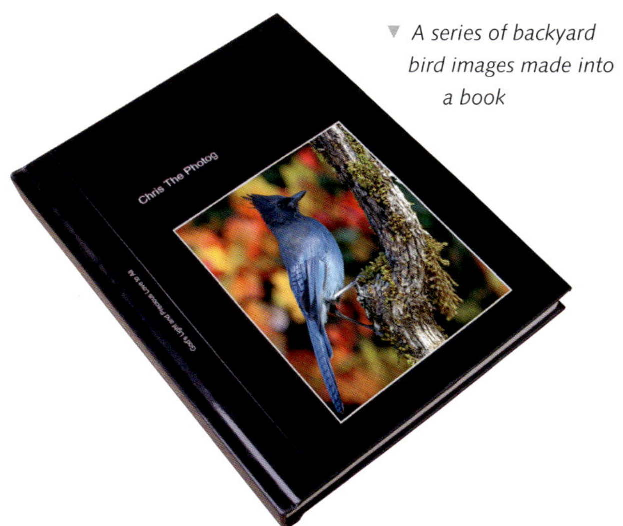

▼ *A series of backyard bird images made into a book*

You can use an online service to create a book. Blurb.com is one of many.

Don't forget entering your images in photography contests, like the Veolia Environment wildlife photography competition. You can also consider showcasing your work in local art galleries and exhibits. Check to see what their framing and exhibition requirements are. Online photo-sharing sites like Flickr, Smug Mug, and Photo Bucket are other options for ways to share your work with others.

For photo-critiques and ways to improve your bird photography, there is no better site than *Birdphotographers.net.* This site has a large number of bird photographers participating on it. It is primarily for images of birds out in nature, but many of the techniques and tutorials you'll find here can be applied to backyard bird photography as well.

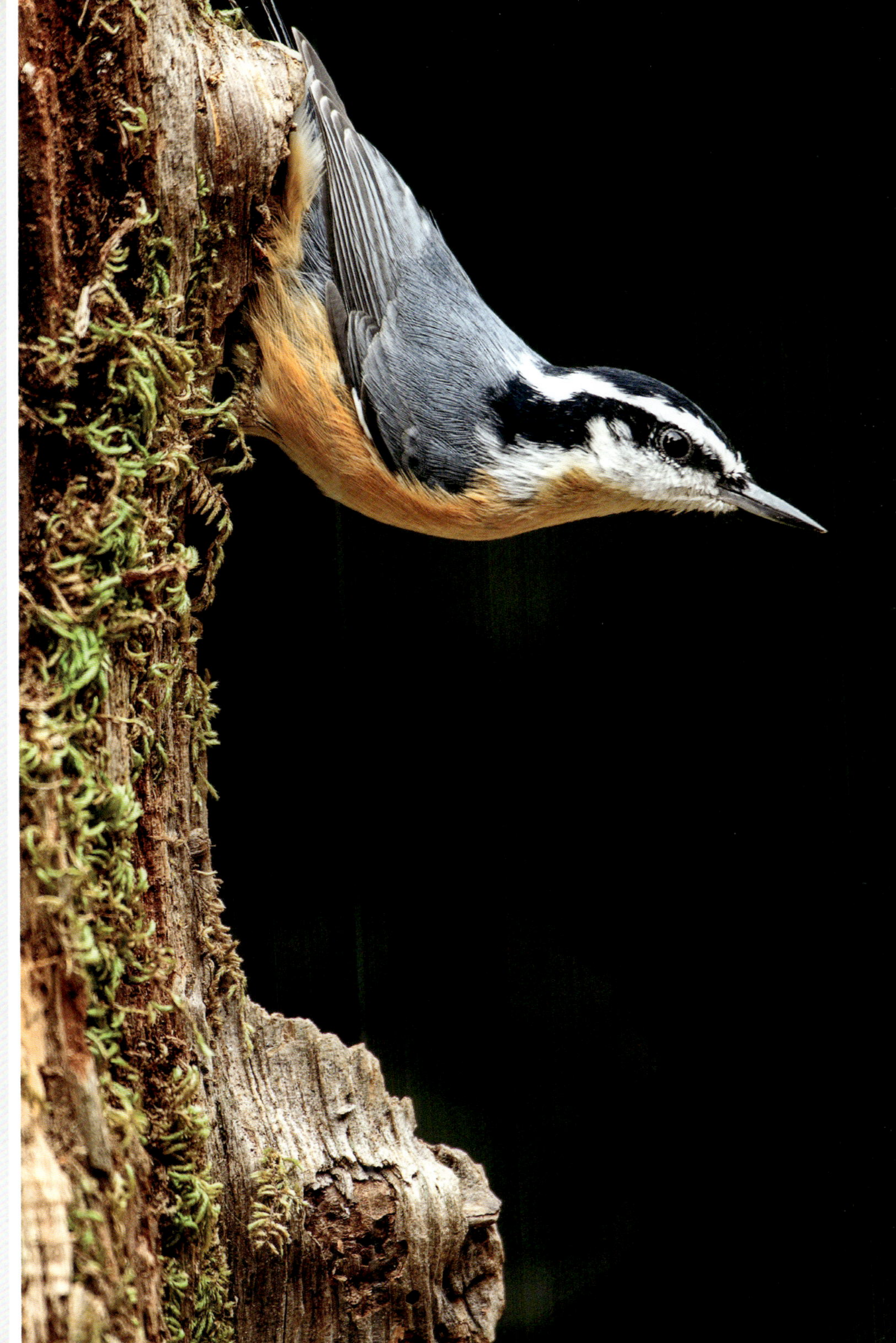

► *Red-breasted nuthatch coming down the side of perch to a platform feeder*

PETER PAN FEEDER

Level: Easy

Materials list:

- Empty plastic jar (I use Peter Pan peanut butter jars) with lid
- Wood screws
- Power drill

One of the simplest ways to get small birds such as nuthatches and chickadees to go upside down or into unusual spots is to put out a "Peter Pan Feeder." I gave it this name because the first one I created used a recycled Peter Pan peanut butter jar. The concept is very simple. Use a drill and bore a small hole in the bottom of a plastic container that has a lid. Make the hole just big enough that seed won't flow out of the container unless a bird picks it out. Then use wood screws to attach it to the back side of a perch. Fill it full of birdseed and put the lid on. Larger jars can be used for large perches and small prescription bottles can be used on smaller perches. Metal containers need to be used where squirrels are a problem because they will chew through the plastic ones.

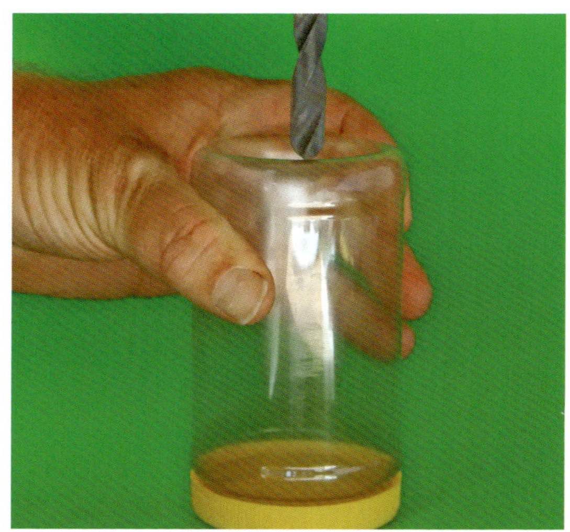

▲ *Step 1: Drill a hole in the bottom of a plastic container. Get it as close to the edge as you can.*

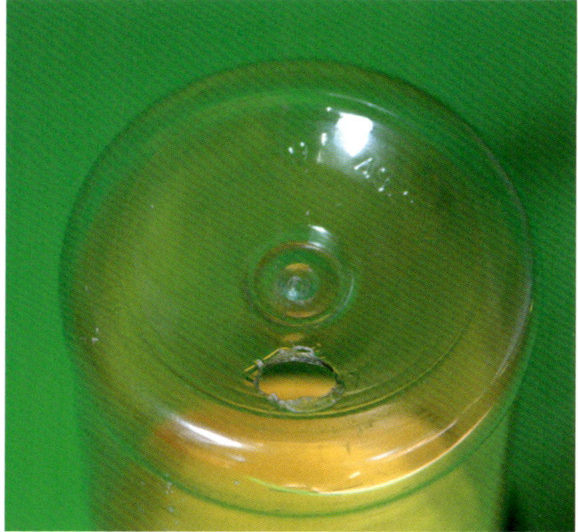

▲ *Yep, it's a hole*

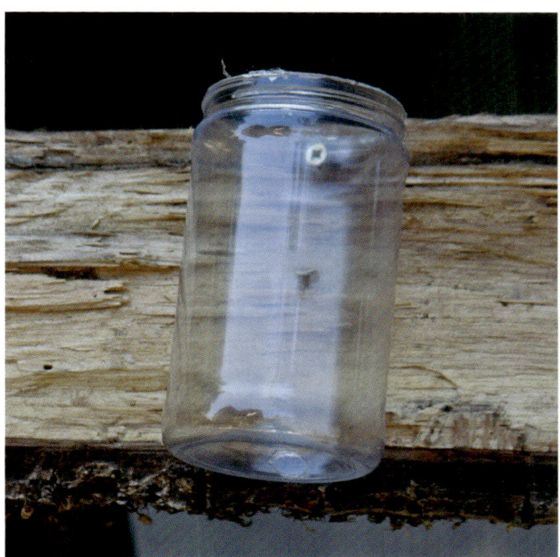

▲ *Step 2: Attach to the back of a likely perch*

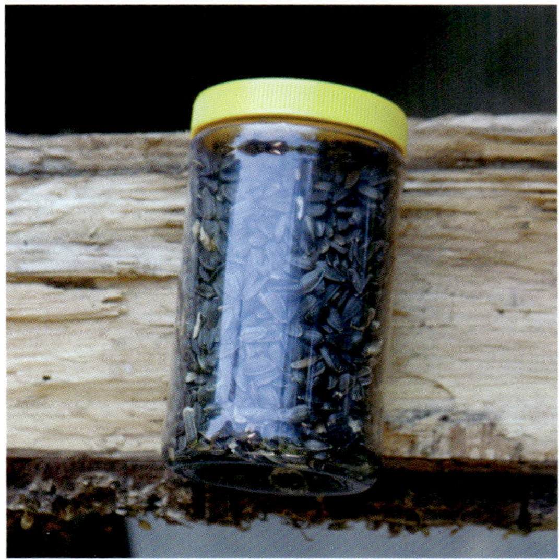

▲ *Step 3: Fill with seed and put the lid on*

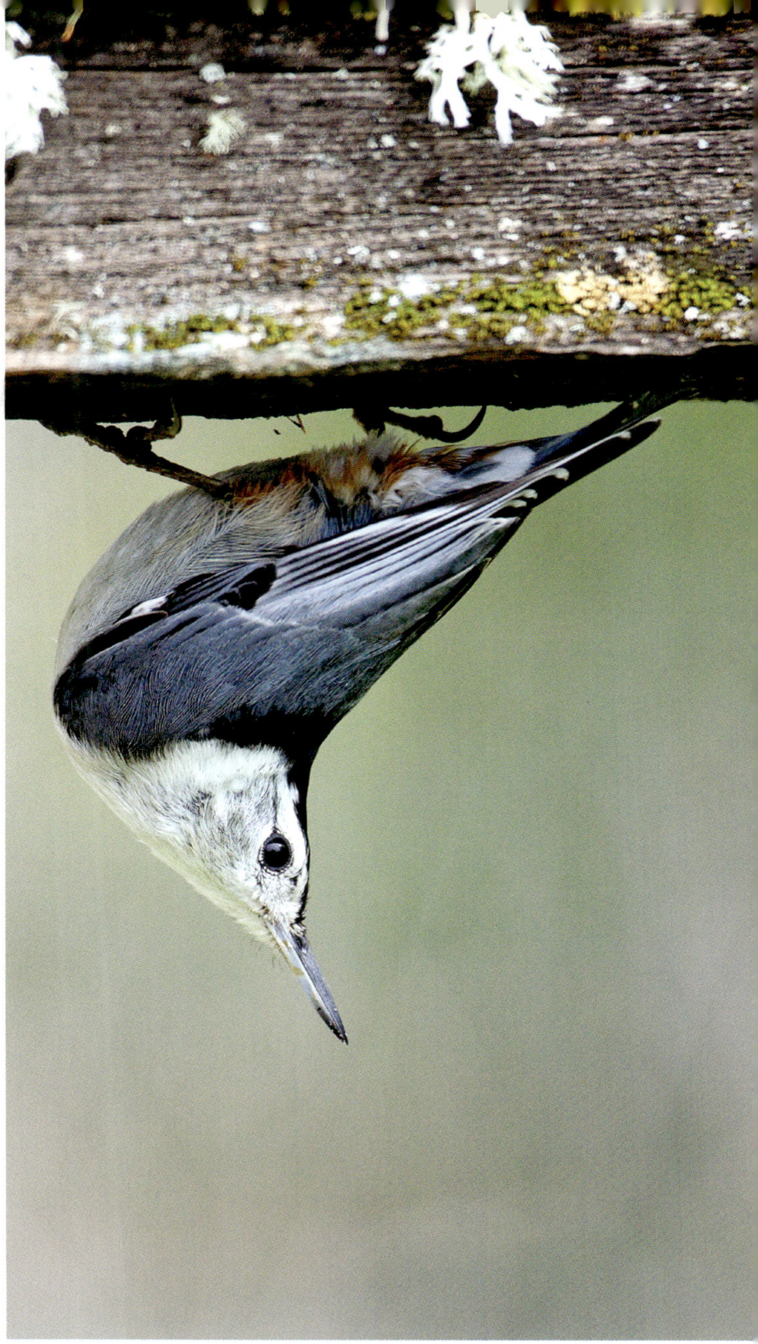

▲ *White-breasted nuthatch hanging upside down from a mossy board to get seed from a Peter Pan Feeder*

A CHANGEABLE PERCH FEEDER

Level: Easy

Materials list:

- Cookie tin
- Floral foam block
- Two wood screws
- Power drill
- 1¼″ or 1½″ spade bit
- Spray paint (optional)

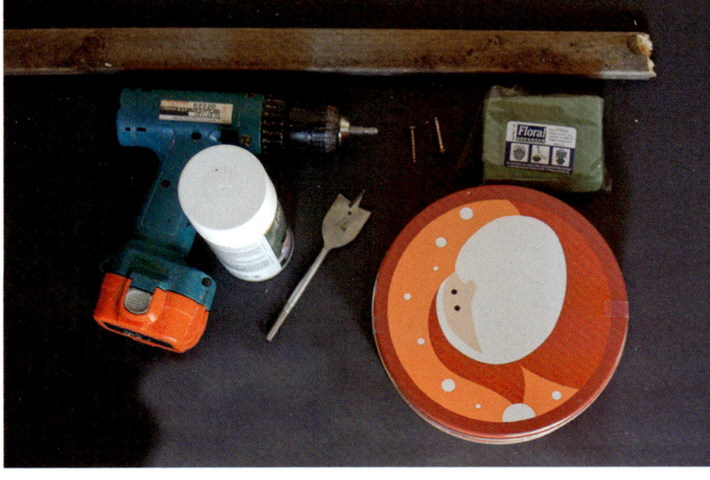

▲ *Basic supplies and tools needed*

Recently I was creating some images of chickadees using small branches with bright red berries on them next to the feeder. I was having a problem with the angle of the branch and the fact that the birds were landing too close to the platform feeder I was using. I knew I needed to try a new type of feeder. First I tried a tube feeder—that solved the issue of the birds landing too close to the feeder. They moved out just far enough onto the branch to make it workable.

There was still the problem of changing the angle of the branch. While perusing goods in the local dollar store, I stumbled upon some floral foam. You can stick a stem into that stuff and it will hold it at any angle. I thought it would be too difficult to put it into a tube feeder, but what else could I use to hold the foam block?

When I got home I discovered two cookie tins that I had purchased from the same store around Christmas time. One of those worked great. I drilled a couple of holes into the tin, and then added the foam block with some black sunflower seed. I screwed it to a scrap of lumber and then added the berry branch to it. It works perfectly for perching birds.

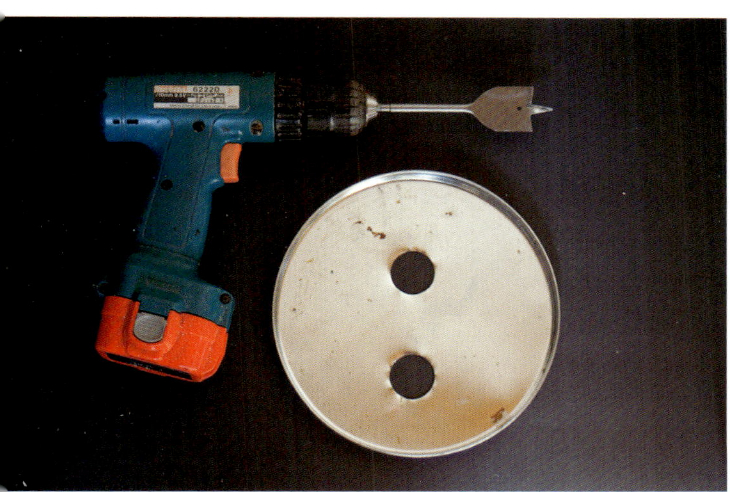

▲ *Step 1: Drill two holes in the lid*

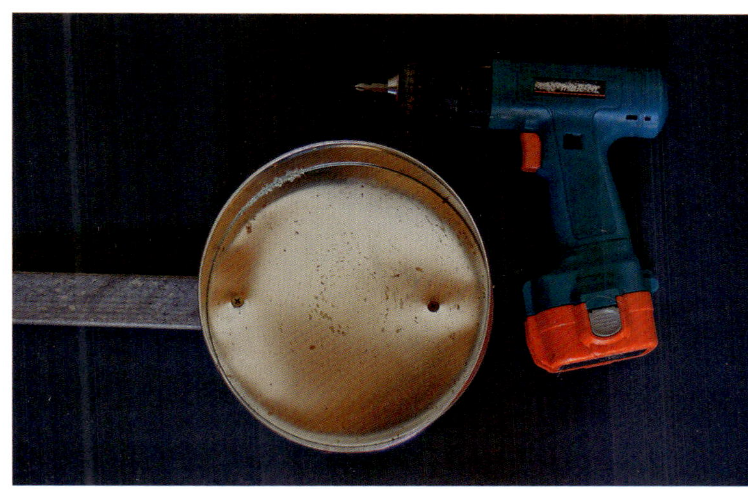

▲ *Step 2: Screw the bottom of the tin to a 1″ × 2″ or similar piece of wood*

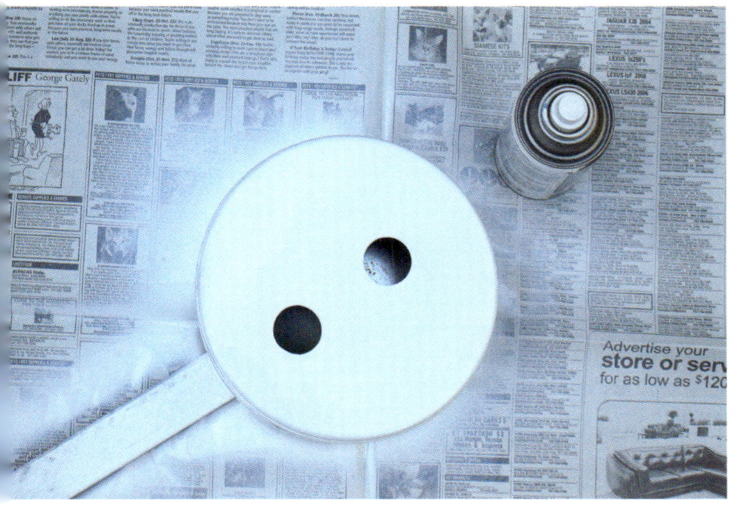

▲ *Step 3: Spray paint the lid (optional)*

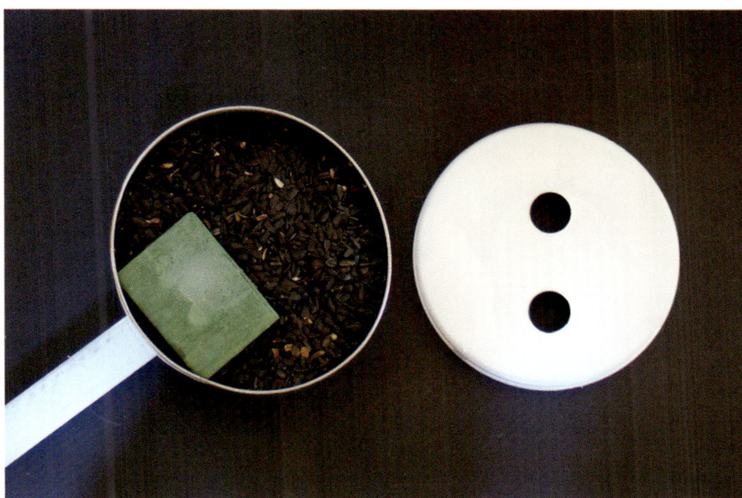

▲ *Step 4: Place the foam block at the bottom and pour seed around it*

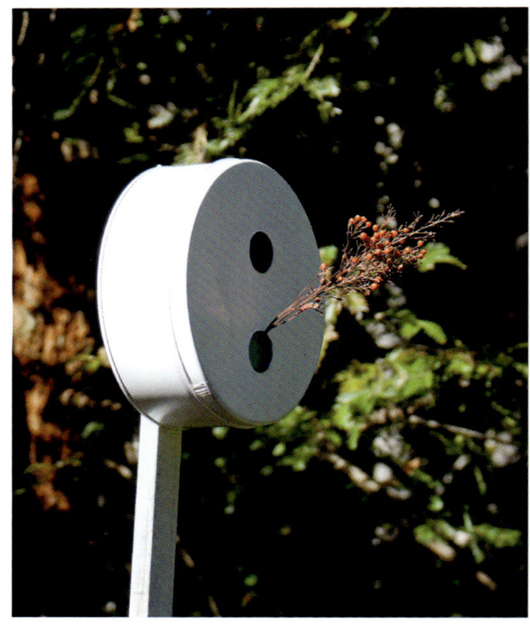

▲ *Step 5: Put the lid on and stick a light perch into the foam block*

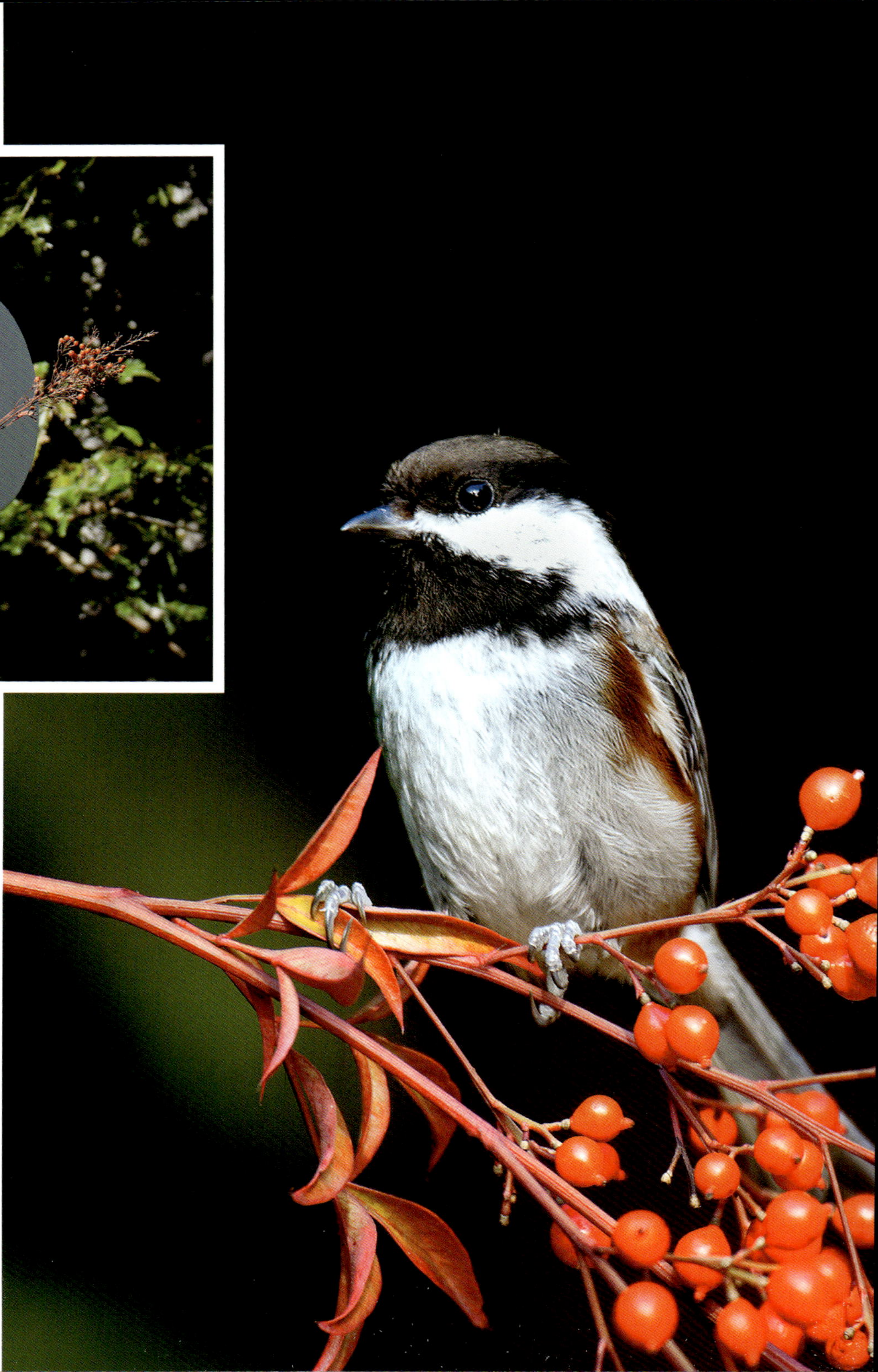

► *Chestnut-backed chickadee tries out the feeder as soon as it is put up!*

SMALL WATER FEATURE: BIRD BATHS

Level: Easy

Materials list:

- A piece of plywood—any shape or size greater than your platter
- Jigsaw
- Plate, shallow bowl, or platter
- Spray paint (black usually works best)
- Natural decorations of your choice

I love to do bird photography during the arrival of spring. That's not to say I don't like doing it at other times of the year, but in the spring, birds are in their breeding colors. Also, because I live in Northern California, all the water sources start drying up as soon as the rainy season ends in March. You know the song, "It Never Rains in California"? With few available water sources, birds start searching for new places to drink and bathe.

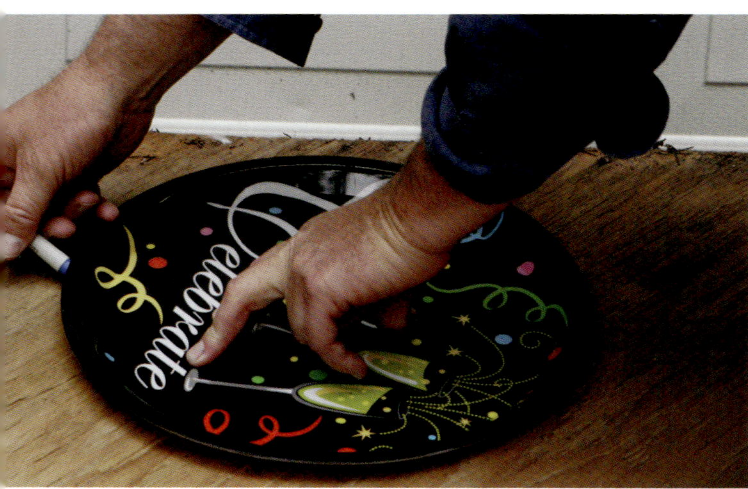

▲ *Step 1: Trace the base of the platter or plate on the plywood*

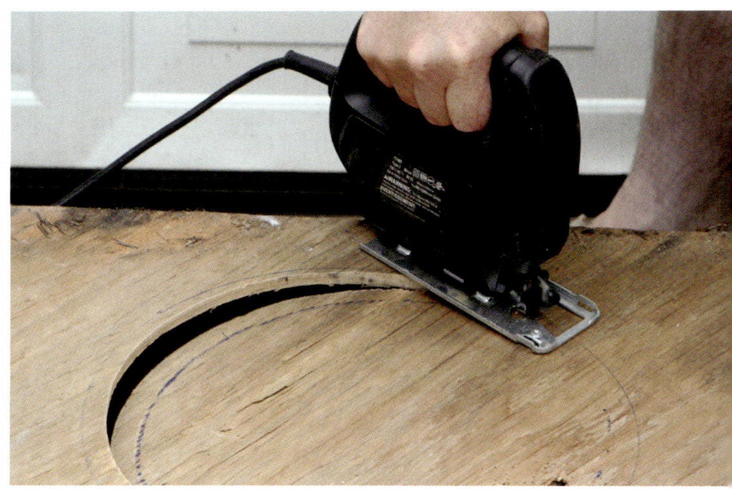

▲ *Step 2: Cut a hole about ⅛" larger than the base of the platter*

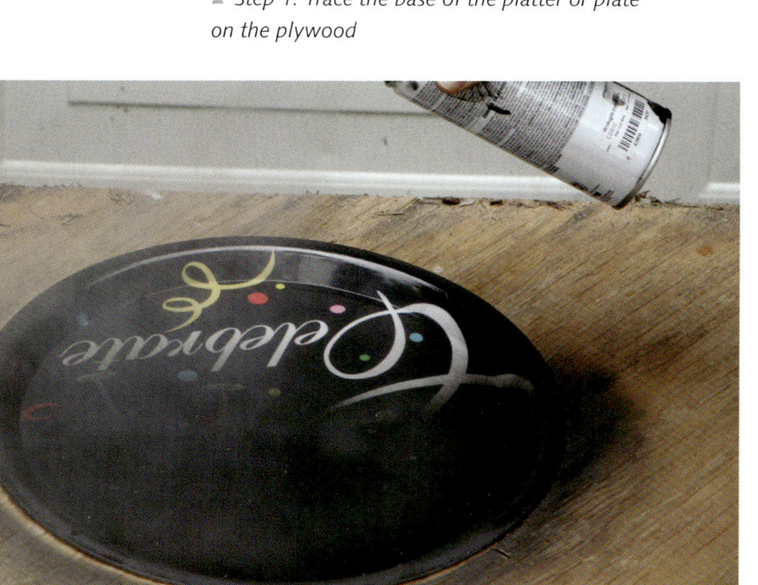

▲ *Step 3: Set the plate or platter into the hole in the plywood and spray paint black*

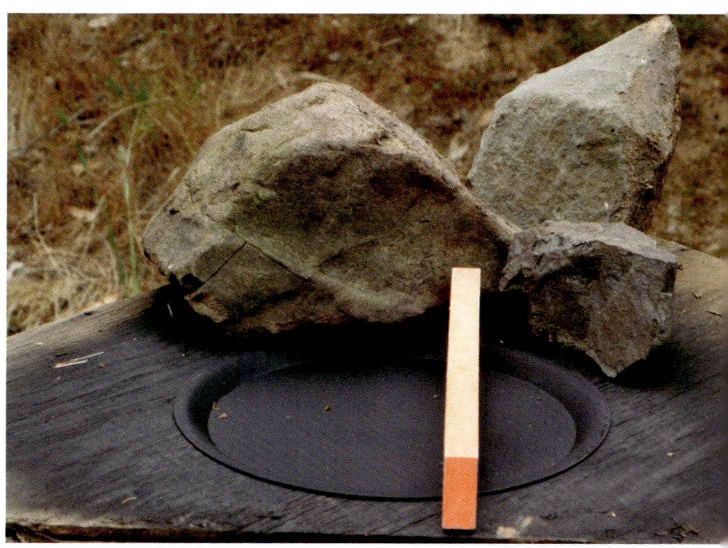

▲ *Platter set within the plywood*

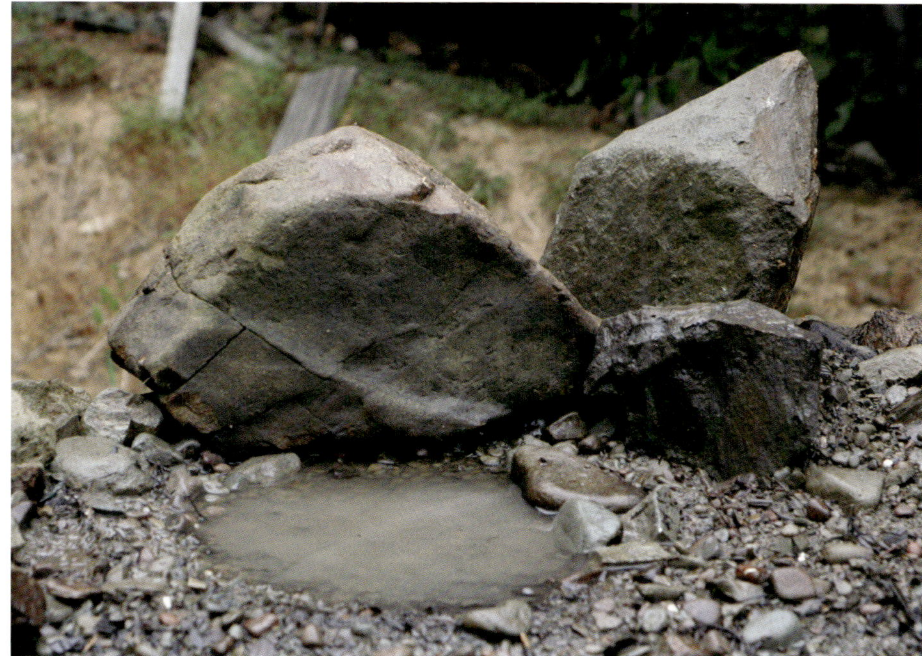

◄ *Step 4: Decorate your birdbath to make it look more natural*

This is where the dollar store comes in handy. They have wonderful flat platters and shallow bowls that work perfectly for birdbaths. Add some rock, sand, and gravel around them, and even some plants, and you have a perfect water set-up to photograph birds drinking and bathing.

Start with scrap plywood and cut a hole about ⅛″ bigger than the base of the platter with a jigsaw. Set the platter in the hole and spray paint it with flat black spray paint. Then find something level on which to support the plywood. Sawhorses or cinder blocks and bricks on a picnic table work very well.

The last and most creative step is to decorate around the outside of the platter to make it look natural. You can use mossy rocks, branches, plants, and leaves. Add some water dripping into it overhead from a hose and wait for the birds. Most of the time I also place a few seed feeders close by. This seems to attract more birds. The last thing you will need to do is set up some sort of blind. Mornings are usually best for lighting, and birds seem to be more abundant at this time of day. On hot days, mid-afternoon seems to work best because the birds are looking for a place to cool down.

THE KNOTHOLE FEEDER

Level: Medium

Materials list:

- An empty can (size dependent on your knothole)
- Piece of thick bark from a chunk of 24″-long firewood with a knothole
- Wood screws
- Plaster of Paris
- Hole saw
- Spray paint (I recommend black)
- 1″ × 3″ × 3′ piece of wood for a post
- Drill
- Natural decorations of your choice

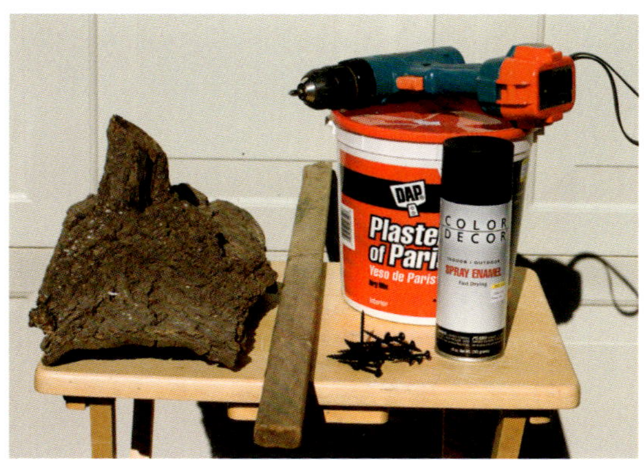

▲ *Materials for a knothole feeder*

Have you ever seen those cool pictures of birds and squirrels poking their heads out of knotholes in trees? The photographer must have spent days following birds around trying to find their nests. When I have actually done that I've gotten some neat shots of birds bringing food to their young. But what do you do when it's not nesting season? One day when I was getting some wood from the woodpile, I came up with a great idea. I picked up a piece of firewood that had a knothole in it, and the bark came right off of the wood! I got to thinking, "why not add a feeder to the back side of the bark?" After a number of attempts using wood, wire, and string, I finally settled upon using wood screws, a coffee can, and some Plaster of Paris.

Basically, it's a simple, messy process. You'll need wood screws, the can, and a 1″ × 3″ × 3′ (or similar) piece of wood for the post.

One of the best ways of imitating a nest hole in the side of a tree is to actually use what would have eventually become a nest hole in the first place. Find a piece of firewood or a section of a downed tree where a branch has broken off and a cavity is starting to form where the dead material is rotting out. Most pieces of wood are too small for a knothole feeder, or the cavity isn't big enough. The solution is to enlarge what's already there by drilling out the hole from the back.

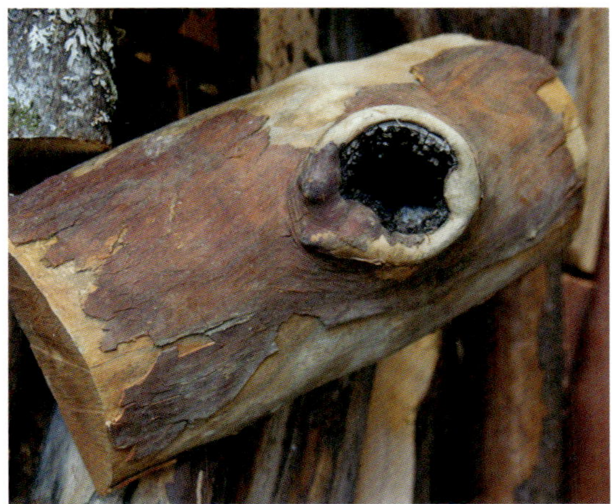

▲ *The hardest part is finding a suitable piece of wood*

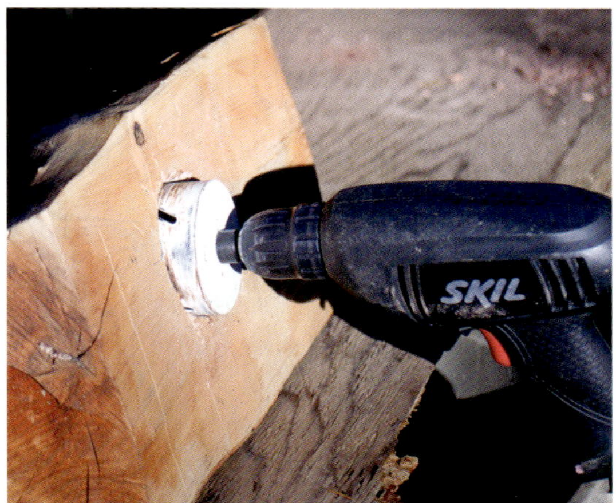

▲ *Step 1: Drilling out the back with a hole saw*

Step 1: Drill out the back side of the bark or wood with a hole saw.

Step 2: Spray paint the inside of the can black.

Step 3: Use wood screws to add the 1″ × 3″ post to the back of the can so that you have something with which to mount the feeder once you're ready to secure it.

Step 4: Put the can opening on the back of the piece of bark, centered over the knothole. Drill a circle of wood screws into the back of the thick bark to fit around the can. Be careful not to go through the bark with the wood screws.

Step 5: Mix up a batch of Plaster of Paris and build up a wedge or ramp around the can onto the bark, making sure to cover the wood screws to hold it all together. Let it set for a couple of hours and you're done.

Step 5 (alternate): If you don't want or need to use plaster, you can simply screw the can to the back of the wood with wood screws. The size of the tin cans will vary depending upon the size of the wood. Using tin snips, make vertical cuts all the way around the top of the can, roughly ½ to ¾ of an inch apart to create tabs. Bend these tabs down with a pair of pliers, and screw them into the back of the piece of wood with wood screws.

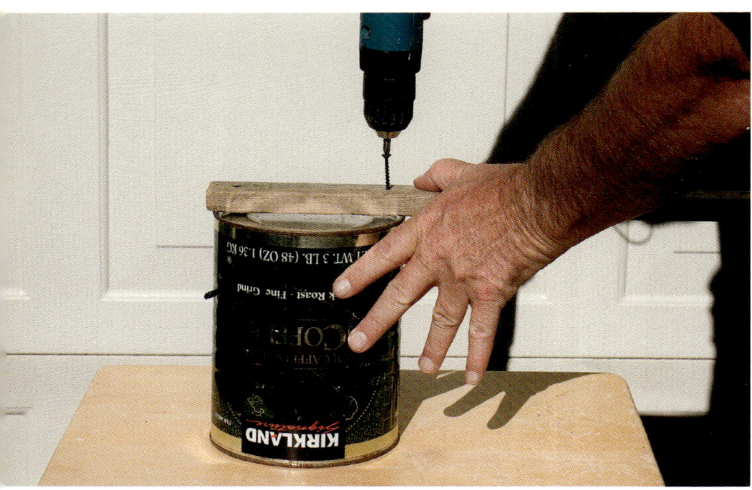

▲ *Step 3: Adding a post to the can*

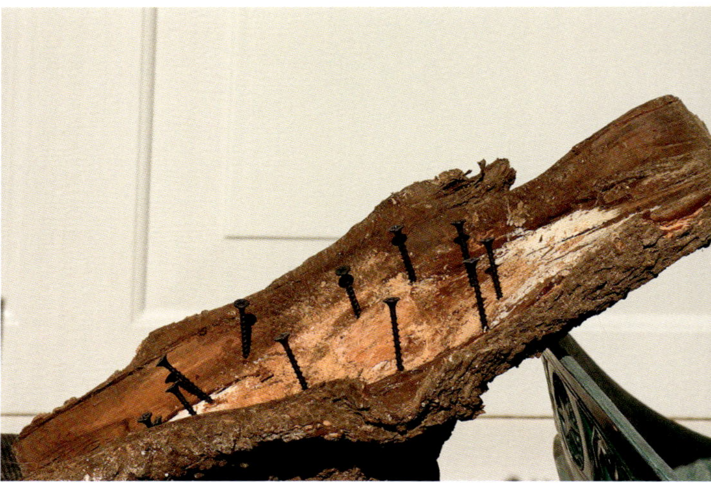

▲ *Step 4a: Drill a circle of wood screws to create a "basket" structure for the can*

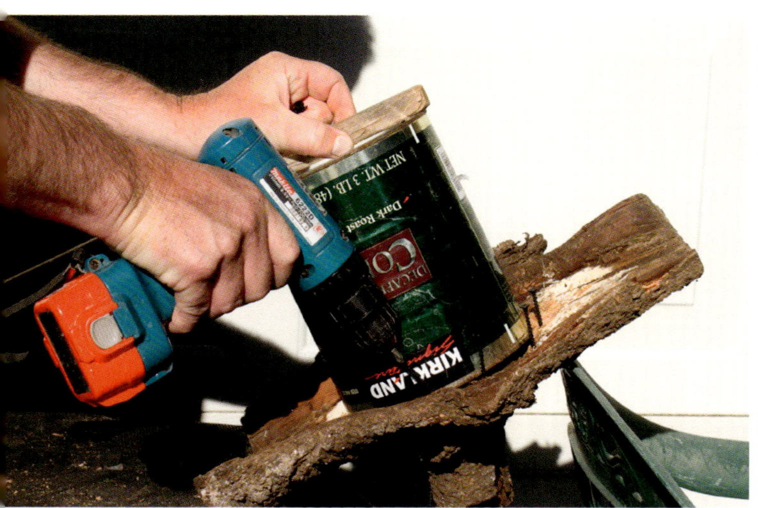

▲ *Step 4b: Place the can within the structure created by the circle of wood screws*

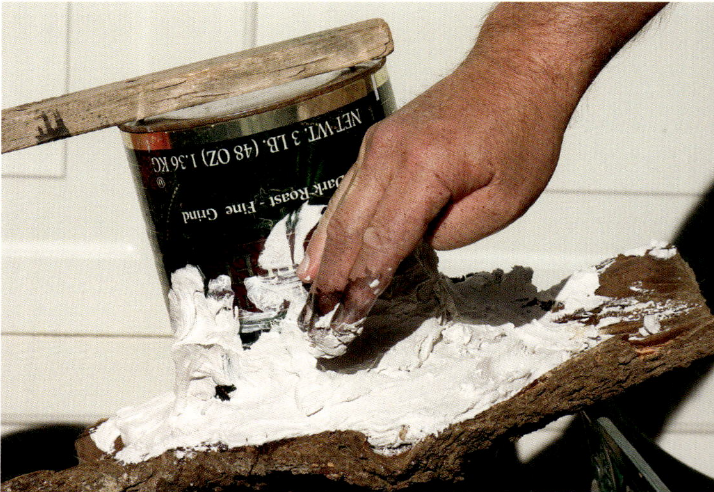

▲ *Step 5: Use Plaster of Paris to anchor the can into the structure of wood screws*

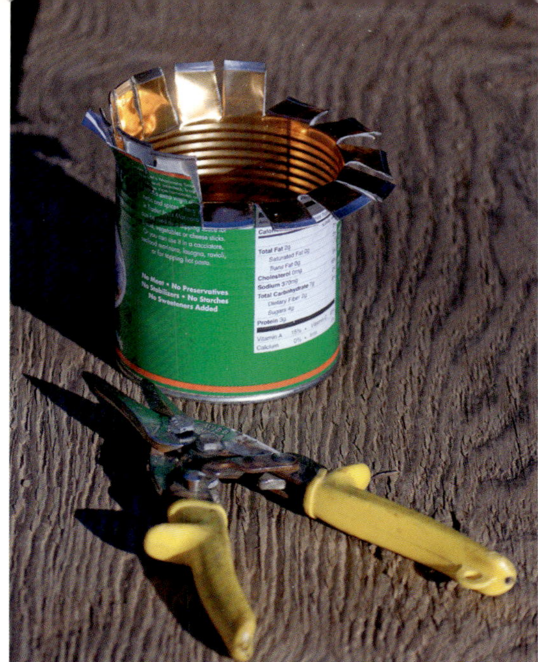

▲ *Step 5a (alternate): Cutting tabs in the can and folding them down*

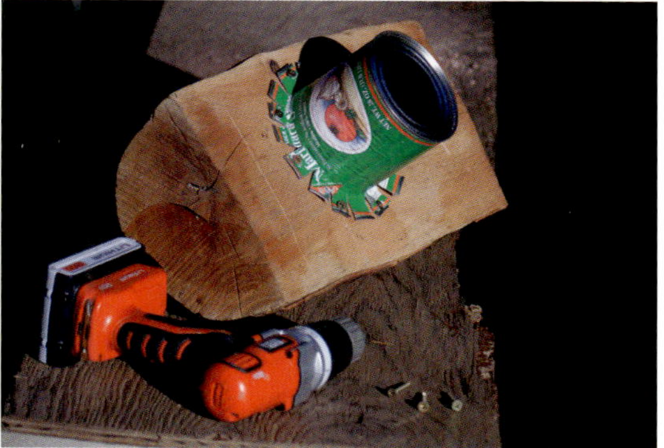

▲ *Step 5b (alternate): Wood screws are used to fasten the can tabs to the backside of the piece of wood*

Step 6: Once the feeder is completed, add seed to the can. Now find a convenient fence or pole on which to mount the feeder. It is best to place it near other feeders to help critters discover the feed that you put inside of it. Be sure to take into consideration what kind of light you want to fall on it. It also helps with birds to place feeders near bushes for cover. They are a lot more comfortable feeding in places where they know they can dive off into safety if a predator comes near. The nice thing about these feeders is they make for an extremely natural looking nest hole.

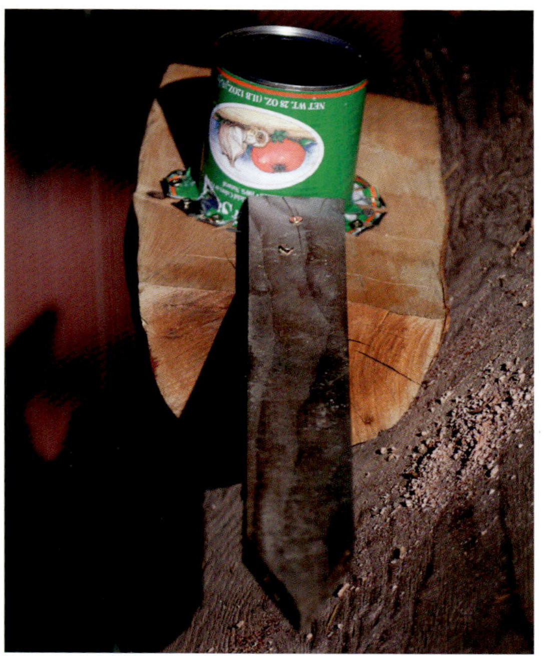

▲ *1″ × 3″ post screwed to the knothole wood in preparation for placement*

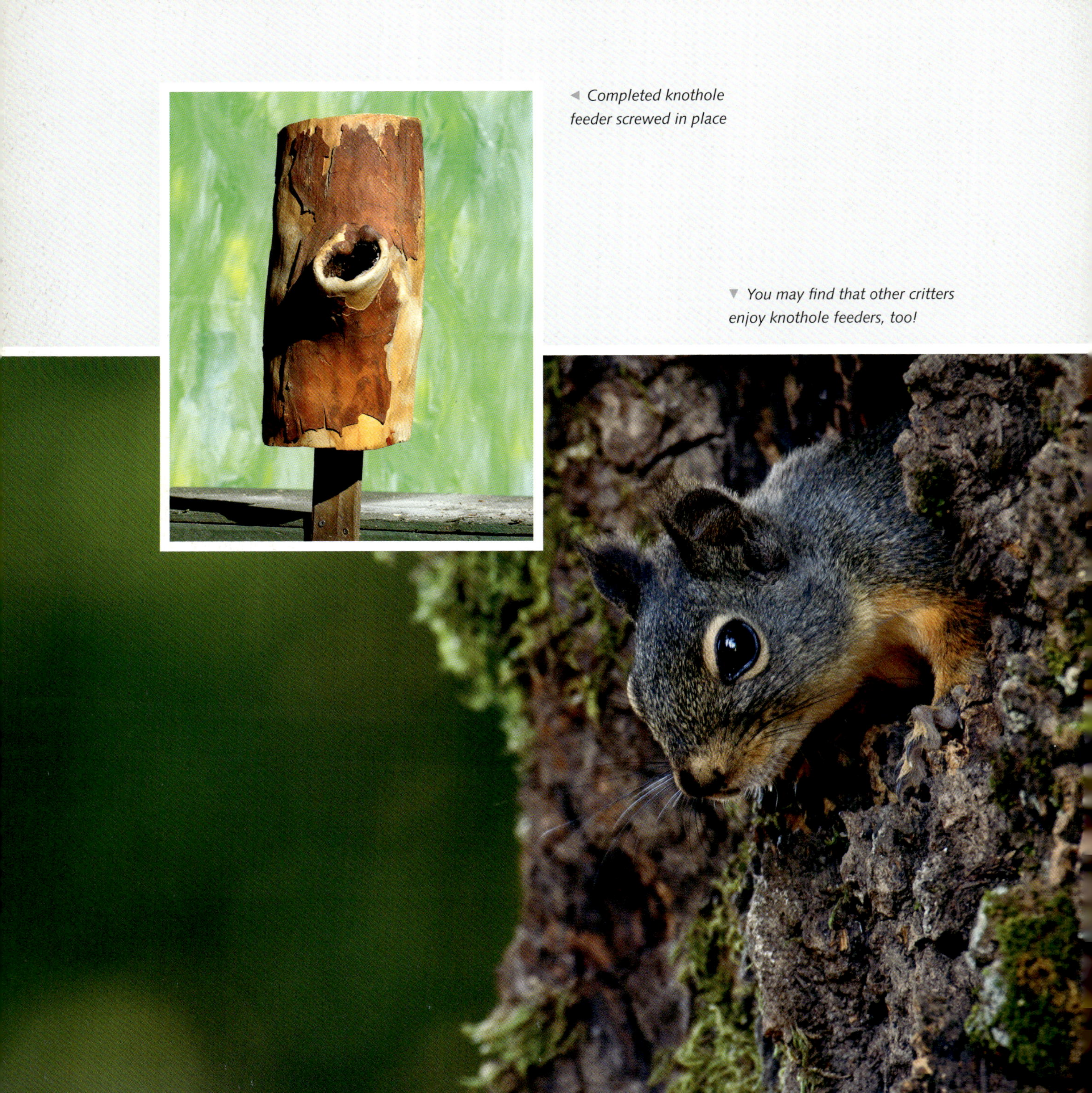

◂ *Completed knothole feeder screwed in place*

▾ *You may find that other critters enjoy knothole feeders, too!*

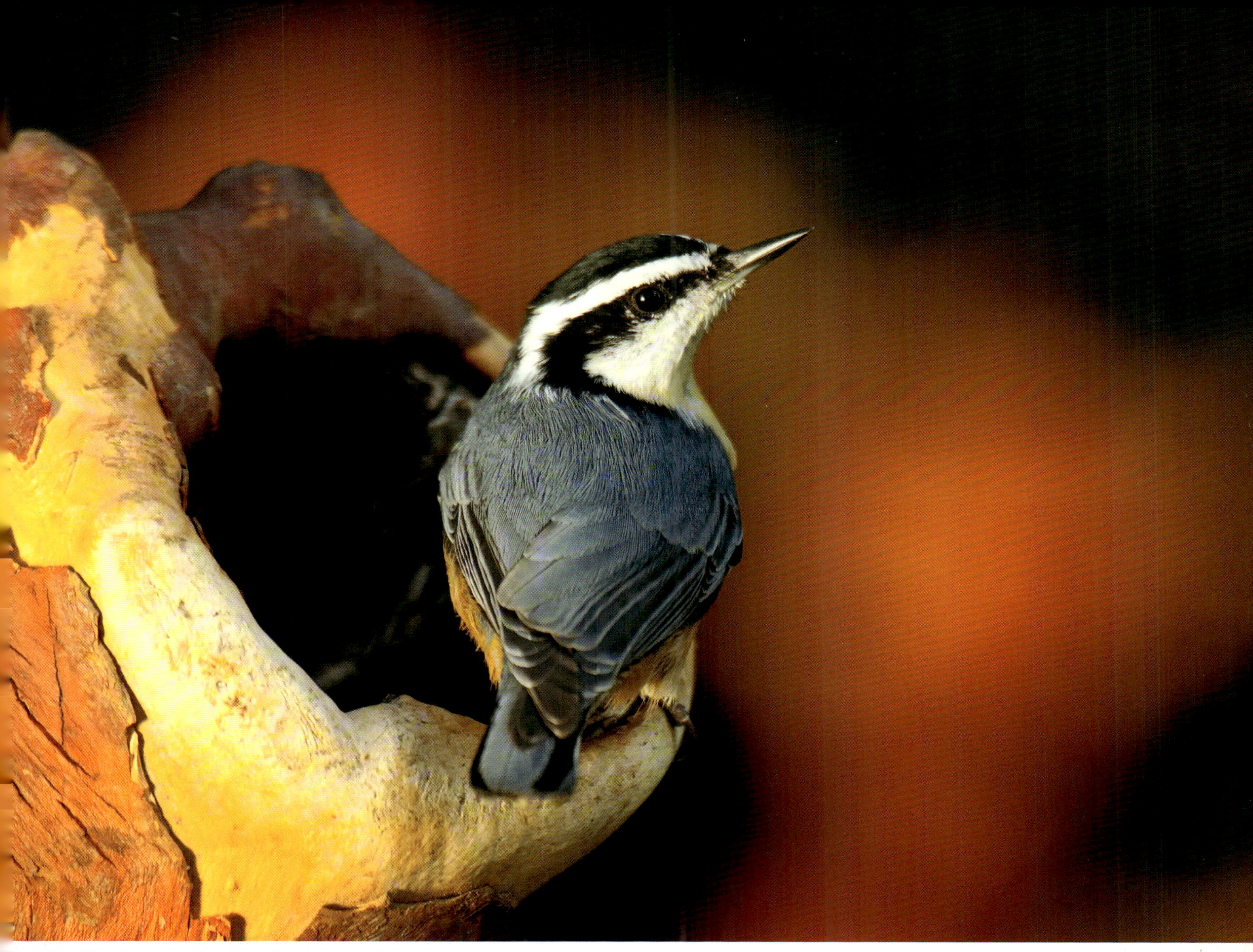

▲ *Red-breasted nuthatch gathering black sunflower seed from the knothole feeder*

BUILDING A WINDOW BLIND

Level: Medium

Materials list:

- ⅛″ Masonite (cut to the size of your window)
- Strips of a towel, enough to surround the edges of the Masonite
- Circular saw
- Tape
- Netting or batting material, cut into 2″ strips
- 1″ × 4″ boards (optional)

Yes, it's true. I have a custom, luxury blind that has a TV, fridge, and a computer with Internet. It's also heated. On top of that it has the most comfortable chair I have ever used in a blind. So before you think I'm nuts, let me say that this blind is the office inside my house. I do a good percentage of my bird photography right out the back window of my house. I place my rolling feeder in appropriate lighting with a good background right next to my office window. There are holes drilled in the rolling feeder so I can place branches of different types as perches for the birds to land on.

Creating a blind out of one of your windows can be as simple as tacking up a piece of fabric with a hole in it for your camera over the window. I like something a little more secure, so I use a piece of ⅛″ Masonite that is cut to the window size.

Step 1: To create the blind, first measure the window and then cut the board to size. Keep in mind when cutting your board that you'll need to subtract ½″ from all sides to accommodate for the frame of towels.

Step 2: Tape strips of towel around the outside perimeter of the pressed hardboard to keep the windowsill from getting scratched up.

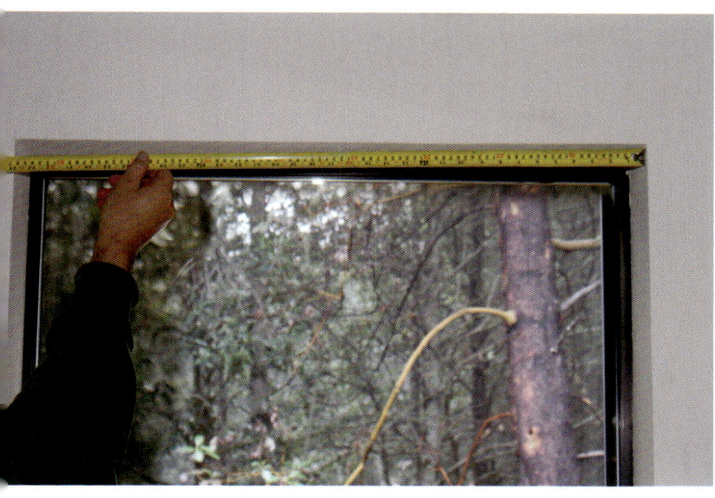

▲ Step 1a: Measure the inside of the window

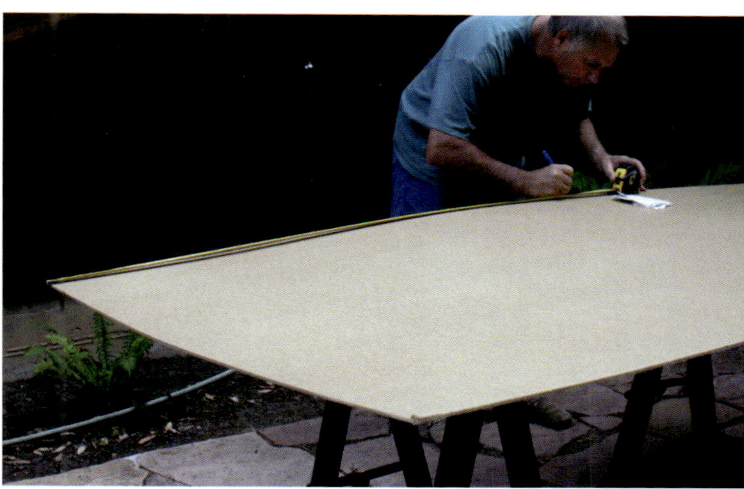

▲ Step 1b: Transfer the measurements to a piece of plywood or hardboard (I use Masonite). Subtract ½" from each side to allow for wrapping the edges in the towel.

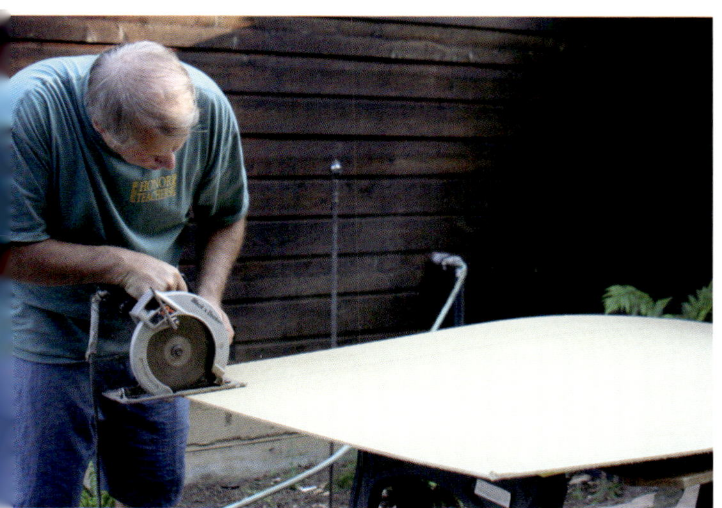

▲ Step 1c: Cutting the sides with a circular saw

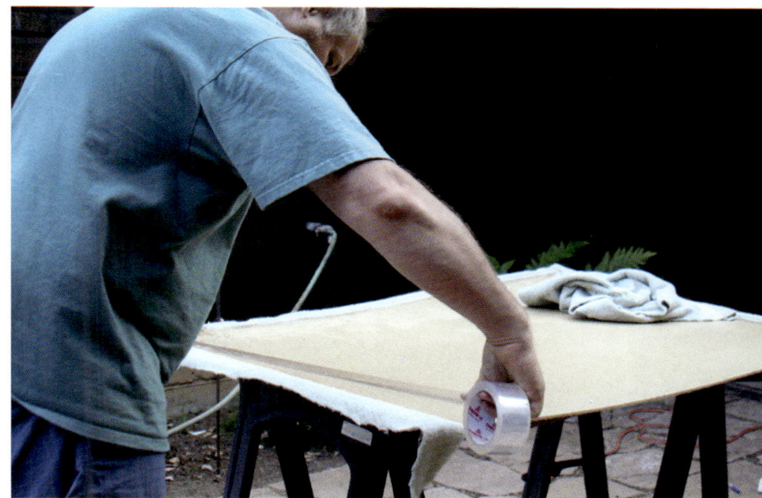

▲ Step 2a: Taping the towel material to the back of the hardboard

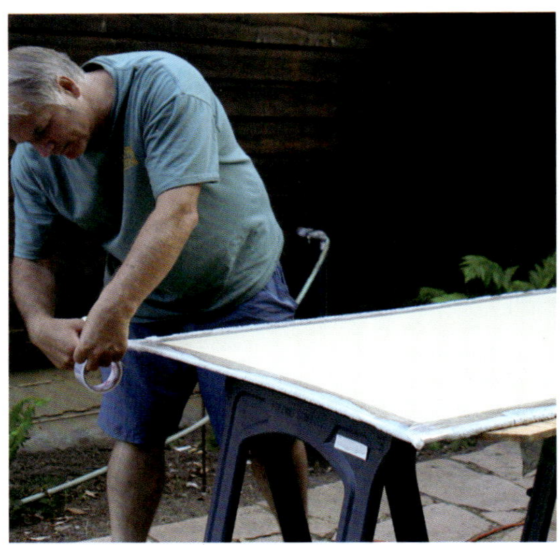

▲ *Step 2b: Taping the front side of the hardboard*

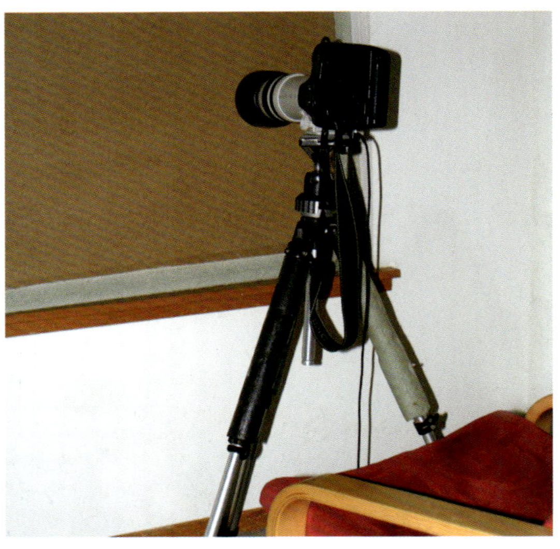

▲ *Step 3a: Checking for the correct window height to cut the opening*

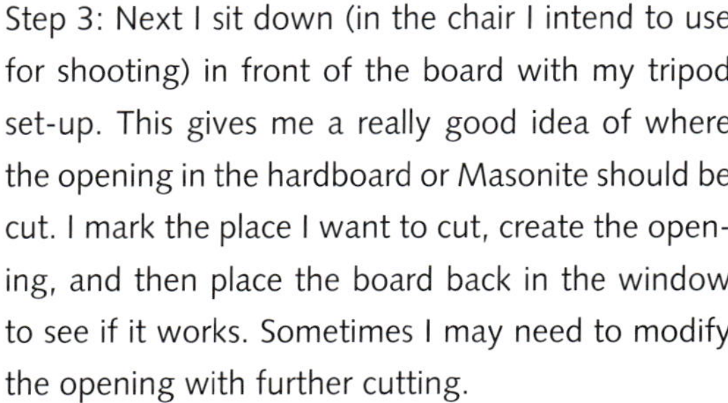

Step 3: Next I sit down (in the chair I intend to use for shooting) in front of the board with my tripod set-up. This gives me a really good idea of where the opening in the hardboard or Masonite should be cut. I mark the place I want to cut, create the opening, and then place the board back in the window to see if it works. Sometimes I may need to modify the opening with further cutting.

Step 4: Tape a piece of netting or batting material to hang over the hole. I like to cut it in strips about 2″ wide.

Step 5: After having used the window blind for a while I reinforced the hardboard by screwing on some 1″ × 4″ boards to the outside edges to stiffen it.

The flat board will fit easily behind a door, or it can be stored in the garage or basement, ready for use. You can cut boards to fit all the windows in your home to allow yourself a variety of shooting locations.

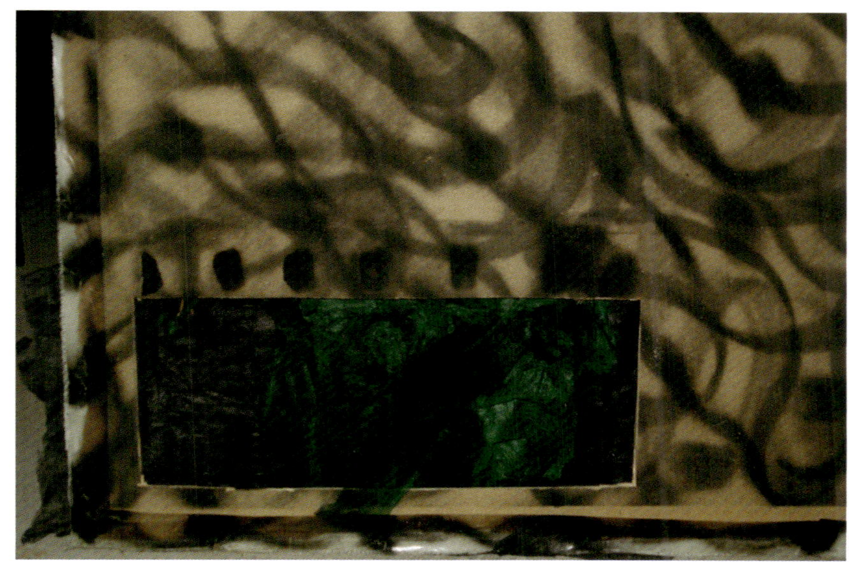

◄ *Step 3b: Cut an opening and spray paint the outside*

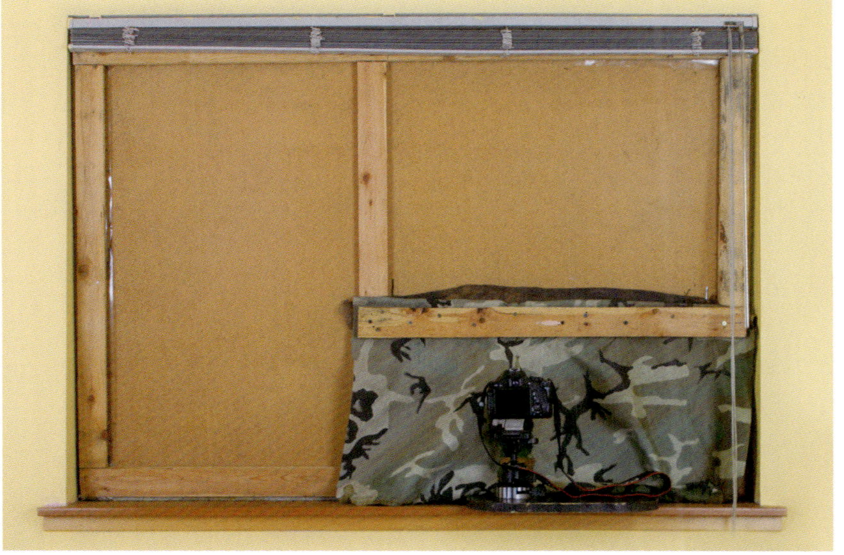

◄ *Completed window blind in place*

GROUND POD FOR SHOOTING FROM A WINDOWSILL

Level: Medium

Materials list:

- Clamp
- Bogen ballhead (or equivalent)
- Scrap board (1″ × 12″)
- ⅜″ carriage bolt
- Epoxy
- Netting or batting material, cut into 2″ strips
- 1″ × 4″ boards (optional)

Over the years I have struggled with ways to photograph from my office window. The main problem is that I can't get up next to the wall because the legs of the tripod are in the way. I've tried using rolled up towels and beanbags to stabilize the camera instead of a tripod, but towels aren't very stable and beanbags aren't very adjustable. The commercial beanbags come with a ¼″ mounting screw on top, and you have to spin the bag to attach it to your camera. These don't allow you to maintain the camera in a locked and focused position.

I finally settled on a solution that works really well—clamping a DIY ground pod to the windowsill ledge.

Step 1: Use an old Bogen ballhead (or equivalent) from a long dead tripod.

Step 2: Drill and mount it to a piece of scrap board (1″ × 12″) with a ⅜″ carriage bolt, and then epoxy the bolt in place. Be sure to check and see what size bolt your tripod head uses before epoxying one into place.

Voilà! A new ground pod is born. It is light and easy to carry with a camera mounted on it. I can easily switch from horizontals to verticals. (Try that with a commercial beanbag pod!) I clamp it to the windowsill of my office (behind the blind) using a large spring clamp, and I'm ready for some bird photography.

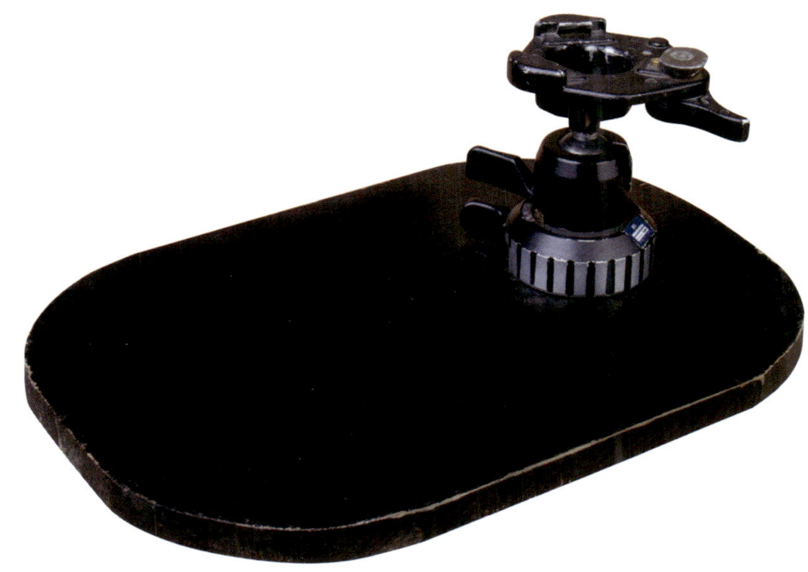

◂ *Ground pod made with a 1″ × 12″ board and a ⅜″ carriage bolt*

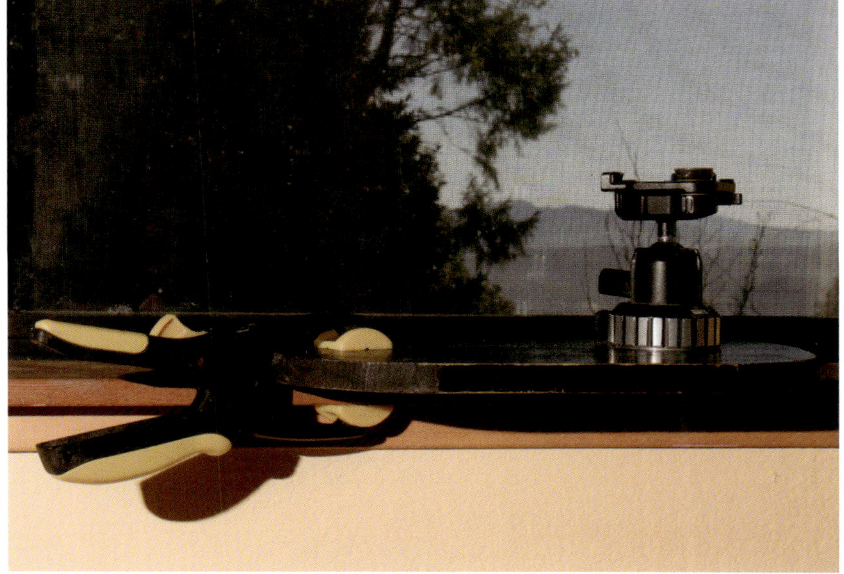

◂ *Ground pod clamped to a windowsill, ready for use*

The following projects are more elaborate and extensive, and require more construction or sewing experience, and materials.

BUILDING A LARGE WATER FEATURE

Level: Complex

Materials list:

- Table (picnic table or similar)
- Qt of sealer or waterproof paint
- 1″ × 4″ × 8′ pieces of wood (2)
- 1″ × 4″ × 4′ piece of wood
- Sheet of 4′ × 8′ plywood, 3⁄8″ or thicker
- 1¼″ wood screws (20)
- Circular saw
- Black plastic sheeting (Visqueen), 10′ × 6′
- Rocks and gravel to line the edge of the pond

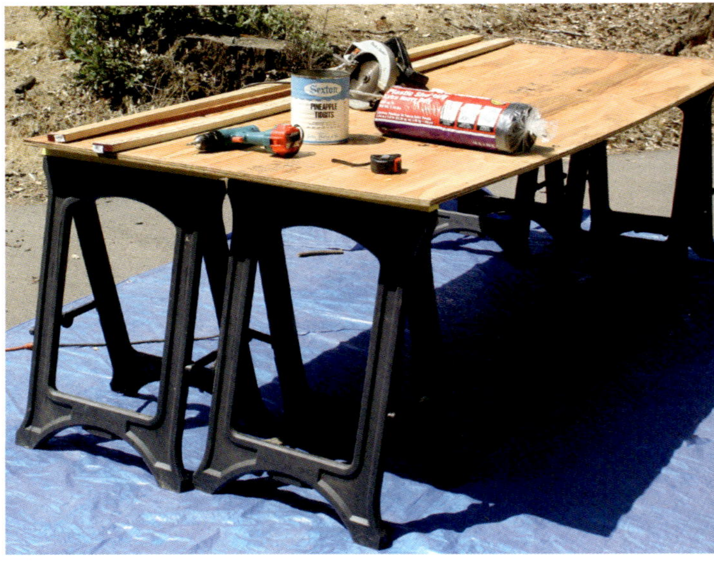

▲ *Step 1: Here are the needed supplies. First, apply a sealant to the plywood.*

This water feature is a project for someone with a yard with plenty of room, as it is 4 feet × 8 feet in size. The birds absolutely love it. You will have birds visiting it throughout the day. The pond is a 4′ × 8′ sheet of plywood set on top of an old table (an old picnic table or a table picked up cheap from a garage sale will do).

Step 1: Seal the sheet of plywood with enamel paint, varathane, polyurethane, or some other type of wood sealer.

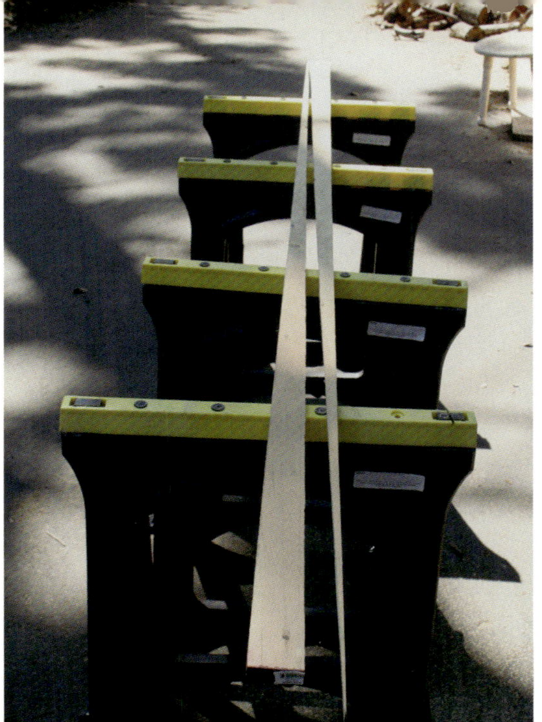

▲ *Step 2: Cut the 1″ × 4″ × 8' in half, diagonally*

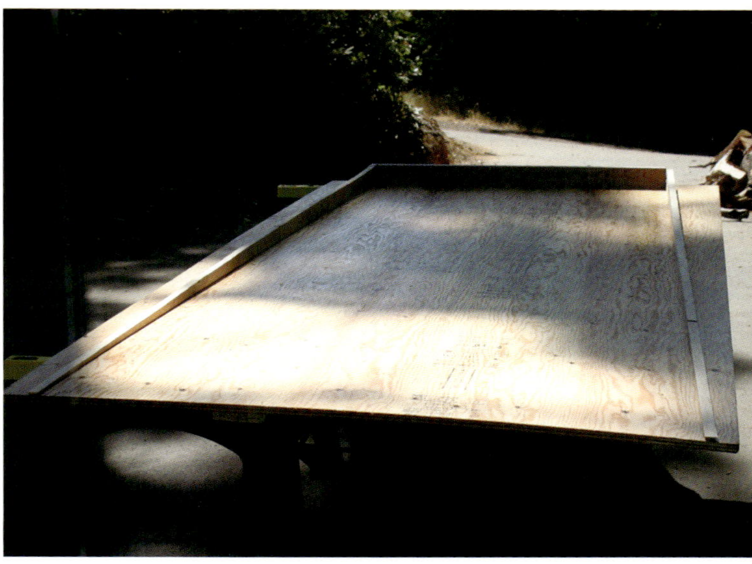

▲ *Step 3: Screw the 1″ × 4″ diagonals and the 1″ × 4″ × 4′ deep-end piece to the top of the plywood*

Step 2: Cut both 1″ × 4″ × 8′ pieces of wood diagonally lengthwise. One set will be used to make the sides for the pond. The other set will be placed on edge lengthwise on the table, and the plywood will set on top of it. The angle of these planks will provide some slope for the pond to have a deep end.

Step 3: Use some 1″ wood screws to fasten the sides (one set of the 1″ × 4″ × 8′ diagonal pieces for either long side of the pond) and the deep-end frame piece of 1″ × 4″ × 4′ to the plywood. This is a little tricky because you have to screw them from the underside of the plywood. Be careful when you get to the shallow end that you don't go all the way through the thin edge of the board with the wood screws.

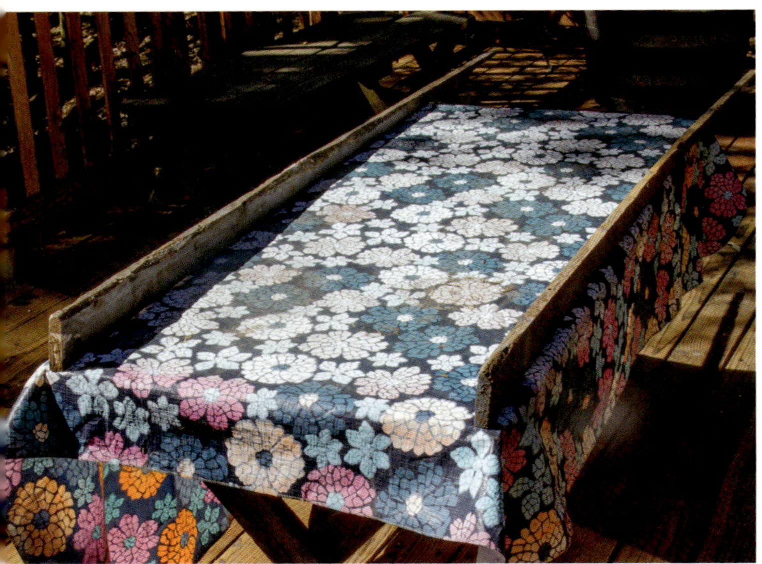

▲ *Step 4: One set of 1-inch × 4-inch boards placed on edge on the top of the table. The edge closest to the viewer will be the shallow end of the pond.*

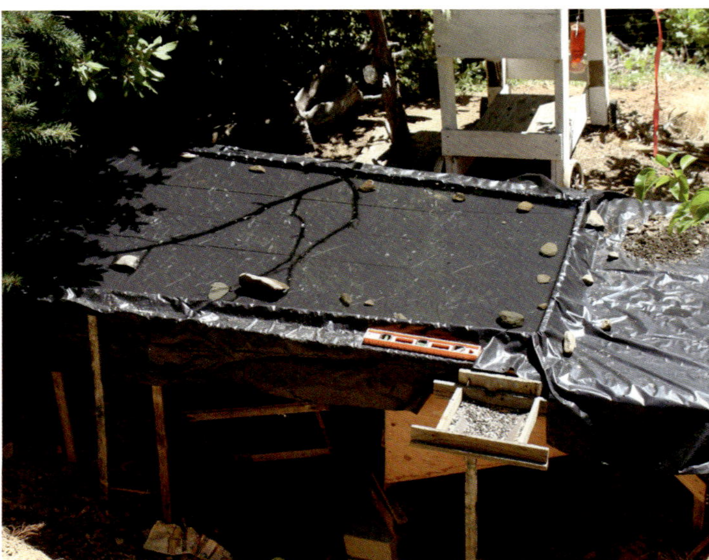

▲ *Step 5: Place plywood at an angle on the table. Cover the pond area in plastic Visqueen sheeting.*

Step 4: Place the other set of diagonal 1-inch × 4-inch boards on edge lengthwise on the table. The thick end will be the shallow end. These do not need to be screwed down because the weight of the water feature holds them in place. It also helps to leave them unscrewed so that they can be moved to help adjust the level of the water in the pond.

Step 5: Set the plywood on top of the 1″ × 4″ × 8′ wood pieces so that the thick ends of the 1″ × 4″ × 8′ pieces on top of the plywood match up with the thin ends of the 1″ × 4″ × 8′ pieces between the plywood and the table. Carefully cover the pond area with black Visqueen plastic.

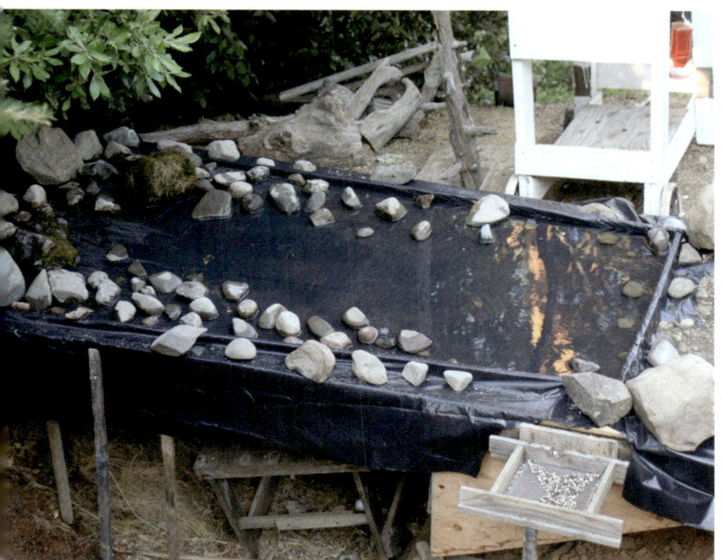

▲ *Step 6: Fill with water and begin placing river rock*

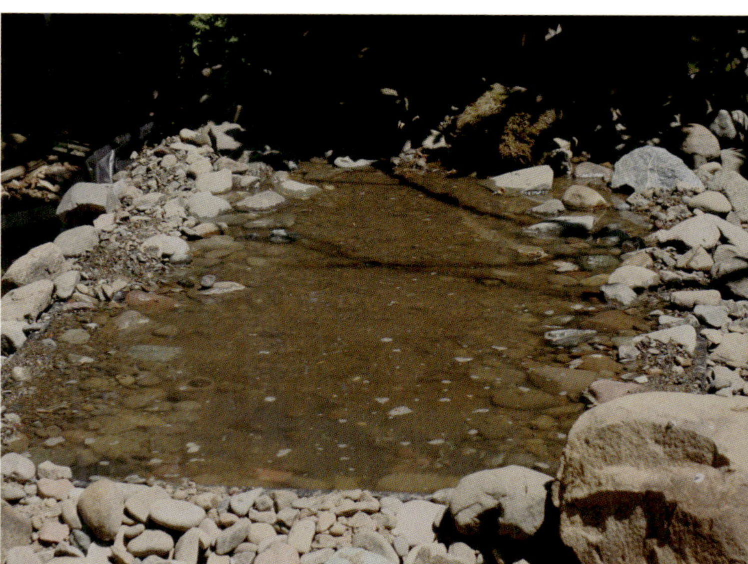

▲ *Step 7: Complete covering the water feature with gravel and sand*

Step 6: Place rocks all around the edges of the pond. Place two of your biggest rocks at the front corners to hide the sides of the pond. Place the rest of the bigger rocks across the back to provide a backdrop. Fill the pond with water so the water level is right at the brim of the deep end of the pond. You can get better reflections this way.

Step 7: The final step is to fill in the pond with rocks and gravel. Place a thin layer of very fine gravel and sand across the middle to cover up the bottom of the pond.

From here you can add plants, sticks, moss, and any other natural-looking items you can think of. I attached a platform feeder to the side of my pond and filled it with black sunflower seed. On the other side, I put a bowl of hen-scratch. I keep this away from the water because otherwise the birds tend to kick it around and knock corn into the pond.

I set up my blind about six feet away from the deep end of the pond and I set my tripod height to about two inches above water level. You can go lower, but the water will sometimes look milky from a lower angle.

What's nice about this project is that you can move it if you have to. First pick of all the big rocks. Then get a flat shovel and shovel the gravel and smaller rocks into five gallon buckets. With someone's help you can easily move the plywood and the table to a new location and set it up again.

One final tidbit: Keep a hose with a small valve and a clear plastic line going from the blind to the pond. If the pond's water level goes down too much when you are shooting, you can add water without disturbing the birds.

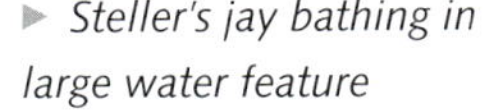

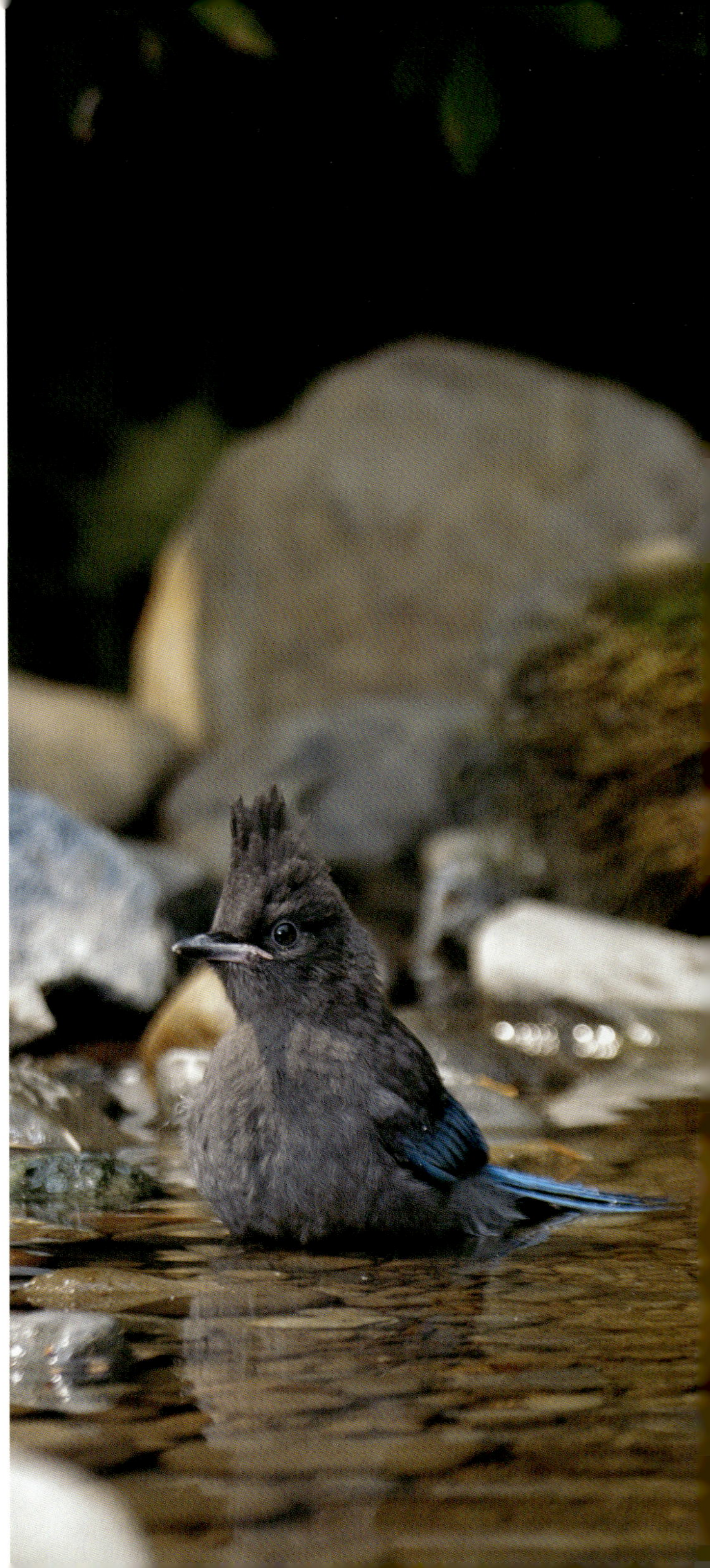

▶ *Steller's jay bathing in large water feature*

BUILDING A CHAIR BLIND

Level: Complex

Materials list:

- Camping chair with canopy
- 4½ yds. of camouflage fabric (or more, if you have a very large chair)
- Black or green thread
- Sewing machine
- ¾″ PVC slip couplings (2)
- ¾″ 90 degree PVC elbows (2)
- Ten feet of ¾″ PVC pipe
- Hacksaw or PVC pipe cutter
- Duct tape

I have been really busy shooting images of birds, turtles, millipedes, and a number of portraits among other things. Through all of this, my burning desire has been to create a new chair blind. I have been using an Ameristep chair blind for a lot of my nature photography; it works really well, but after much use I have found that it lacks a few essentials for photographers, since it was designed as a hunting blind. The biggest problem with it is that the front of the blind is too far away from the seat (it was designed with a rifle barrel in mind). Another problem is limited side-visibility. Finally, these types of blinds are fairly heavy. With those thoughts in mind, I set out on a quest to build a reasonably cheap chair blind.

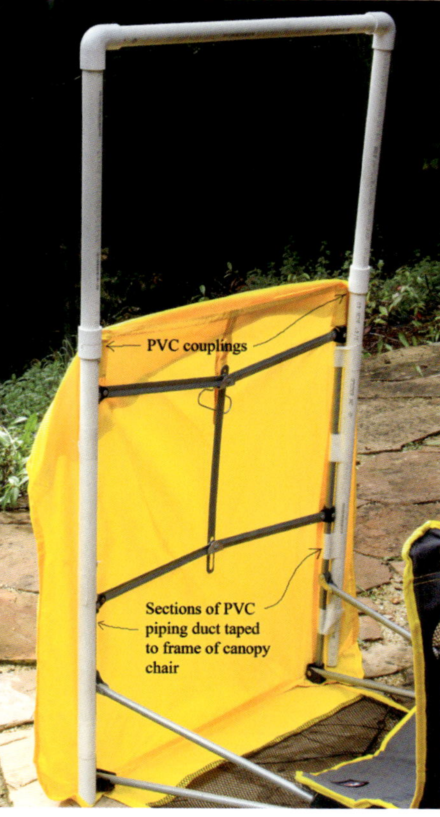

◄ *Step 1: Underside of canopy showing PVC frame taped to canopy frame*

A good chair is the most important aspect of this project. The best thing I found was a folding camping chair with a canopy sunshade at a local store for 23 bucks.

Step 1: Tape a piece of ¾″ PVC pipe and a slip coupling to the canopy frame with duct tape. The length of PVC will vary depending upon canopy chair used.

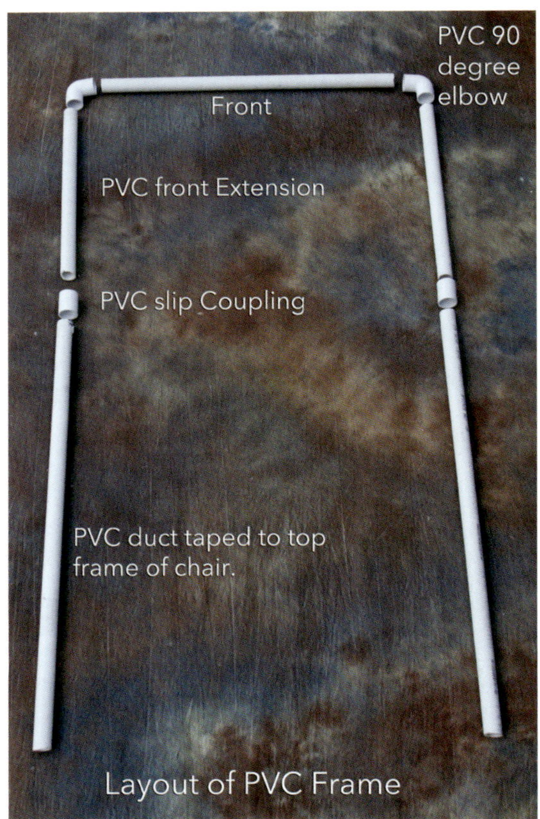

▲ *Step 2: Layout of PVC to be duct taped to chair blind canopy*

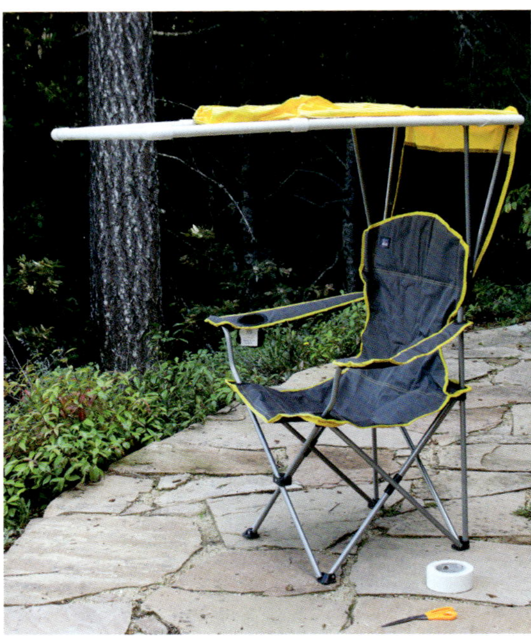

▲ *PVC frame duct taped to the sides of the chair blind canopy with white duct tape*

Step 2: Make a U-shaped extension with 3 pieces of PVC pipe and a couple of 90-degree elbows. This will fit right into the slip couplings on the piping already attached to the canopy. I don't glue mine so the blind is easy to break down and transport.

Step 3: Set the chair up. You'll need to measure your chair so that you know how much fabric to buy. Measure from the front of the chair to the back, so you know how deep the chair is. Then measure from the bottom of the left side of the chair up over

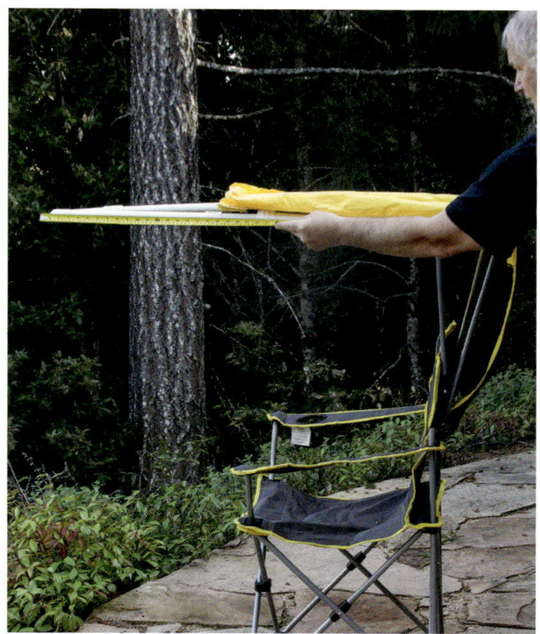

▲ *Step 3: Measuring the left side of the chair blind for fabric.*

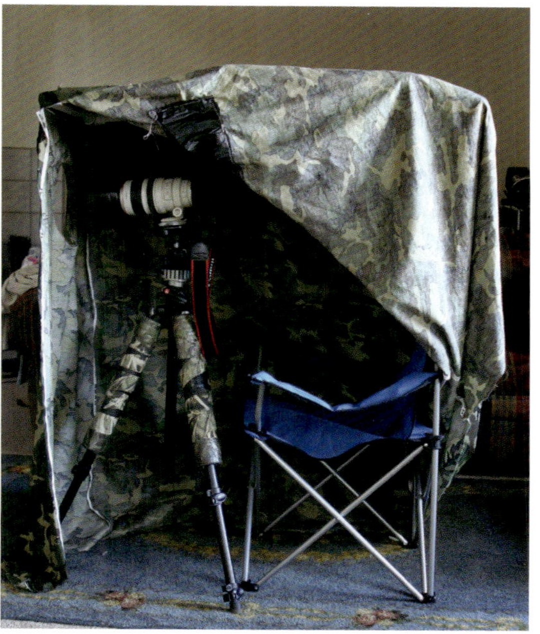

▲ *Inside the chair blind*

the top, and down the right side of the chair to the ground. These will be the dimensions of the piece of fabric that will drape from the bottom of the left side of the chair over the canopy and down to the bottom of the right side of the chair.

Step 4: The pieces of fabric that will cover the front and back of the chair should be about the same size. Measure the chairs height and width, so you'll know how much fabric you'll need for these panels.

Step 5: Add ½″ to the measurements of the fabric on all sides to make room for the seams. Purchase fabric and cut three panels: two panels for the front and back of the chair, and one long panel to cover the left, right and top of the blind. See the chair blind pattern.

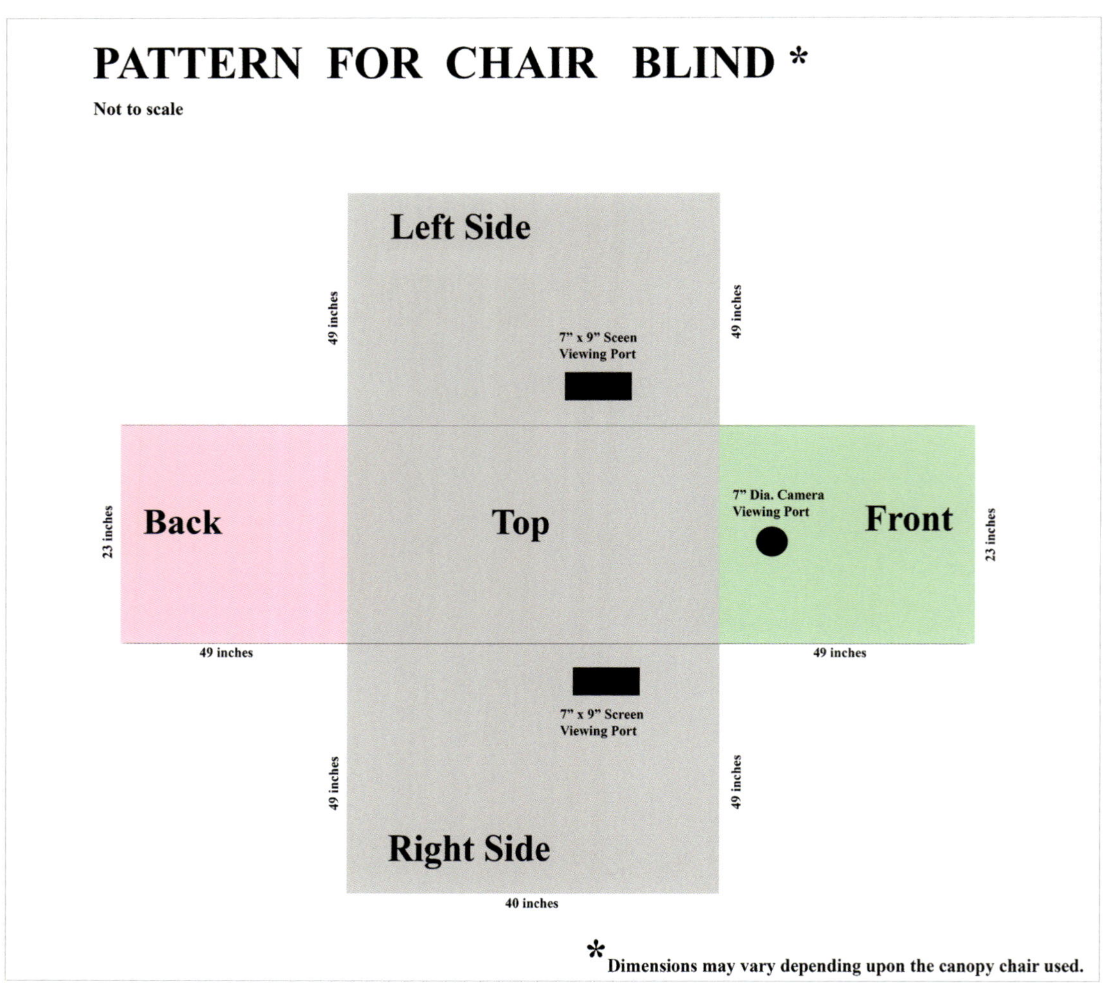

▲ *Sewing pattern for chair blind*

Step 6: Drape the long piece of fabric over the chair so it falls from the top of the chair to the ground on both sides. Pin or baste the top of the front and back panels to the roof section of the blind. When you are satisfied with the way the blind fits over your chair, sew the pieces together, attaching the top edges of the front and back panels to the appropriate places on the long piece of fabric.

Step 7: Sit in the blind with your camera, lens, and tripod, and mark where the openings for the lens port and viewing ports should be on the fabric.

Step 8: Cut the lens port and sew a flap to cover it. Cut the viewing ports and cover them by sewing mesh over the openings.

Step 9: Sew the edges of the blind together so the right front corner and both back corners are completely stitched together from top to bottom. The fabric should create an enclosed box except for the front left edge, which will be left open.

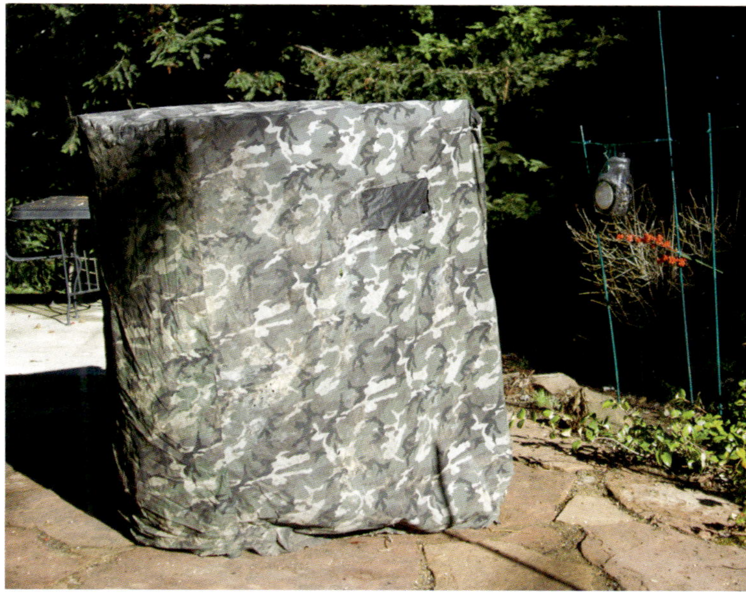

▲ *Chair blind set up in the backyard*

Step 10: Use a snap tool and add black metal snaps to the front left corner of the blind to create an access point to get in and out of the blind.

There you have it! A chair blind that is lighter and far more camera-friendly than a commercial blind, at half the cost.

A PERMANENT BLIND

Level: Complex

Materials list:

- 3⁄8″ plywood, 48″ × 48″ (4) (these are the three sides and the floor)
- 3⁄8″ plywood 40 5⁄8″ × 48″ (this is the back door)
- 3⁄8″ plywood 48″ × 60″ (this is the roof)
- 3⁄8″ plywood 13½″ and 5″ × 48″ (2) (these are the upper left and right sides)
- 3⁄8″ plywood 16¾″ × 48″ (this is the upper front piece)
- 3⁄8″ plywood 12″ × 12″ (this is the back door slider)
- 2″ × 4″ × 48″ studs (10) (for framing)
- 2″ × 4″ × 41″ studs (2) (for framing)
- 2″ × 4″ × 45″ stud (for framing)
- 2″ × 4″ × 10″ studs (2) (for framing)
- 1″ × 2″ × 45″ furring strips (4) (frames for sliders, right and left sides)
- 1″ × 2″ × 38″ furring strips (4) (frames for sliders, right and left sides)
- 1″ × 2″ × 41″ furring strips (2) (frames for front sliders)
- 1″ × 2″ × 34″ furring strips (2) (frames for front sliders)
- 1″ × 2″ × 13″ furring strips (4) (frames for back door sliders)
- 1″ × 2″ × 40 5⁄8″ furring strips (2) (for door frame)
- 1″ × 2″ × 46½″ furring strips (2) (for door frame)
- 1″ × 6″ × 11½″ planks (tongue and groove) (24) (sliders)
- Hinges (3)
- Wood pallet roughly 48″ × 48″
- Roll of landscape cloth

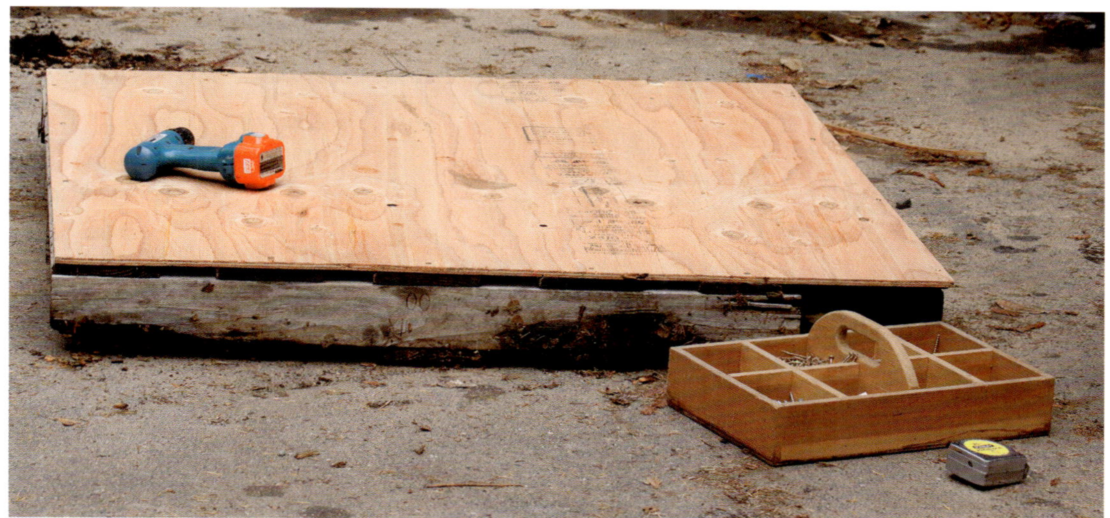

▲ *Step 1: Cover the pallet with plywood*

Winter can be a difficult time to photograph birds. Depending upon your geographical location, it can be windy, rainy, or snowy, which has the potential to make photography quite miserable. However, if you are prepared for heavy downpours and snowstorms, these conditions give you the potential to create some incredible bird images. Most canvas or cloth blinds are fairly waterproof, but they will only put up with so much water and wind, which is why building winter or permanent blinds can be such a good decision. Permanent blinds are snug, dry, and exceptionally useful for photography.

To create my permanent blind, I started off by going to the lumber yard. I picked up a 4′ × 4′ pallet. I just asked nicely, and they gave it to me for free (they get tons of them daily). Other possible places to get these are discount and warehouse stores, or anywhere that gets supplies delivered by truck. Please note that not all pallets are exactly 4′ × 4′ so some of the dimensions given may vary depending upon the pallet you choose.

For this project you need to have some basic carpentry skills. I'm not a skilled woodworker, but I do know how to use basic tools. If you aren't very confident with this sort of thing, just get someone who knows what they're doing to help you.

Step 1: Cut plywood to fit your pallet, and screw it down to the top of pallet.

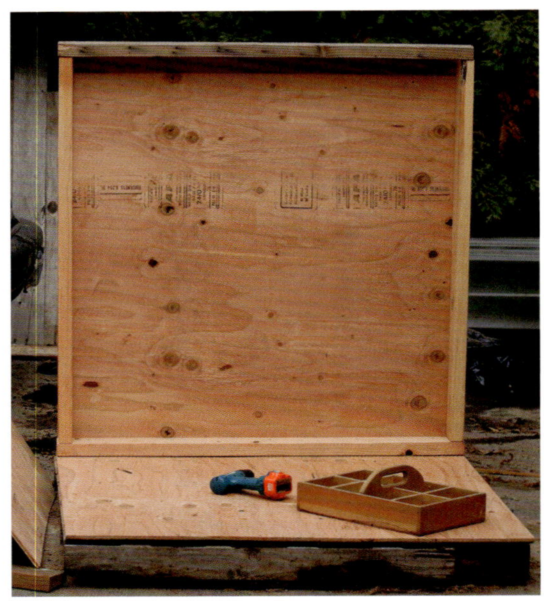

▲ *Step 2a: Cut and frame up one side and screw it down to the base*

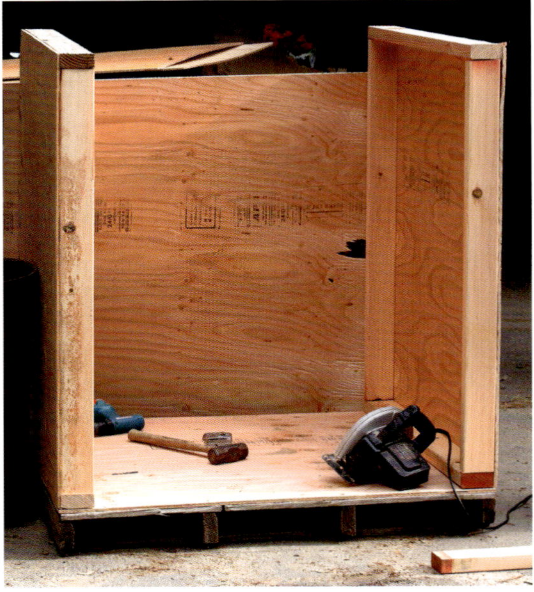

▲ *Step 2b: Cut and frame the other side and screw it down to the base*

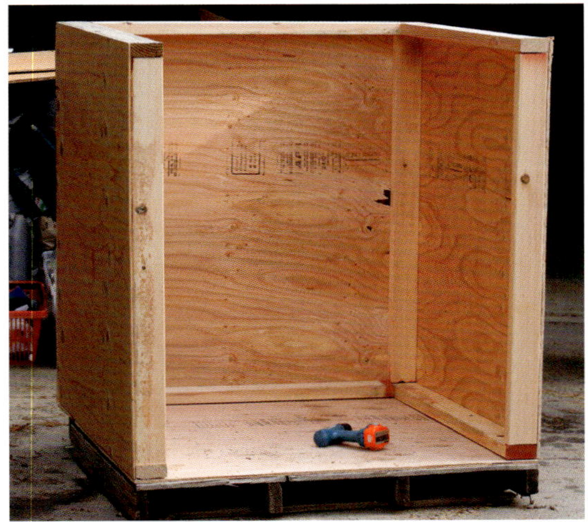

Step 2: Frame up the right and left sides of the blind using four 2″ × 4″ × 48″ studs and four 2″ × 4″ × 35″ upright studs. Add the framed side panels by screwing them down to the pallet. Frame in the back of the blind by toeing in two 2″ × 4″ × 41″ studs between the two sides on the top and the bottom. Screw on the plywood to the back frame. The final step to the lower framing is to screw one 2″ × 4″ × 48″ stud across the top of the front, between the two sides.

◀ *Step 2c: Cut and frame the back and screw it to the base*

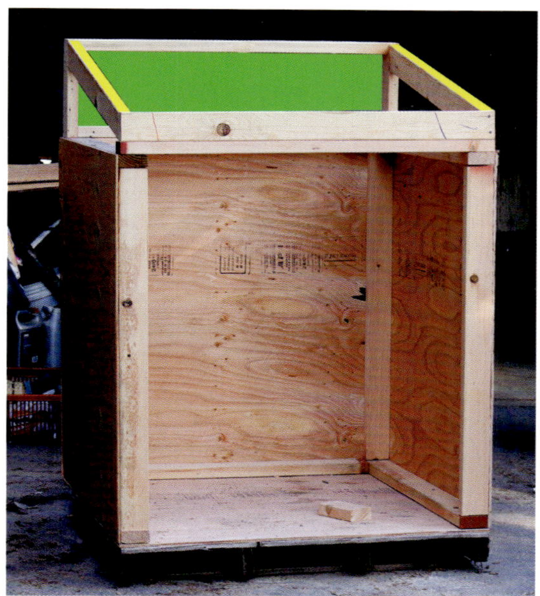

▲ *Step 3: Frame up the roof*

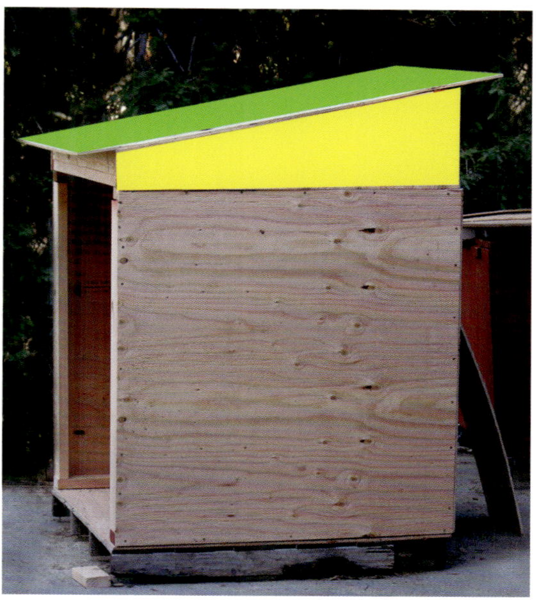

▲ *Step 4: Cut the sides and top of the roof section and screw them to the framing*

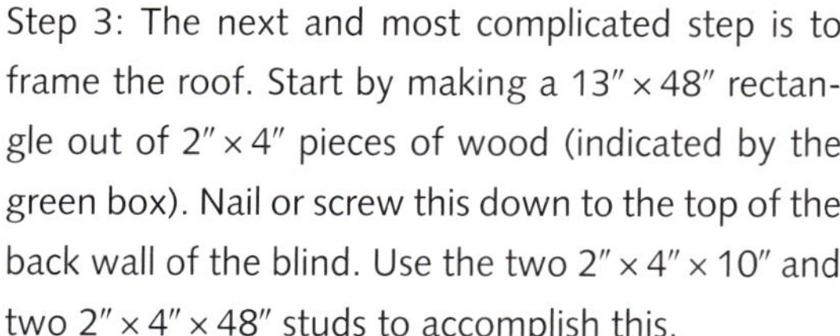

Step 3: The next and most complicated step is to frame the roof. Start by making a 13″ × 48″ rectangle out of 2″ × 4″ pieces of wood (indicated by the green box). Nail or screw this down to the top of the back wall of the blind. Use the two 2″ × 4″ × 10″ and two 2″ × 4″ × 48″ studs to accomplish this.

Next, use a 2″ × 4″ × 48″ stud, and nail or screw it in (on edge) to the 2″ × 4″ × 48″ stud above the front door opening. Be sure to screw or nail it in from the underside. Following that is the most difficult part. Measure and cut two pieces (size 2″ × 4″ × 48″) to create a triangular frame (in yellow) between the rectangular frame above the back wall and the 2″ × 4″ above the door. The easiest way to do this is to hold a 2″ × 4″ up in between these two points and mark the length and angles for the cut with a pencil. Make the cuts and toe in the last of the framing with screws or nails.

Step 4: To keep it all nice and dry, cut out a piece of plywood, 48″ wide by 60″ long, for the roof (in green). Screw the roof down to the top section of the roof frame. Cut a 16¾″ × 48″ piece of plywood to cover the rectangle of 2″ × 4″s that is above the front wall of the blind. This piece should overlap the plywood below to keep the blind dry inside.

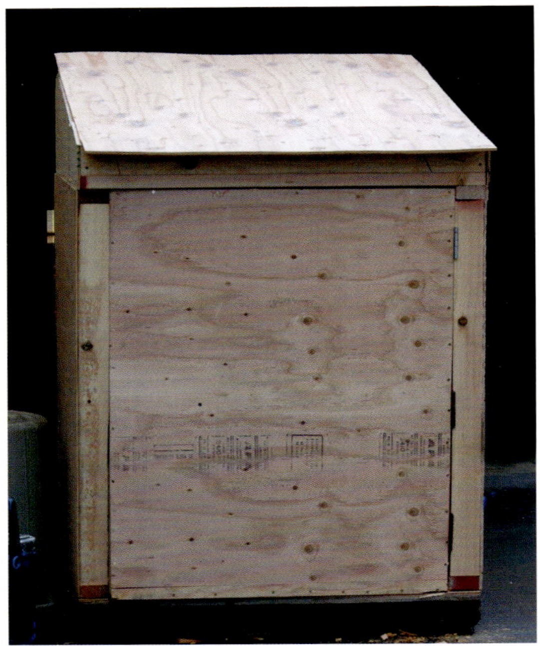

▲ *Step 5: Frame the door with 1″ × 2″ lumber. Install hinges and hang the door.*

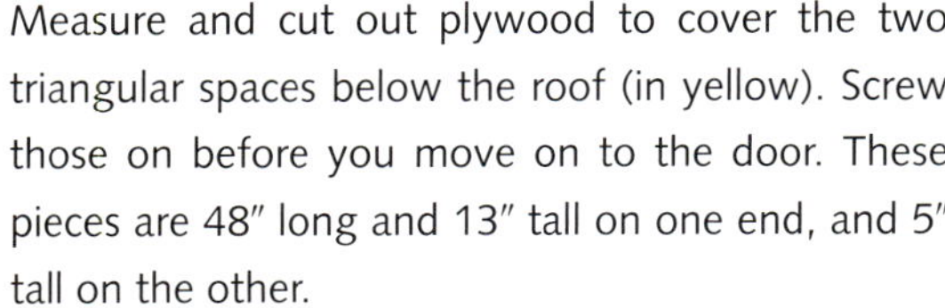

Measure and cut out plywood to cover the two triangular spaces below the roof (in yellow). Screw those on before you move on to the door. These pieces are 48″ long and 13″ tall on one end, and 5″ tall on the other.

Step 5: You'll need to be able to get in and out of the blind, so frame the door with 1″ × 2″ lumber. Use the two 46½″ and 48″ pieces, and add hinges to one side. Hang the door.

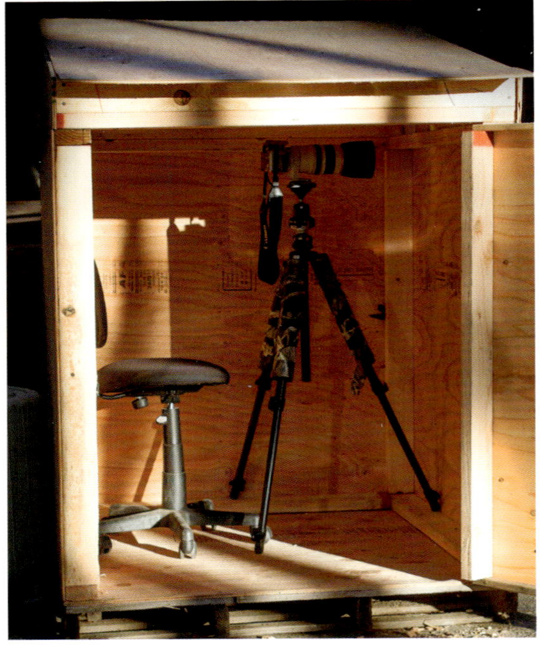

▲ *Step 6: Set up the tripod, and cut a hole for your camera*

Step 6: Set up a tripod and camera to figure out a comfortable camera height. Mark and cut out the window openings on the wood.

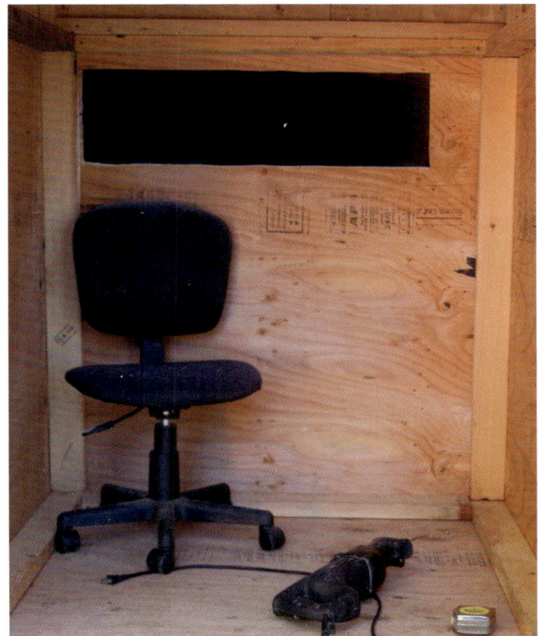

▲ *Step 7: Cut rectangular openings for the sides and back*

Step 7: Cut the window openings in the sides and the back of the blind. Please note that the opening is cut 6½ inches from one edge to allow for room to take the sliders (see next step) in and out. Cut a 10″-diameter circular opening in the back door for the camera. The left and right openings are 38½″ long and 9½″ high. The front opening is 35½″ × 9½″.

Step 8: Install the slider guides for the windows. The slider guides are made of 1″ × 2″ furring strips. Two 1″ × 2″ pieces are screwed together to make an "L" shape. This is the guide at the bottom of the window. Two pieces are screwed together to make

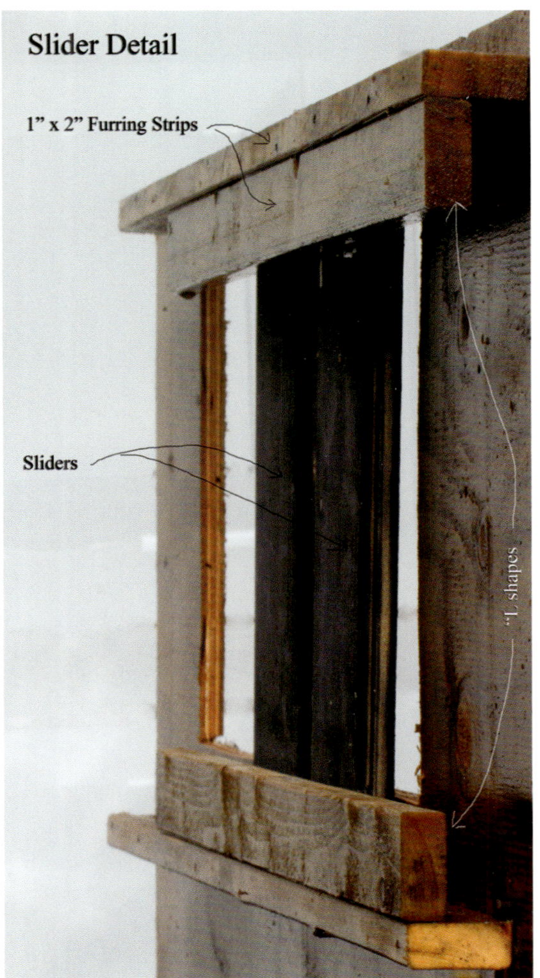

▲ *Step 8: Mock-up of a slider to show construction details*

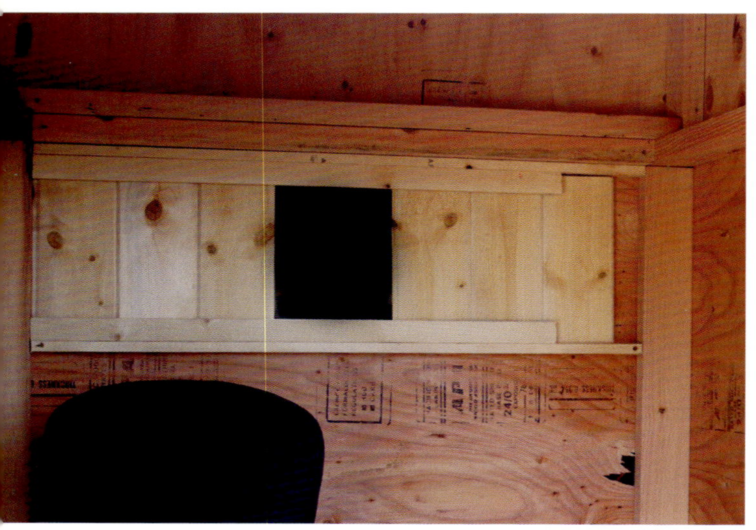

▲ *Slider assembly*

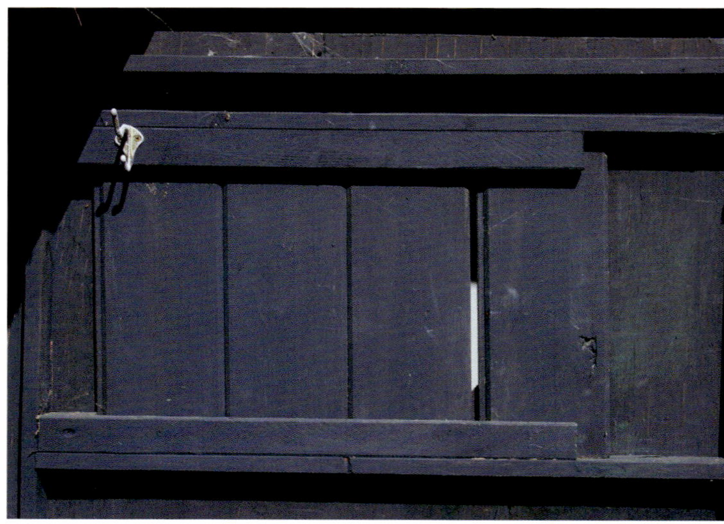

▲ *Slider assembly in detail*

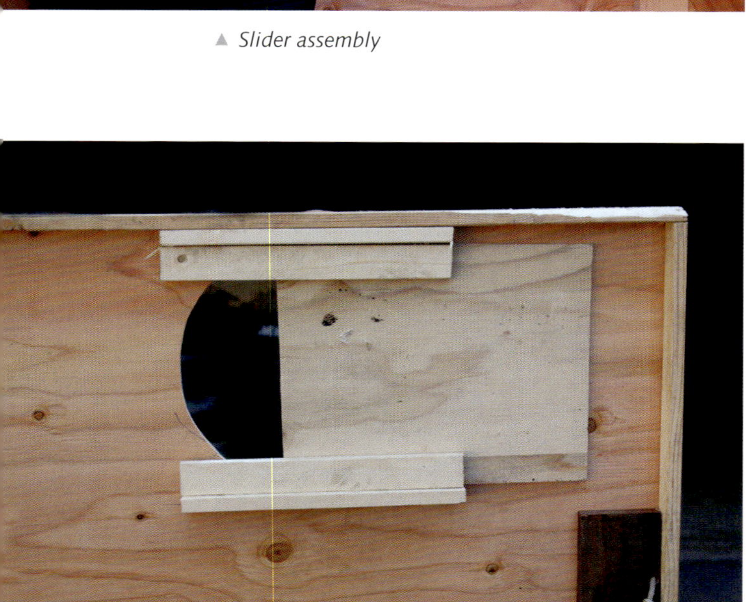

an upside down "L" shape above the window. Screw these pieces to the blind from the outside. The longer pieces of the pair go at the top and bottom for the guides. It is best to have someone help you at this stage by putting the sliders between the guides and holding them in place while the guides are being screwed on from the outside. The sliders should have plenty of free room to be able to slide from side to side. Check the materials list to see which pieces go with which window opening.

◀ *Slider over the door opening*

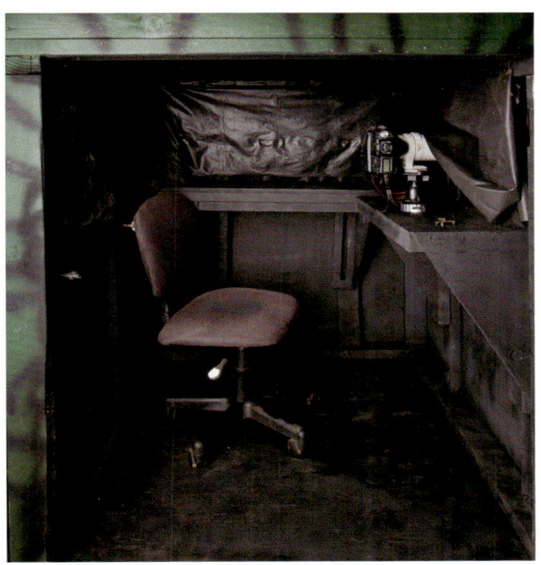

▲ *Interior of photo blind with shooting shelves and window coverings— interior is painted black to mask movement*

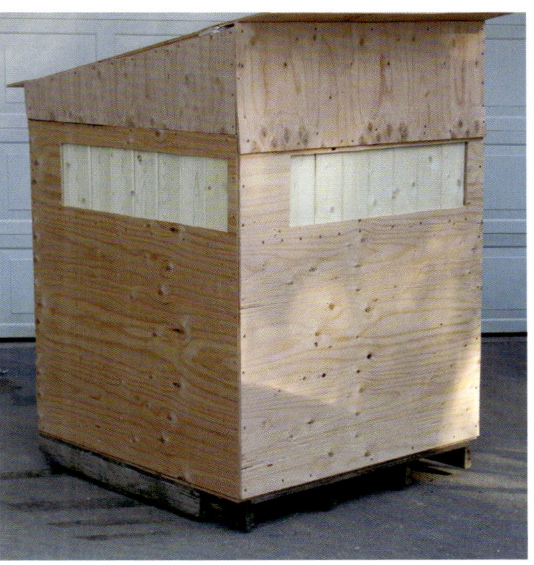

▲ *Complete unpainted photo blind*

Step 9: Create and install a shooting shelf (see "A Shooting Shelf for a Permanent Blind").

Step 10: It's a good idea to paint the inside of the blind black.

Step 11: Next, install the window coverings. I used landscape fabric, which is both waterproof and mildew proof. It has the advantage of being transparent enough to see through, but still opaque enough to hide your movements from outside the blind.

Step 12: The last step is to paint the outside with colors that will blend in with your yard.

The primary disadvantage of a permanent blind is that it is designed to stay in one place, and can be difficult to move. I put a set of wheels under one end and attached some two by fours to the side (like a wheelbarrow) for when I needed to move mine. It was a difficult job, so remember that proper placement of your blind is critical. Some people choose to scout a location first, and build the blind in place.

A SHOOTING SHELF FOR A PERMANENT BLIND

Level: Complex

Materials list:

- 2″ × 2″ × 8′ stud
- 12″ × 16″ piece of ⅜″ plywood cut into two triangles
- 12″ × 41″ piece of ⅝″ plywood
- 1″ × 2″ × 2′ furring strip
- ⅜″ dia × ¾″ bolt
- ½″ dia × 2″ bolt
- ½″ dia × 5″ carriage bolts (2)
- ½″ wing nut (2)
- ½″ flat washer (2)
- 12″ × 2″ × ¼″ channel iron

I believe that one of the best features that a permanent or semi-permanent blind can have is a shooting shelf. A shooting shelf is an adjustable platform to support your tripod head so you don't have to use a tripod in your blind. The shelf also frees you from having to fight with tripod legs, while still giving you a stable platform to shoot from. It also allows you to place your camera closer to the lens opening of the blind.

The shelf can easily be adjusted to the desired camera height by loosening two wing nuts, then raising or lowering the shelf and tightening the wing nuts again. A swing arm ballhead support on the shelf allows the photographer to move the camera position closer or farther from the window sliders as well as to the right or left. Additionally, the swing arm can be moved to the far end of the shelf to enable shooting from the side window sliders. To make full use of the side sliders, the shelf can be repositioned to those windows by undoing the wing nuts and moving the shelf.

The combination of the shooting shelf, swing arm ballhead, and the window sliders make a blind very comfortable and easy to shoot from. If you are planning on building a blind or want to make a nice addition to one you already have, consider this key, additional feature.

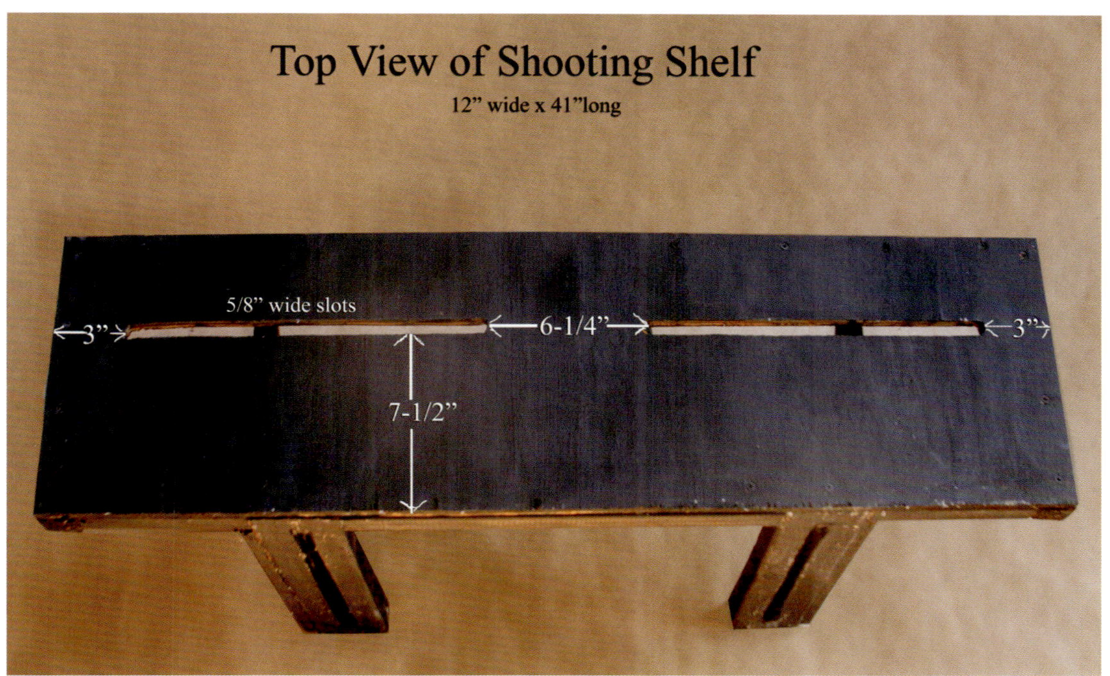

▲ *Step 1: Finished piece of plywood*

Step 1: Start with a 12″ × 41″ × ⅝″ piece of plywood. Cut two horizontal ⅝″ wide by 14⅜″ long slots, 3″ in from the outside 12″ edge. The slots should be 7″ from the back edge and 3″ from the right and left sides. Please see the top view of the shooting shelf.

Step 2: Cut two 2″ × 4″ pieces of wood, 18″ long. Cut a ⅝″ slot down the center of both of them, 1½″ from each end.

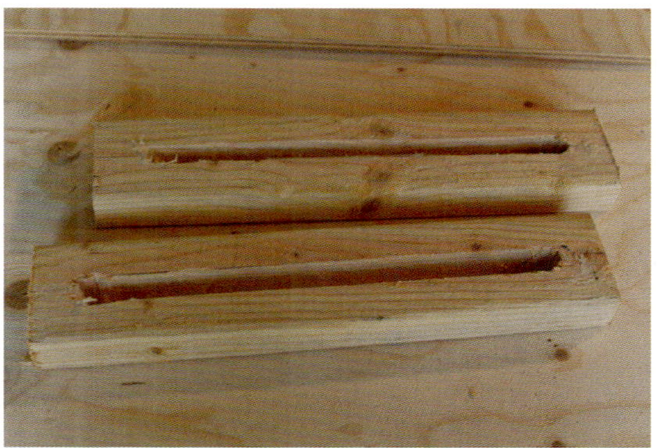

▲ *Step 2: 2″ × 4″ pieces of wood with cuts down the center*

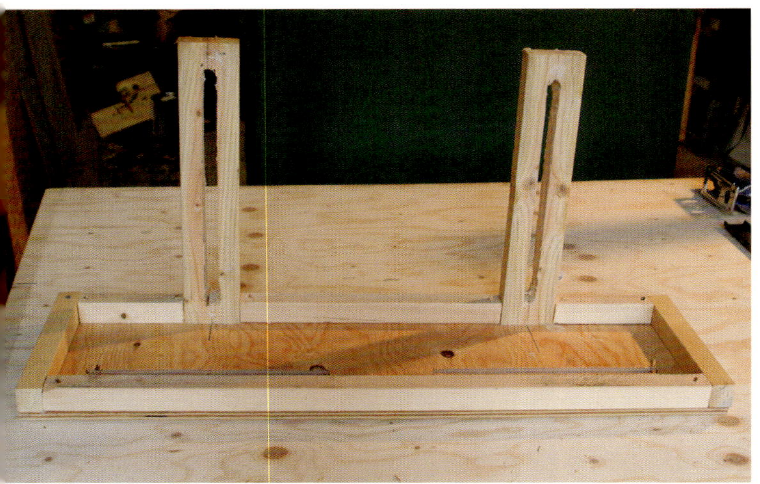

Step 3: Screw the end of the 2-inch × 4-inch pieces to the underside of the plywood and frame them in with 2-inch × 2-inch pieces. The outside edges of the 2-inch × 4-inch pieces should be 8¼″ from the outside edge of the plywood.

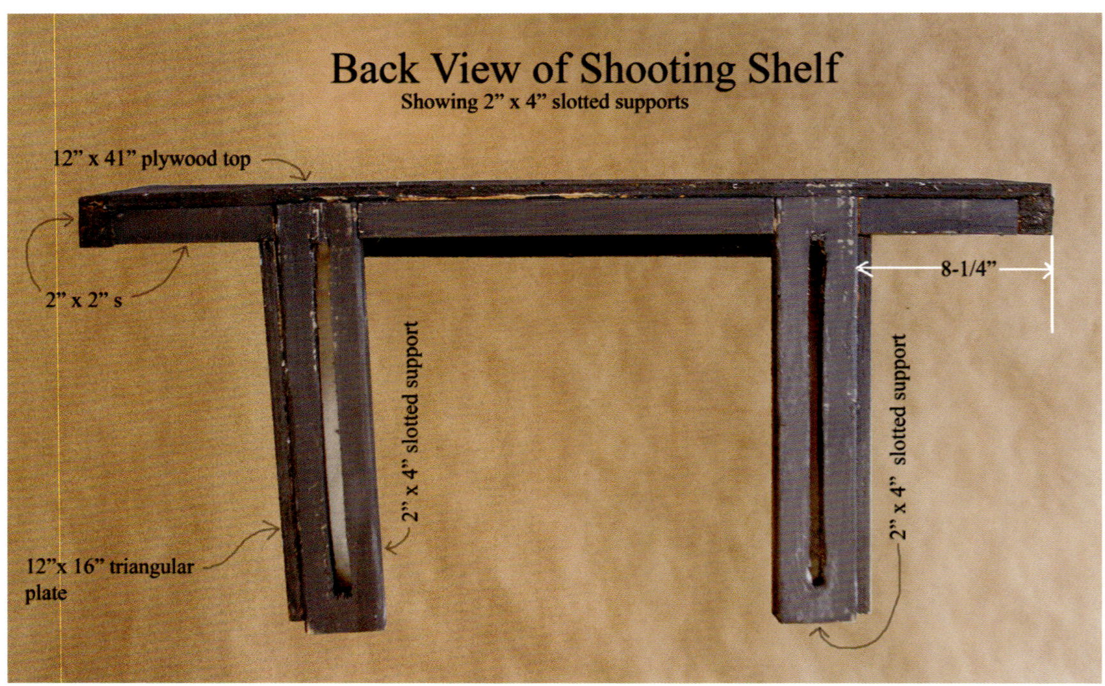

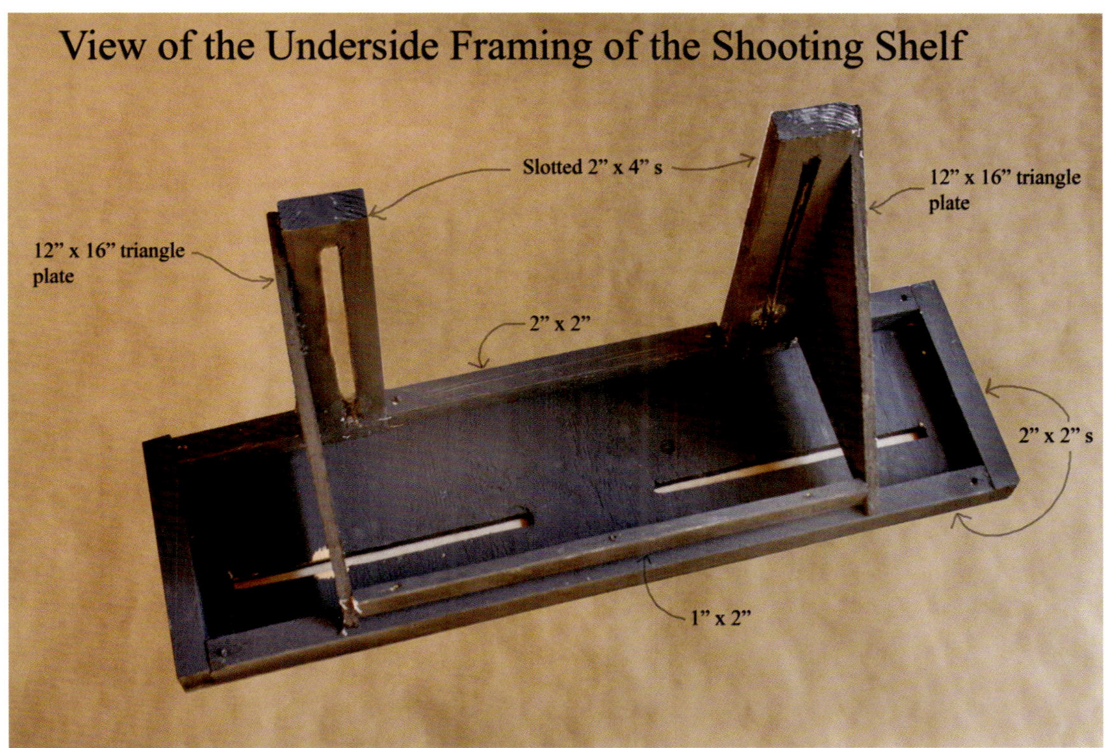

▲ *Step 4: View of the underside framing of the shooting shelf*

Step 4: Brace the 2-inch × 4-inch pieces with 12″ × 16″ plywood triangles, with the 16″ edge of one triangle screwed (at a perpendicular) to the 18″ × 2″ side of the 2″ × 4″. Add a 1″ × 2″ × 24¼″ piece of bracing wood in between the two triangle corners on the bottom edge of the shelf.

Step 5: In the photo blind, choose the wall you are most likely to photograph from. Add two vertical 2″ × 4″ supports centered the same distance apart as the slots in the 2-inch × 4-inch pieces on the shelf. Drill a ½″ hole 6 inches down from the top end of each 2″ × 4″. Put a ½″-diameter carriage bolt (5″ long) through the hole from the outside of the

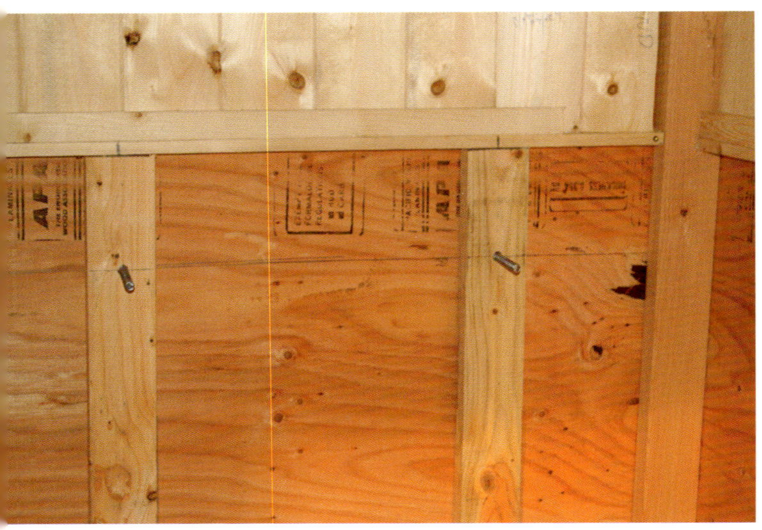

▲ *Step 5: Thread the bolts through the outside of the wall*

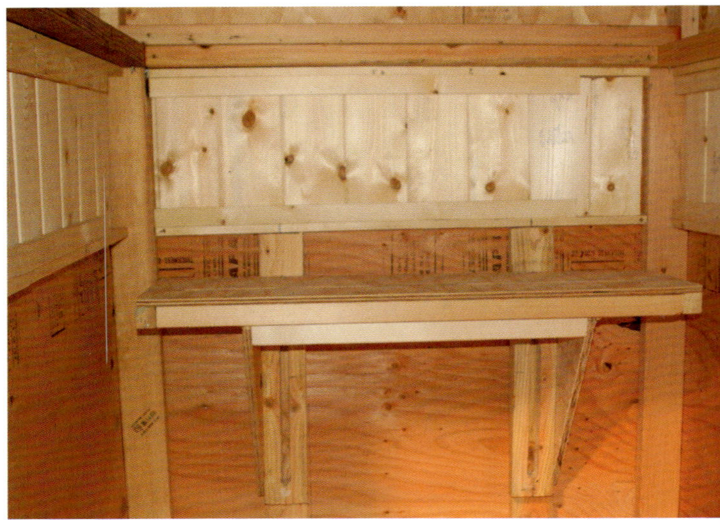

▲ *Step 6: The secured shooting shelf*

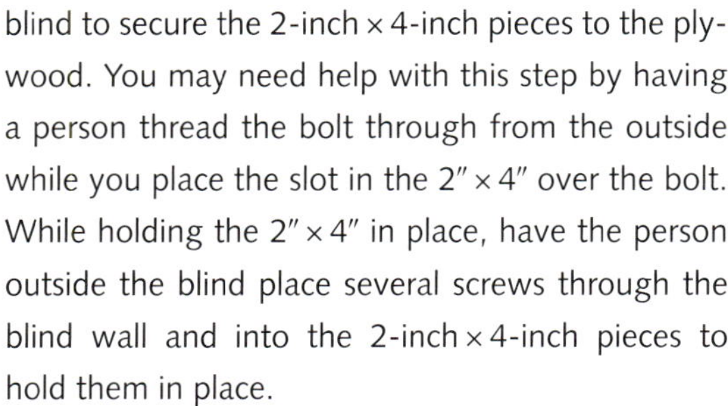

blind to secure the 2-inch × 4-inch pieces to the plywood. You may need help with this step by having a person thread the bolt through from the outside while you place the slot in the 2″ × 4″ over the bolt. While holding the 2″ × 4″ in place, have the person outside the blind place several screws through the blind wall and into the 2-inch × 4-inch pieces to hold them in place.

Step 6: Secure the shelf to the bolts with two ½″ wingnuts. Adjust the shelf to a comfortable photographing height and tighten the wing nuts at that level. You can always reposition the shelf height once you have placed your camera on it.

Step 7: Drill a ⅜″ hole 1½″ from the end of a 12″ × 2″ piece of channel iron, and drill a ½″ hole ¾″ from the other end.

Step 8: Tack weld a ⅜″ × ¾″ bolt into the ⅜″ hole. Then tack weld a ½″ × 2″ bolt into the ½″ hole in the channel iron as shown, with the threaded sides opposite one another. Any welding or machine shop should be able to do this for you quite cheaply.

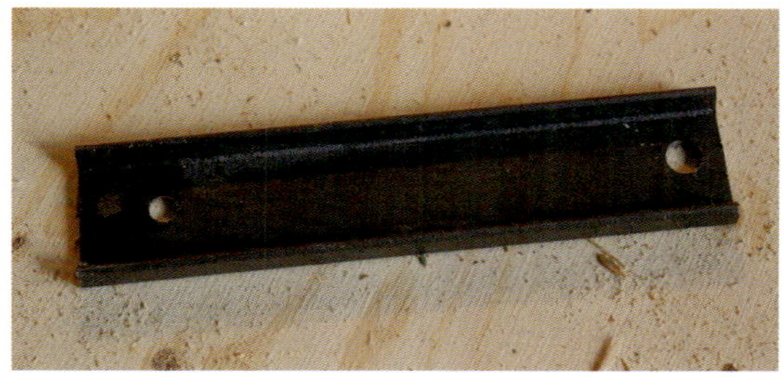

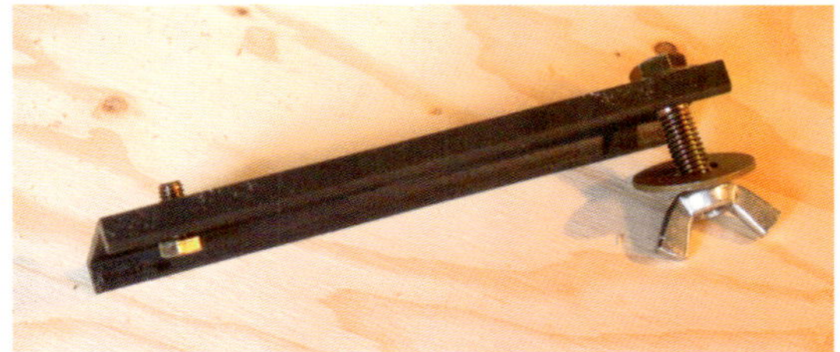

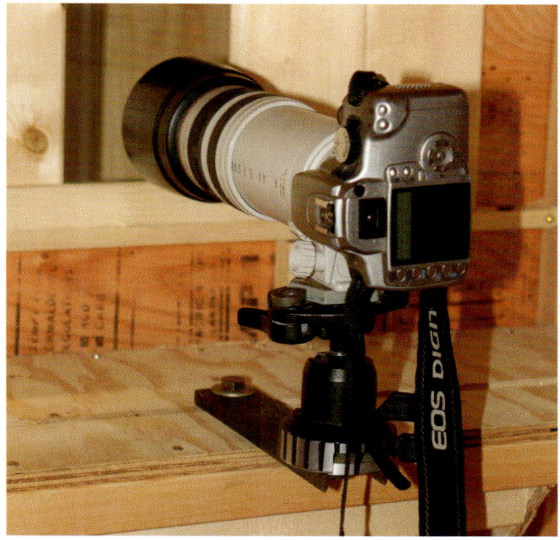

▲ *Step 9: Swing arm secured in place by a wing nut with a camera and ballhead mounted on it*

Step 9: To attach the swing arm to the shooting shelf, put the ½″ bolt side of the channel iron into the slot in the plywood and tighten it up to the underside of the plywood with a flat washer and a ½″ wing nut. To attach a tripod head, screw the tripod head onto the ⅜″ stud sticking up from the channel iron. Please make sure the tripod head is tight and secure!

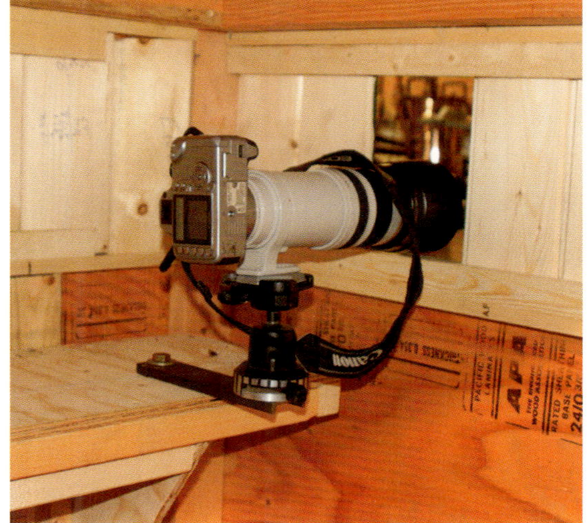

► *Camera mounted to photograph out the side of the photo blind*

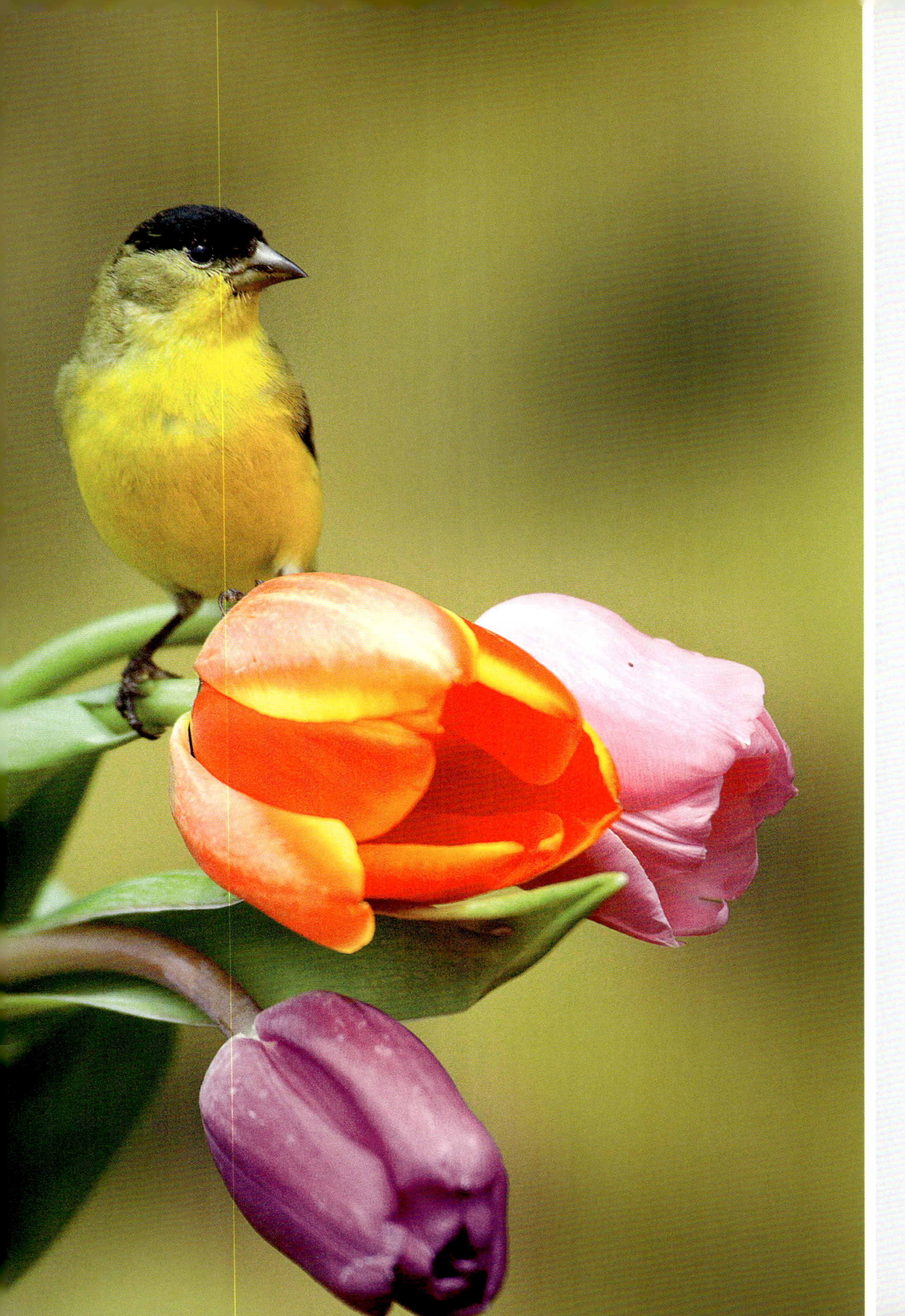

◀ *Goldfinch on tulips waiting for the feeder. There is a tube feeder just out of the frame to the right.*

Resources and Suppliers

Photo Blinds:

Ameristep
ameristep.com/blinds/doghouse.html

Cabelas Outfitters
cabelas.com

Bass Pro Shops
basspro.com

Dicks Sporting Goods
dickssportinggoods.com

Bird Feeders – Brands:

Opus

Perky Pet

Droll Yankee

Heritage Farms
heritagefarms.biz

Stokes
stokesbirdsathome.com

Camera Equipment Suppliers

B+H Photo and Video
420 9th Avenue
New York, NY 10001
Bhphotovideo.com

Adorama
42 West 18th Street
New York, NY 10011
Adorama.com

Hunts
Huntsphotoandvideo.com
(Multiple locations on the US East Coast)

KEH, Inc
4900 Highlands Parkway SE
Smyrna, GA 30082
keh.com
World's largest supplier of used camera equipment

Bristol Cameras Ltd
47 High Street, Bristol, BS1 2AZ
Bristolcameras.co.uk/contact_us.php

Recipes for Suet

Basic Suet Mix

- 1 cup peanut butter
- 1 cup shortening
- 1 cup flour
- 3 cups cornmeal
- 1 cup cracked corn or hen scratch

Slowly melt shortening and peanut butter in a large saucepan on low heat. Stir in other ingredients slowly. Pour into aluminum pie tins and let cool.

You can add one small handful of black oil sunflower seeds and/or mixed seed (optional).

Birdy Suet Mix

- 1 cup chunky peanut butter
- 2 cups ground oatmeal
- 2 cups oatmeal
- 1 cup shortening or rendered suet
- ⅓ cup sugar
- 1 cup white flour

Melt the shortening or suet and peanut butter on low heat until melted in a large saucepan. Stir in the other ingredients one at a time. Pour into aluminum pie tins and set aside to cool.

For variations on these recipes add peanuts, berries, or dried cut fruit pieces to the mix in small quantities.

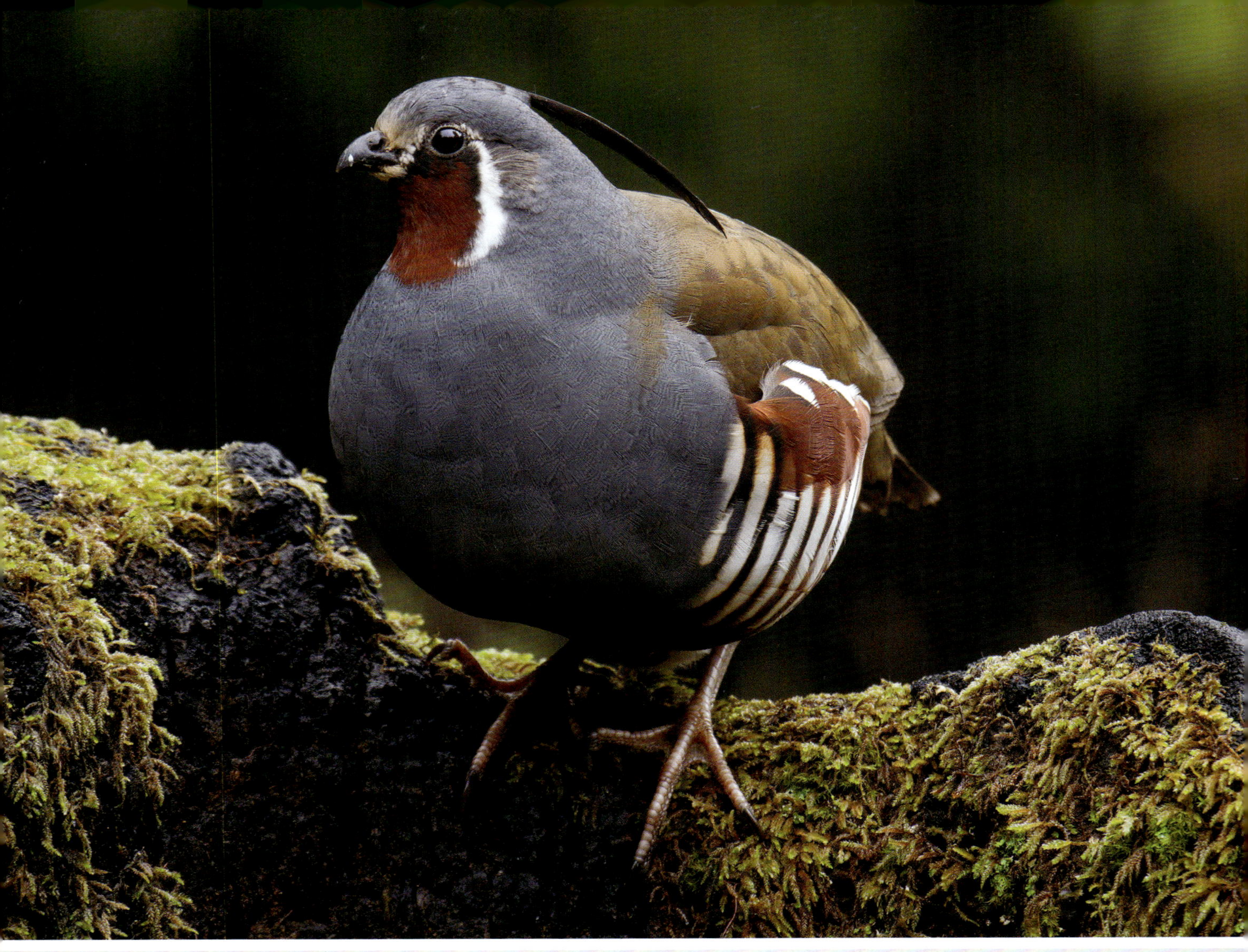

▲ *Mountain quail on a piece of burned redwood burl with moss. There is a feeder cup filled with black sunflower seed on the backside of the burl.*

Conclusion

It has been over three years since I began writing *Secrets of Backyard Bird Photography*. To complete this book, I drew on my years of experience, but it was still a learning process. Along the way I was able to create and compose some beautiful bird images using the techniques covered in this book. I feel privileged to be able to pass along these projects to you!

You now have a wide variety of techniques and projects available to you for the creation of some quality backyard bird images, including the secrets to using blinds, feeders, perches, and set-ups. We have covered information on types of bird feeders and seed, and how to effectively hide birdseed so it does not appear in the image. We have looked at many different kinds of photo blinds, be it a room in your house, a purchased blind, or a permanent photo blind for your backyard that you created from raw materials.

Remember the importance and fun of creating a beautiful set-up in your yard. Be creative! You can use any combination of interesting items, including flowers, gnarly branches, twigs, mossy rocks, and other natural materials to create attractive perches in your pursuit of images of backyard birds. You can choose from a wide variety of backgrounds, both man-made and natural, to position behind your perches for an awesome image. You also have the knowledge to capture the best bird images with great composition. Remember that a good head angle and a catch light in the eye will make for an aesthetically pleasing image of the birds in your yard.

I hope these tips and tricks will help you to find satisfaction and joy in photographing the wildlife in your backyard. I wish you the very best in your pursuit of bird photography. Now gather up some gear and go out and create some beautiful bird images!

J. Chris Hansen

Contact Information

You can follow my photographic exploits on my photoblog: *Chris the Photog*

http://christhephotog.blogspot.com

I am very open to hearing from you if you have questions about backyard bird photography. You can leave a note in the comment section of my photoblog on the most current blog entry, or you can email me with your questions directly at: chrishansen@instawave.net